4-19-05

4/05

Who

She Was

My Search for
My Mother's Life

SAMUEL G. FREEDMAN

SIMON & SCHUSTER
NEW YORK   LONDON   TORONTO   SYDNEY

SIMON & SCHUSTER
Rockefeller Center
1230 Avenue of the Americas
New York, NY 10020

Copyright © 2005 by Samuel G. Freedman

SIMON & SCHUSTER and colophon are registered trademarks of
Simon & Schuster, Inc.
For information about special discounts for bulk purchases,
please contact Simon & Schuster Special Sales at
1-800-456-6798 or business@simonandschuster.com
Designed by Karolina Harris

Manufactured in the United States of America

10 9 8 7 6 5 4 3 2 1

Library of Congress Cataloging-in-Publication Data

Freedman, Samuel G.
    Who she was : a son's search for his mother's life / Samuel G. Freedman.
        p.   cm.
    1. Freedman, Eleanor, 1924–1974. 2. Jews—New York (State)—Biography.
3. Cancer—Patients—New Jersey—Highland Park—Biography. 4. Hatkin family. 5. Bronx (New York, N.Y.)—Biography. 6. Highland Park (N.J.)—Biography. I. Title.
F128.9.J5F74 2005
974.7'043'092—dc22   2004063396
[B]

ISBN 0-7432-2735-2

The author gratefully acknowledges permission from the following sources to reprint
material in their control: Forward Association, Inc., for excerpts from "The New
Year," published September 13, 1939, and "Treblinka: Now He's Telling What He
Lived Through There," published November 19, 1944; Hal Leonard Permissions for
"Prisoner of Love," words and music by Leo Robin, Clarence Gaskill, and Russ
Columbo, copyright 1931 (Renewed), Edwin H. Morris & Company, a Division of
MPL Music Publishing, Inc., Colgems-EMI Music, Inc., and Leo Rubin Music, All
Rights Reserved; Music Sales Corporation for "Ikh Bin A Mame" (I Am a Mother),
lyrics by Jennie Goldstein and Morris Rund, music by J. Jaffe, copyright © 1975 (Re-
newed) by Music Sales Corporation (ASCAP), International Copyright Secured, All
Rights Reserved; Warner Bros. Publications, Miami, FL 33014, for "They're Either
Too Young or Too Old," words by Frank Loesser, music by Arthur Schwartz, copy-
right © 1943 Warner Bros. Inc. (Renewed), All Rights Reserved, and "My Yiddishe
Momme," words and music by Jack Yellen and Lew Pollack, copyright ©1925 Chap-
pell & Co. and Ager-Yellen-Bornstein Inc. (Renewed), All Rights Reserved, and

Page 338 constitutes an extension of the copyright page.

For you, Carol
Some comfort, I hope,
in another sorrowful season

Contents

There is no present or future—only the past
happening over and over again.

EUGENE O'NEILL, *A Moon for the Misbegotten*

Who She Was

Prologue

ON A WINDSWEPT, darkening afternoon in December 2000, I brushed the snow away from the marker of my mother's grave. With each sweep of my gloved hand, the raised lettering of the simple plaque gradually became visible, showing her name, ELEANOR FREEDMAN, and the inscription our family had chosen: A SPECIAL PERSON. It had taken me some time to find the marker, even with a map from the cemetery office and a computer printout designating the exact location like the block-and-lot number in a suburban subdivision. I had not visited the grave in twenty-six years, since another December afternoon, when my family buried her.

I could still see, after so many years, the tears sliding out of my father's unblinking eyes. I could still hear my sister's howls of grief. But my memories of my mother herself had grown vaguer and less distinct over time. I could not remember the timbre of her voice or the pattern of her inflections. I could not summon her face without a photograph. What I did recall in all its shameful detail was the only visit she made to me at college, and my command that she sit rows apart from me in my classes, that we pretend to be strangers until we were safely blocks away from the classroom building. I was just eighteen then, two months into my freshman year a thousand miles from home, and in the full thrall of this new independence. She was already dying of cancer, pulling me back in love and obligation to the excruciating spectacle of her demise. From that day until this one, my memory of her illness, of our family's deathwatch, had eclipsed all the other memories of her existence.

Now I was forty-five, the same age my mother had been when a doctor found that first lump in her breast. I was only five years younger than she had been at her death. I was more than a decade into my marriage, as she had been in hers. I was the father of two children who looked at me, as I had looked at her, only as a parent, not someone with a whole autonomous life, most of which had preceded their arrival. And, as if my own wish during college were taking revenge on me, I had discovered that my mother was more and more a stranger to me. Besides having been my mother, besides having been my father's wife, besides having been someone who died miserably and died young, I did not know who she was.

In the quarter century since our family had interred her ashes, I had become my father's son, by choice and by default. My stepmother had been part of our family, and my life, for more years than my mother was. I had not even gone to the cemetery this bleak afternoon with the intent of visiting her grave. I was there instead for the burial of my father's sister Clara, a devoted anarchist from childhood until her dying day. On her part of the family tree, the Freedman part, lives were lived in bold political engagement. My grandfather and namesake had been sentenced to death as a teenaged radical in Poland; he fled from prison to England during a workers' uprising and bought a steerage ticket to America on a ship called the Titanic before deciding to sell it to a friend. Out in the Jersey farmlands, he raised his children in an anarchist colony with its own experimental school, and every year I attended the reunion, soaking up the tales of strikes, May Day parades, and Woody Guthrie concerts. That my grandfather Samuel died fourteen years before my own birth made him only more vivid, nearly mythological, in my imagination. My mother's people, the Hatkins, formed the conventional part of the family tree, the scufflers and schleppers in an East Bronx walk-up, relieved to make the rent every month. Fluent only in Yiddish, and disinclined to wear her hearing aid, my grandmother Rose had proven an impenetrable figure during my childhood. Sol, my grandfather, fussed and doted too much; my strongest memory of him was a day when I was eight or nine and he took me sledding, and kept insisting I rest between plunges down the hill. Years later, as a journalist, I had chanced upon a word to describe the whole clan, a bit of black slang, of all things. *Drylongso* was the term, meaning something that has been left dry for so long it is now ordinary as dust.

An odd thing had happened, though, during the previous few months. In conversations and occasional speeches, I found myself mentioning stray details from my mother's life—her pride when Bess Meyerson was the first Jew chosen as Miss America, her dancing in the streets when the United Nations voted statehood for Israel. I wasn't even aware at first of how often I was telling these stories until an old friend pointed it out. "I've known you twenty years," he said one night. "This is the first time I've ever heard you talk about your mother." His words jolted me. I had to ponder what my reflex to speak of her meant. I carried that mystery with me from place to place over the weeks, and eventually I came to an answer. I realized that, at last, I wanted to discover my mother's life. I wanted, almost literally, to claw at that frozen cemetery ground, to exhume the soil flecked with her residue, and from it to conjure the past.

She and I had been complicit in the sin of forgetting. For my part, I had built an identity on the rejection of my mother, on the imperative of denying all the softness in myself. On my first day of kindergarten, a block short of the schoolyard, I had ordered my mother to turn around and let me arrive alone. I spent an hour getting home that day, crossing the same few streets again and again, delirious in my show of autonomy. A straight line ran from that day to the day at college. The same straight line ran through every day when I so easily could have visited the grave and never did. The only way I could rationalize my mother's death at fifty, the only way I could make it bearable, was to transform it into some kind of precondition for my own adulthood, as if her coffin were my chrysalis.

When I eavesdropped on my wife talking every day to her mother, when I read novels like *Anywhere But Here* and watched movies like *Tumbleweeds,* I marveled in a judgmental and superior manner about mothers and daughters and their limitless capacity for entanglement. Love or hate, or both at once, the passion flowed, and it flowed without cease. What I understood firsthand was distance. I dared not remember my own dependence, feeling homesick at sleep-away camp or needing my mother's help with my algebra homework. I had delivered the main eulogy at her funeral, and yet I no longer could recall what I said, only the fatalistic line I quoted from Omar Khayyam: "The moving finger writes; and having writ, moves on." One night about two years after my mother died, I treated my college girlfriend to dinner at a fancy restaurant, and as we took our seats in our let's-pretend dress clothes, I realized I had eaten in the same place with my mother during her visit. I began to cry, as I never had cried at her death or funeral or burial. I have cried since then for others—for a friend's older brother killed in an Air Force training flight, for an editor and mentor felled by AIDS—but I never have let myself cry again for her.

My mother, I was sure, would have wanted my tears. She would not, I was equally certain, have wanted me to explore her past. While I rarely had asked about her life before marriage and motherhood, neither had she ever volunteered the information. I knew she had been some kind of ace student, because her jewelry box held a few academic medals. I knew in a general sense that she had been the family rebel, but I had no clue as to how and at what price she had purchased her freedom. Growing up, I had seen how she treated her father with patient indulgence and her mother with brusque contempt, which was more than returned in kind. During one of my grandmother's rare visits, my sister innocently walked into a bathroom to find the old woman methodically breaking every tube of lipstick my mother owned. One day when I was in eighth grade, my mother and I were stopped at a traffic light on the way home from Burger King. She met my eyes in the rear-view mirror, the same way she had a few years earlier when she explained the facts of life to me, and said offhandedly, "Did I ever tell you I was married before Dad?" I said no, and the subject was dropped, never to reemerge.

The same kind of ignorance, perhaps willful or maybe just lazy, alienated me from my mother's parents, too. It closed me off from all the history and heritage they embodied, all the experience, all the knowledge. From my mother's example, I absorbed a sense that Rose and Sol were insignificant, irrelevant in all ways except the genetic, not worth my curiosity or my questions. I accepted without elaboration the explanation my mother offered for my grandmother's leathery disposition: *Bubbe lost her whole family in the war.* Not even the simplest Jewish folkways reached me. On Rose's visits to our house, she often brought homemade blintzes, which she had wrapped in foil, frozen for preservation, and loaded by the dozen in a small cardboard box. All through my childhood, I gnawed them straight from the freezer like ice-cream pops, completely unaware that blintzes were meant to be cooked and eaten hot. When I first noticed blintzes served that way, at the sole Jewish deli near my college campus in Wisconsin, I inwardly snickered, thinking this was one of those Midwestern atrocities against ethnic food, like shrimp and pineapple on pizza.

My mother died three weeks before I was hired for my first job as a professional journalist, interning on a small daily newspaper. I learned first how to report events I had witnessed or that had occurred only hours or days before, the robberies and ball games and Board of Ed meetings. Gradually, over decades, I taught myself the kind of research a historian practices, the method of recapturing vanished times and remote lives. I had utilized those skills to write about other families in other books. Now, shivering in the December twilight, fingers and toes going numb, I decided to apply them to my own flesh and blood. My mother's two siblings were still alive. I knew the names of three or four of her girlfriends from high school, as well as a couple of beaus, although I had no way of knowing who lived where or was even alive. Some time in the previous few years, while rummaging through a storage area beside my childhood bedroom, I had stumbled onto a milk crate containing a half-dozen short stories, autobiographical in tone, each bearing a rusty paper clip and a rejection letter from *The New Yorker* or *The Saturday Review*. She had written them, evidently, for a class at The New School. As far back as I could recall, she was always taking a class in something—painting, sculpting, classical guitar, creative writing. Or she was until her illness required her to keep her days available for the oncologist.

For most of my childhood, we lived in a spacious brick house with a slate roof, sun porch, and two-car garage in the suburb of Highland Park, New Jersey, a bedroom community for Rutgers University. Like an odd cross between Horatio Alger and Alexander Berkman, my father David had grown from anarchist origins into a successful capitalist, building a storefront machine shop into an international corporation manufacturing microbiology equipment, much of which he designed himself. He and my mother read *I.F. Stone's Weekly*, canvassed for Gene McCarthy, and signed petitions for SANE, the ban-the-bomb group. They also firmly believed marijuana led to hard drugs and rolled their eyes at the white professors on the next block who subscribed to the Black Panther newspaper. Their marriage was better than some and worse than others; they argued but always managed to reconcile, if only out of shared commitment to their children. I was the oldest of three, with a sister, Carol, only eleven months behind me, and a brother, Ken, three years my junior. Until her cancer changed everything, my mother had led a Cub Scout troop, sewn Halloween costumes, baked birthday cakes in the shape of spaceships or choo-choo trains, and hopped the Penn Central to Manhattan for Broadway matinees.

She also descended, in rare and unpredictable times, into bouts of rage or gloom. When I was ten, our family was attending a potluck lunch at the local branch of the Workmen's Circle, a Yiddish cultural organization, when one of us children accidentally knocked several plates of food off the table. My mother stormed out and did not rejoin us at home for hours. Tucking me in that night, my father explained that she'd been moody since quitting cigarettes a few months earlier. It had taken a case of pneumonia to scare her off a three-pack-a-day habit. Occasionally at night I would find my mother asleep at the kitchen table, face down in the *Times*, a glass beside her. Once or twice, pulling a coat from the hall closet, my hand brushed against a cool cylindrical shape on a back shelf. Upon further inspection, the object turned out to be a flip-top canned cocktail. I returned it to its niche and said nothing to anyone.

I was fourteen years old on the summer Sunday my father first told me about my mother's diagnosis. She had begged him not to, but I was the eldest child, the one most able to accept the burden, the one who would have guessed soon enough that something was wrong. After I heard the news, I got on my bike and rode for a long time alone through the Rutgers campus, a pretty empty place at that time of year. Behind my impassive eyes, I imagined my brain exploding into a mushroom cloud.

On many nights in the weeks to follow, when I should have been asleep, the agitated voices of my parents seeped out of their bedroom and down the hallway into mine. Laying in bed, beneath my Mets pennant and Abbie Hoffman poster, I gathered what the dispute was all about. My father was pressing my mother to have a mastectomy. She was resisting. They had already lost valuable time, he warned her, all those months the gynecologist had been assuring them that the lump was benign. They had to act now, and they had to act radically, before the cancer spread. "I can't do it," my mother said, her tone distraught. "I will not be mutilated. I will not be disfigured."

Eventually, she compromised on submitting to a lumpectomy. As a family, we always had maintained a relaxed, casual attitude about the human body, shuttling through the main bathroom and the upstairs hallway in various stages of undress. Now, however, my father took me aside to explain that I must be careful never to barge in on my mother. She was ashamed of the scars on her breast. There was no convincing her she was still attractive. And even at the cost of her vanity, the lumpectomy soon proved quite literally too little, too late. That year, my sophomore year of high school, I learned the word *metastasize*. My mother commuted into Manhattan for rounds of chemotherapy and radiation. When I was a junior, she underwent a hysterectomy, in the hopes that stanching her hormones would slow the advance of the disease.

Throughout, my mother wanted nothing more fervently than for her family to ignore the battle even as she fought it. When she went into the city for treatment, she brought me back containers of beef stew from Macy's for school lunches. Within two months of the hysterectomy, she resumed playing tennis, hot flashes be damned. She worked part-time as a sales rep for an educational publisher, a job that could be fit around medical appointments. In the summer of 1973, my last summer before college, our family traveled to Greece, the country she always had longed to see. She hiked through the Parthenon and Delphi and exulted in our al fresco dinners of souvlaki, stuffed vine leaves, and ouzo. When my father grew a mustache on the trip, she chided, "Dave, you look like Nasser."

Three days after returning home from Greece, I left for college. At my insistence, I flew alone from New Jersey to Wisconsin to move into the dorm and register for classes. I put my mother on a quota of one letter and one phone call a week, which she promptly came up with reasons to break. One letter wistfully recalled that first day of kindergarten, and another confessed, "I wanted to throw myself in front of that plane and keep it from whisking you away." I shuddered that my roommate, a product of small-town Wisconsin with a Marine poster over his bed and the nickname Buck, ever would glimpse those words. I wore the armor of sophistication—my heroes were Lenny Bruce and Clarence Darrow—but inside it I felt incompetent at life. I was a virgin; I didn't yet need to shave. I shriveled amid the burly farm boys and the hirsute revolutionaries who were the campus's divided soul. Mostly, though, my mother wrote about the daily dross, how Carol was doing in the high school play and Ken on the track team, how a neighbor girl got a pet raccoon, never anything about her disease. From my father came a different set of letters, unsparing assessments:

Last week Mother went to have an X ray scan of her hip . . . for the detection of possible cancer in that area. . . . The tentative results appear to be that there may be some positive cancer activity in her bone tissue. . . . She seems quite depressed about the whole matter, which you can understand.

And several months later:

The X-ray group took a lot of her head & neck to see if there has been any spreading to her neck and skull bones.

And later still:

Regarding Dr. Escher's and Dr. Zucker's comments, I have asked them the very same question you have asked a number of times. Their answer is very simple—they just don't know and don't have any idea. It is really not possible for them to predict what the future will be, but that we must understand the nature of her illness and that it is serious and that it is not curable.

In the spring of 1974, my mother set about planning her own fiftieth birthday party. The Saturday night closest to the actual date happened to fall just between my week of spring break and the onset of summer vacation, and I complained that I didn't want to make yet another trip home. My mother, wisely, did not push the issue with me. It fell to my father to apply the correct pressure. "She bemoans the fact you might not be there," he wrote me, "even though it may be her last birthday." And, of course, that was the real issue. In an almost physical way, I felt my mother's disease pulling me back home, some giant magnet dragging me from my parallel universe of willful undergraduate oblivion. I wanted to put off the reckoning as long as possible.

As it turned out, the party was a blast. The house hummed with company, three generations of relatives and a lifetime's worth of friends, and everybody got looped on my uncle Ziggy's champagne-and-Cointreau punch. I found a different uncle, this one a painter, smoking pot in the laundry room, while in another corner a cousin by marriage was making out with somebody's husband. My mother had designed the invitations herself, with the silly doggerel, "Be thrifty, no gifty, to rhyme with fifty." She cooked up platters of moussaka, her new favorite since our trip to Greece, and draped herself in a print gown. Beneath it, hardly anyone knew, she had a cracked rib, the latest consequence of her cancer. Sometime well after midnight, the bacchanal wore itself out. I never saw my mother look so joyful again.

A few weeks after the party, I came home for the summer, and in some ways the summer of 1974 never has ended for me. It seared into my brain the sight of a broken woman—depleted, defeated, desiccated—to whom as a loyal son I was shackled. It seared into my brain every guilty effort I had made at escape, especially that day on the Wisconsin campus when I pretended not to know her. In the years since, friends have told me that I judge myself too harshly. They have told me any mother would have understood a teenaged son's display of emancipation. As a parent myself, I could accept these explanations at a cerebral level. In my soul, though, I still carried the stain. All those friends who had offered me reassurance—no, expiation—had grown into adulthood with mothers still alive and available for reconciliation. I stood frozen in the posture of rejection, frozen by my mother's early death, the eternal punctuation.

As I beheld her grave in December 2000, I wanted so fiercely to know who else she had been. I wanted to know about the family and the home and the neighborhood and the world in which she had grown. What did it mean to have come of age during the Depression, World War II, the Holocaust? I no longer could settle for the routine answers—*We were poor, but everybody was poor. . . . Bubbe lost her whole family.* What did those giant forces, forces that shook a planet, mean to my own mother? How did they shape her, or misshape her? I harbored no desire for cheap sentimentality or easy solace, but neither did I seek a bill of indictment, a lurid litany of dysfunction. The questions that seized me were of a more quotidian sort. Who was my mother before she became my mother? Whom did she love? Who broke her heart? What lifted her dreams? What crushed her spirit? What did she want to be? And did she ever get to be it in her brief time on earth?

My mother should have lived long enough to write her own story, the story she was groping toward in those yellowing pages I had discovered in the storage area. She was smart enough. She was skilled enough. She was young enough, young enough that she still should have been alive now, a graying grandmother in her late seventies, taking literature courses at Elderhostel. The duty never should have fallen to me, and yet I welcomed it, having failed in so many other filial duties. After all my years of rejecting her in life, after all my years of posthumous neglect, I finally had found the means of penance.

As dusk settled over the cemetery, I picked my way between the headstones and back toward the mourners still at Aunt Clara's grave. It was time to leave. It was time to pick up the tools of my craft, the pens and notebooks, the telephone and computer. I thought of them now as an archaeologist's instruments, as if I were scraping up the dirt of antiquity one spoonful at a time and sifting it through wire mesh to find what chip of pottery or fragment of bone might remain. As I collected the pieces and tried to assemble the skeleton, I told myself I wanted only one thing: to see my mother clear and true.

Fannie, Sol, Seymour, Rose, and Eleanor Hatkin,
Crotona Park, Rosh Hashanah, September 1939

One

Becoming

[1938–1941]

ELEANOR HATKIN AWOKE on the morning of her
first day of high school. She was three months shy of
fourteen years old and sharing a narrow daybed and
single blanket with her younger sister Fannie. Some-

times, especially lately, her world felt just as cramped and confining.

The first spears of daylight were striking the slit of a courtyard that divided the six-story tenement at 1461 Boston Road from its companion building at 1459. It was twenty-one degrees and still dropping outside, and the northwest wind swirled in the concrete gap and squirmed through the open kitchen window of Apartment 24, the Hatkins' home. The chill made Eleanor and Fannie more reluctant than usual to relinquish the covers, but their parents, Sol and Rose, were convinced that fresh cold air guaranteed health, even if the same prescription had given Eleanor double pneumonia in infancy.

Sol Hatkin had crept out of the apartment an hour earlier into the six o'clock darkness, heading from the East Bronx to Lower Manhattan for a day's piecework at the LeValle shoe factory. Because he had some work, he could spring two cents for the *Daily News,* and as the Third Avenue El lumbered along, he looked over its front-page headline, NAVY CHIEF LISTS PERILS TO THE U.S. That meant, of course, perils from Germany, Italy, and Japan, though much of Congress was convinced the warning was just more of Franklin Roosevelt's trickery to drag America into Europe's war.

Meanwhile, Rose had pinned back her hair under a kerchief, laced up the corset for her bad back, and tugged on a tattered housedress and a worn, oversized pair of shoes. They were Sol's old ones, large enough to spare her bunions and corns. She clomped into the sole bedroom, jostling seven-year-old Seymour from the cot beside her and Sol's bed, and then rousing Fannie and Eleanor in the parlor that tripled for living, dining, and sleeping. "Drink," she commanded, and the children made their way separately to the kitchen table.

Rose fetched a pail of milk from the windowsill, her secondary icebox in the winter months. The milk's surface was frozen across. For Fannie and Seymour, Rose set out soft-boiled eggs and bowls of lumpy farina. Then each reported dutifully for a spoonful of cod-liver oil. Everybody in the house knew better than to expect Eleanor to consent. Breakfast was just one more occasion for rebellion. She pulled the bobby pins from her hair and shook it free into waves. She went into the apartment's lone closet for first choice of the several dresses she and Fannie wore, $1.69 specials from Alexander's bought with their own babysitting money. Only then did she cross the foyer to the kitchen and serve herself bread and cheese.

This morning, of all mornings, offered the proof of her independence. A week ago, she had graduated from junior high school; today, February 1, 1938, she was entering Morris High School. Because the school was so crowded with the children of the East Bronx's Jewish immigrants, it admitted incoming classes twice yearly, and ran them on the later half of its split session, beginning at 10:25 AM. So when Fannie left for Junior High School 40 at eight o'clock, and Rose walked Seymour to Public School 61, Eleanor had the apartment to herself. There was nobody to object when she switched on the radio at a quarter past nine and tuned it to WNEW and her favorite show, "The Make Believe Ballroom."

It was not as if the family challenged her. The family adored her. She was the unquestioned star. She could fling herself across the couch with a book in one hand and a jar of peanut butter in the other and not move again until she had consumed them both. She was learning to play the piano at a settlement house. She led the Sabbath table in the Yiddish songs she and Fannie learned at the Arbeiter Ring. *Eins und tsvei and drei und fier. Vus mir zeinin, zeinin mir, One and two and three and four, What we are is what we are.* In junior high, she'd been the class treasurer and editor of the student newspaper. A classmate, signing her autograph book, addressed her not as "Eleanor" but as "Brilliance." And whenever Fannie, a year and a grade younger, had a book report due, she copied one of Eleanor's old ones, the surest route to an A.

The neighborhood used to seem capacious enough for all her joys and longings. She roller-skated down the Bristow Avenue hill. She jumped rope double-Dutch on the sidewalk. A tailor gave her extra bits of fabric and buttons for her dolls, and when the shoemaker saw her skipping past his window, he called out, "That's right, darling, skip, skip. You'll wear your shoes out faster that way." On Monday and Friday afternoons, Rose's times for doing the laundry and preparing for the Sabbath, she gave the children three pennies apiece, and Eleanor spent hers on a bagful of *arbislach,* chick peas, dripping with butter. She was friends with Fannie's friends, Ruth Klekman and Hilda Saltzman and Clare Abramowitz, and most of all she was friends with Fannie. Summer after summer, they tilled garden plots in Crotona Park, growing carrots and beets and Swiss chard, learning the names of flowers and birds from a lady named Riley who wore khakis and a pith helmet.

As Eleanor stepped out onto Boston Road alone in midmorning, defiantly hatless in the piercing wind, the familiar remained predictably in place. Just up the block, on the ground floor of 1465, Kopelov's candy store whipped up egg creams and Charlotte Russes, and had a phone where you could get calls for two cents. Across the way from Kopelov's stood Consolidated Laundries, sending the tang of chlorine and soap powder into the air. Down the street from Consolidated was the Loew's Boston Road, a second-echelon movie house offering free dishes on Monday nights; the marquee was being changed from the weekend double feature of *A Damsel in Distress* and *Fight for Your Lady* to *The Bride Wore Red* and *Fifty-Second Street*. Along the steel rail embedded in the street's cobblestones clattered the Boston Road trolley, sparks flicking off its electric pole.

All were, in certain ways, reminders of what lay out of reach, or what required painful sacrifice. Five cents for a Charlotte Russe, a nickel for a streetcar ride—those were luxuries beyond the Hatkin budget. The children knew not even to ask. To see a dime movie at the Loew's Boston Road, Eleanor would collect milk bottles for the three-cent deposit. She didn't begrudge her parents the constraints. She could barely remember a time before the Great Depression, a time when Kopelov's storefront had contained a savings and loan branch with marble floors, before it was felled by a run on the bank.

Eleanor walked south on Boston Road, her shadow etched sharply on the pavement. The cloudless sky poured light unforgivingly on the dirt-streaked windows of empty stores, the sagging unkempt awnings of the struggling shops, the signs admitting PRICES DOWN TO THE BOTTOM! or STORE FOR RENT—SUITABLE FOR ALL PURPOSES. There were people in the neighborhood who shared eyeglasses to save money. Dentists did two-dollar fillings on 25-cent installments; their patients stuffed cotton in the drilled-out cavities until they were done paying for the bit of silver to be tapped into place. A summertime vendor in Crotona Park sold the lyrics to hit songs—not sheet music, just the handwritten words—for a nickel apiece. "I cash clothes," chanted the local peddler who dealt in hand-me-downs. Old men with violins or accordions plied the alleys and vacant lots, warbling Yiddish ballads for whatever coins some pitying housewife might toss out the window.

In the brick tenements that lined the street, this was an especially desperate day, the first of the month, the day rent was due. Eleanor knew her own parents rarely got their forty-two-dollar rent in on time. But at least they got it in. It was commonplace at the juncture of months to find belongings piled on the sidewalk—hutch, valises, mattresses, radio—and a dispossessed family silently bearing a tin cup for handouts. Not that the landlords were making out, either. Apartments dangled shingles with offers of "concession," meaning a free month or two or three in the hope of landing a paying tenant. Some families jumped from one concession to the next, stealthily decamping in what were known as "midnight moves."

Still, even amid deprivation so widespread it passed for normality, Eleanor could not help but know the sensation of wanting. Lately she had been asking Rose why their family couldn't eat steak on Sunday and turkey on Thanksgiving, like Americans did. On the shopping strip of Fordham Road, Freed's was featuring girls' dresses with "smart bolero effects," a style inspired by the gown Wallis Simpson had worn to marry a king. When the Hatkins visited their better-off relatives, Eleanor noticed how the Osders had an electric mixer, the Schneers had a refrigerator. And these were the same Schneers who had been living in 1461 only a few years earlier. Depression or no, they'd escaped the walk-up for an apartment house with an elevator, paid for with the take from father Harry's hat store.

Eleanor's aspirations went beyond the material. She imagined becoming a bacteriologist and considered Madame Curie her personal hero. She dreamed of crossing the river to Manhattan for something besides the bargain table at S. Klein with its dresses piled like animal hides. A boy who'd gone to Morris, Clifford Odets, had a hit play on Broadway right now, *Golden Boy*. Eleanor devoured the novels of Charles Nordhoff, adventure tales of the South Seas. While Nordhoff was best known for *Mutiny on the Bounty*, Eleanor most loved *The Hurricane,* a vision of Polynesia through the eyes of a French doctor.

These days, a palpable divide was growing between herself and Fannie, and their distance was only partly the function of nineteen months' difference in age. Fannie drew comfort from the commonplaces of household and neighborhood that now bored Eleanor. Dutiful and undemanding, she was content with the meals, the markets, the relatives, the religion. Her best friends lived within a block or two of 1461, and her world needed to stretch no farther to provide happiness. Fannie admired Eleanor's will without feeling the faintest temptation to imitate it.

Eleanor had her own separate social life with her own separate friends. Two blocks to her right the pavement gave way to Crotona Park and all the way across it, in connected buildings on Fulton Avenue, lived Vicky Behar and Lillian Golden. With Eleanor, they called themselves "The Three Musketeers." They could spend hours on parkside benches, watching Joe Lempert glide past standing on his bicycle seat because he had such a crush on Vicky, rolling their eyes when fancy-pants Leon Mandelbaum tried to lecture them on the glories of classical music. Propping her elbows on a pillow in her kitchen window, Vicky's mother gazed benevolently on the antics. Sometimes she looped twine through a dozen of her special donut-shaped cookies—*biscochos,* a specialty of Sephardic Jews from her native Turkey— and lowered them to the girls. "In Vicky's house,"

Eleanor would say accusingly on her return to 1461, "they're always laughing."

Eleanor's other group called itself "the Union Avenue Gang" for the street she was just now crossing on her way to Morris. The gang passed summer nights on the stoop or in the hallway of the building that was home to four members, the Goldfarb brothers Sol and Sidney and the Adler sisters Regina and Monikou, Czech Jewish refugees. Eleanor's oldest friend, Marion Herzog, was part of the crowd, mooning over Artie Fluger. Regina Adler was old enough at sixteen to be going out with boys, and the rest spent hours practicing flirtation, weighing the risks of a goodnight kiss on a first date, asking about whether they should "do sex" or not, as if any of them had the slightest idea what it was.

Meanwhile on this morning, Eleanor pushed farther down the blocks of Boston Road, each thoroughly known. At McKinley Square, where 169th Street and Franklin Avenue converged, the carved granite masks of Comedy and Tragedy hung over the McKinley Square Theater, where Rose took in Yiddish shows. Just around the corner beckoned the Morrisania branch of the public library, more like a mansion with its arched windows and elegant staircase. Eleanor had grown up borrowing books there six at a time. A narrow dingy store across the street sold used books and magazines, and for a treat Sol would go there to buy Eleanor the Bobbsey Twins and Outdoor Girls series. Eleanor herself had been avoiding the place since the time she planted her palm in a pool of rat piss on a counter. A few blocks further down Boston Road, nearly all the way to Morris, the Jackson Democratic Club, the machine's legation in the Fourth Assembly District, held forth behind the plaster pillars of a second-floor office. Sol was a regular.

The biggest change of all for Eleanor had begun two autumns ago, when she first noticed the red stain in her panties. She stayed home from school, sure she was slowly bleeding to death, until Rose finally teased out the cause. "You're not dying," she said. "You're just sick. You'll get sick every month and you'll get better, too." Then Rose shredded an old pillowcase into a sanitary napkin and spoke nothing more of symptom, cause, or meaning. It was up to Eleanor herself to figure out that this monthly catastrophe, this private disgrace, had something to do with her ripening of her body and the nascence of desire.

She stood five-foot-six already, taller than either of her parents. She had glossy hair to her shoulders and skin such a deep olive that even among Jews it seemed exotic. When she parted her lips a bit, tilted her head forward, and widened her brown eyes, she broadcast a sense of expectancy. But her overcoat covered a thickening middle, the product of peanut butter and milk, bread and cheese, all those cheap staples. Worse, she had just gotten glasses, with hideous pink frames. To other girls, there was nothing wrong with Eleanor's looks; they'd have been amazed to learn how desperately, even irrationally, she feared swelling into a size 18. Guys were the only reliable test of allure. On those afternoons when Eleanor

lay splayed across the daybed with a book, she waited
for a knock on the door from Kopelov's errand boy with
the word that somebody, somebody male, was on the
phone for her down in the store. And the summons never
came. "They're jealous, that's why," Rose explained of
the nonexistent suitors. "You're too smart for them." It
was hard to say which was worse for Eleanor, the feeble
excuse or getting it from her mother.

What Eleanor knew of romance she knew from the
movies. For months now, she had been stuck on *Rosalie*. Nobody told Eleanor Powell she was too smart to
have a boyfriend. There she was on the screen, a Vassar
coed lounging in silk pajamas, and secretly a European
princess besides, and she had Nelson Eddy as the football star of West Point, Nelson Eddy with blond hair
and rolling shoulders, serenading her from outside the
dorm window in his operatic baritone. And that was
only the first reel. When Rosalie returned to her country, unhappily betrothed to a prince, her football star
flew across the ocean like Lindbergh to woo her and
wed her. *Rosalie* was all around. In just a week, Eleanor
Powell would be doing her tap-dancing act at four
moviehouses in the Bronx. The title song had climbed
onto the Hit Parade, and it spoke right to a different
Eleanor's fantasies.

Rosalie, my darling
Rosalie, my dream
Since one night when stars danced above
I'm oh, oh, so much in love

For now, Eleanor continued on her route beneath fire escapes and beer signs, past trucks delivering loads of coal or eggs, across sidewalks chalked with grids for potzie or skelly, beyond newsstands with their racks of papers riffling and snapping in the wind. The walk that would become her daily routine—fifteen minutes, three-quarters of a mile—was nearing its destination, and no longer was Eleanor solitary. Off the trolley and down the side streets tumbled her impending classmates, by the dozen, by the score, by the hundred. They wore bar mitzvah suits and shined shoes for this moment. They wore starched dresses with matching hair bows. They stepped, most of them, anyway, with alacrity.

Above them all, at the intersection of Boston Road and 166th Street, loomed Morris High School. Stretching 312 feet across, rising 179 to a crenellated tower, adorned with terra cotta trim and cathedral windows and gabled corners, it both intimidated and uplifted the scuffling streets that fell so literally in its shadow. Morris embodied an architectural style known as English Collegiate Gothic, one immeasurably alien to a community fresh from *shtetl* and steerage, and yet the school's designer, C. B. J. Snyder, had envisioned his creation as one both elite and democratic. He called Morris "the people's college." In that same spirit, the president of Columbia University, Nicholas Murray Butler, had declared on Morris's dedication day in 1904, "If our city is to be great and memorable it will be because we succeed in placing it by the side of Jerusalem, Athens, and Rome as the intellectual and spiritual capital."

At the foot of the tower, Eleanor Hatkin mounted a half-dozen steps and stepped through a graystone archway into the center hall. There the light glowed from fixtures built to resemble chandeliers. Already the world was growing larger, large enough, perhaps, to accommodate her ambitions.

Even at noon on a brilliant winter day, Apartment 24 stayed a dusky place. Its three rooms were Rose Hatkin's domain, her portion of America after nearly twenty years. She presided over an icebox, a gas stove, a tub for both bathing and laundry, a cabinet holding separate sets of meat and dairy dishes, a buffet storing linens in the absence of sufficient closets. When the superintendent was ready for the day's garbage, he banged on a pipe and Rose shoved the family trash into the dumbwaiter. From the hallway she could hear the footsteps of neighbors, plodding at routine intervals to and from their jobs as tailors, cutters, pressers, painters. The kitchen window admitted its sliver of southern light as well as the judders and squeaks of a horse-drawn vegetable cart and the occasional howls of wife-beating somewhere across the courtyard.

Rose treated her territory with selective attention. She washed the floors so tenaciously that she stripped off the varnish and turned the sodden planks black, and yet she piled clothes and sheets on furniture like so many *shmattes*, like rags. Nearing forty, she appeared just as careworn. Her skin was ruddy, her face rutted and creased, her thin lips drawn downward, so that on those occasions when she smiled, the effort pushed her eyes into a squint, as if pleasure went against her nature. "Happiness," she often told her children, "isn't important."

The few sentimental objects in the apartment rested within a china chest that had been acquired in better times. It contained an inkwell lined with tiny seashells, a souvenir of Rose's honeymoon with Sol at Niagara Falls. A small blue glass, painted with a picture of Shirley Temple, held spare change when there was any. One shelf bore a growing collection of Eleanor's academic medals and prizes. On another stood two brass candlesticks, religiously polished, that Rose had carried with her from Poland on the S.S. Susquehanna in December 1920. They told her where her heart belonged.

Rachel Markiewicz, as she was born in 1899, had never wanted to come to America. She had never chosen to come to America. No, the process had been more like conscription, more like involuntary servitude. The Markiewicz family had uprooted itself once already, moving from the Polish town of Kalnik into the burgeoning industrial center of Bialystok. Yehuda Ariyeh, Rose's father, may have taught in *cheder* in the time-honored way, but his seven children were moderns, almost to the one. They lived in a city of textile mills and department stores and landscaped parks for weekend strolls. Bialystok throbbed with Zionism, the Bund, and the one-world dream of Esperanto, a language invented in the city. Among the Markiewiczes, one son went underground to make revolution, another joined a theater troupe, and a sister married into a family that owned a beauty salon. There teenaged Rose learned to style hair, and how to bob her own. When she posed for portraits, she wore a pearl necklace, whether costume or real, and belted dresses that showed her buxom figure to advantage.

She was not ignorant of the risks of being Jewish in Eastern Europe, having once had a tsarist soldier tear her earrings off as war booty. During World War I, Russian troops had pillaged and razed scores of Bialystok's factories, and entering the 1920s, 40 percent of the work force remained unemployed. In a protest against the anti-Semitism of the restored Polish regime soon to govern their city, Bialystok's Jews boycotted the municipal elections of 1919.

So as the youngest child in the Markiewicz family, and the only one unmarried, Rose received the role of savior by default. She was assigned to travel across the ocean to earn money to bring over her brothers and sisters. A maternal aunt already in New York put forward the ship's ticket and arranged a job making hairnets. Two years later, Rose attended the wedding of her cousin Rachel Gartenberg, who was marrying a hatmaker appropriately named Jacob Hatkin, and there she encountered a man she had met before in passing, the groom's brother Sol. On June 10, 1923, awash in tulle, ribbons, and appliqué, Rose spoke her own bridal vows. Within two months, she was pregnant.

The Hatkins lived in the Jewish slum of Brownsville, Brooklyn, with the provocative company of Sol's mother Sarah, at whom Rose once heaved her treasured candlesticks. Two daughters arrived, Eleanor in April 1924 and Fannie in November 1925. Sol worked steadily enough in shoe factories to sit with Rose for a studio portrait that captured him with pocket watch and fob, her with a plunging neckline. More importantly, several months before the stock market crash of 1929 and the onset of the Depression, the family moved to the Bronx. The borough's rocky elevation, Sol had been reliably assured, would ease the rheumatism afflicting Rose in damp, low-lying Brooklyn. Subway and El lines, newly extended northward from Manhattan, made for a convenient commute to the Lower East Side's sweatshops. The apartment houses, even in the working-class districts, boasted marble lobbies, tiled halls, cornices. Moving to the Bronx meant getting up in the world. "Mama, darling," Al Jolson had put it in *The Jazz Singer,* "if I'm a hit in this show, we're going to move up to the Bronx. A whole lot of green grass up there and a whole lot of people you know. The Ginsbergs, the Guttenbergs, the Goldbergs. Oh, a whole lot of Bergs."

Now, nearly a decade later, Rose indeed resided among plenty of familiar names. The thirty-seven apartments in 1461 harbored Cohens, Friedmans, Berkowitzes, Sarnoffs, Novicks, Stephinskys. The Bronx counted nearly 600,000 Jews; in the neighborhoods south of Tremont Avenue, among them the Hatkins' district of Morrisania, the population was 80 percent Jewish, more thoroughly Jewish than Bialystok. For all that, the Bronx had brought Rose neither material nor emotional comfort. It had only sharpened her nostalgia for the old country and whetted the longing from an heirloom into a weapon.

"Nothing is as good as it was there," she pronounced with regularity. She said it of the bread and of the rabbis and of Passover. When she saw the kosher certification on packaged food, she sniffed, "It's a business here." She dismissed the movies as junk for *Amerikanesher dopesht,* American dopes. She read no American newspapers, only the Yiddish *Forverts* when she could borrow a copy, and often she wept over the advice column, *Bintel Brief,* especially the letters from exploited boarders and unappreciated parents.

In many ways, Rose was just a typical Bialystoker. Maybe other Eastern European Jews, the rabble, saw America as the *Goldeneh Medinah,* the Golden Land, their deliverer from poverty and persecution. Bialystokers lamented immigration as exile. They even used the biblical word for it, *golus.* Bialystok was the *muter shtot,* the mother city, or the *Mutterland,* the motherland. As émigrés like Rose Hatkin sent millions of dollars to support their relatives abroad, philanthropy that by its very definition attested to the untenable conditions back home, they improbably romanticized their beleaguered birthplace. "Our hearts beat as strongly for little Bialystok as for the whole world," wrote one contributor to *Bialystoker Stimme,* Voice of Bialystok, a monthly magazine published in New York. "[F]or in Bialystok one felt in a way which was impossible to feel anywhere else." One of Eleanor's classmates, first in junior high and now at Morris, had a grandmother from Bialystok. She concluded every letter to her relatives there with the same words. *"Gevalt! Rottevetmir! M'gehtimir bagroben tvishen die goyim."* Help! Save me! They're going to bury me among the gentiles. That cry could have been Rose's own.

But there was something beyond fealty to Bialystok in Rose's temperament, something more like a willful resistance to Americanization, a retreat from modernity itself. She waited sixteen years after immigrating to apply for citizenship. She spoke English so poorly even after a decade in New York that a census worker in 1930 recorded Rose's daughters' names as Helen and Hanah. Only by copying an example written by her children could Rose sign her name on their report cards. She feared 1461's superintendent, Mr. Libby, a German immigrant eager to tout all the jobs and roads Hitler was creating. She feared the Italian Catholic lady in the building, Mrs. Profeti, who joked, "Your kids are better looking than mine. I think they switched them at the hospital." When a neighbor's boy was bitten by a dog, Rose advised cutting some of the animal's hair and having the child smell it. She was becoming more of a peasant than she'd ever been in Poland.

What resourcefulness she had, she reserved for two causes and two families—keeping her own off home relief and getting that of her favorite sister far from the Nazis. Rose conceived of relief as humiliation rather than sustenance, and in that conviction she was not entirely wrong. Lillian Golden, Eleanor's friend, had seen her own mother sob when the home relief inspectors showed up unannounced, rifling through every drawer and closet to make sure she wasn't a chiseler. A caseworker checking up on the Klekmans, whose daughter was part of Fannie's crowd, treated four cups of chocolate pudding cooling on a windowsill as incriminating evidence. Rather than endure the indignity, Rose cut corners until there was no middle left. She stored potatoes under her bed. She patched underwear. On the Thanksgiving when Eleanor wished for turkey, Rose managed tuna fish. When Seymour returned from dinner at a friend's house raving about beef, a new dish for him, Rose dismissed it as "junk, junk." She bought the family's food at the Jennings Street market, a warren of pushcarts and herring barrels, crates of produce and tubs of pickles, the most renowned of them presided over by Jake and his wife, who thrust her hand, diamond ring and all, into the brine to fill orders. To save pennies, Rose plucked chickens herself and carried home live carp for gefilte fish, letting them swim in the bathtub until being dispatched with a rolling pin. "You have two days ago bread?" she asked the baker. "Stale bread? Cheaper?" And when there just plain was not enough money, Rose picked through the market garbage for bruised tomatoes and peppers, the discarded outer leaves of cabbage, the shorn tops of carrots. These she chopped and mashed into vegetable cutlets, the household staple that made Eleanor groan in protest. The Hatkin table proved the Yiddish proverb that said, "When a poor man eats a chicken, one of them is sick."

Somehow, Rose managed to scrounge money to send abroad. She bought tickets to Yiddish musicals at the McKinley Square Theater and sold them at a slight markup, a common fund-raising technique among Bialystokers. She skimmed change from Sol's pockets and hid it in a sack tucked amid the box springs. Or else she bargained for used clothing from the Bathgate Avenue peddlers, sending it overseas for her relatives to sell. The object of all these efforts was Ester Dina, the poorest sister among the Markiewiczes and the most traditional, married to a Talmud scholar named Alter David Kaczkowicz. In 1928, with the United States virtually closed to immigration, Rose pulled together $70, the equivalent of several weeks' pay for Sol, to purchase Alter David a steerage ticket to Uruguay. Six years later, with $150 from Rose, Alter David's two eldest children, eighteen-year-old Judis and seventeen-year-old Julius, rode a train across Europe and boarded the cargo ship Belle Isle in Le Havre to join their father in Montevideo. Distant though it was from both New York and Bialystok, Uruguay was a sensible destination, a country that espoused an American-style commitment to the melting pot, strictly separated church and state, and, most usefully of all, did not charge a fee for a visa. But three younger Kaczkowicz children remained in Bialystok, and with them Ester Dina, Rose's blood. Every letter to the Bronx from over there, every postcard, every snapshot, carried the same parting phrase: "*Oyf aybig gedenken*," Forever remembering. As if Rose could possibly forget.

She found relief and recognition at the McKinley Square Theater more than anywhere else. There were Yiddish theaters elsewhere in New York, especially on Second Avenue on the Lower East Side, that performed adaptations of Shakespeare or contemporary dramas by the likes of Sholom Asch. The Adlers starred on those stages; Boris Aronson designed for them. The McKinley Square Theater was not such a place. It specialized in the melodramas and musicals known as *shund* theater, trash theater. The thespians of McKinley Square trafficked in flailing arms and tremulous arias, and the audience could be counted on to flagrantly weep or guffaw as the plot required. The heroine of *shund* theater was the immigrant mother, martyred and long-suffering, afflicted by ungrateful children, ridiculed as an Old World vestige. For three-night runs, the McKinley Square mounted shows like *Sins of Mothers, Mothers and Children, My Mother's Lullaby, A Mother's Heart.* The songs of Yiddish musicals consecrated "A Mother's Worth," "A Mother's Wish," "A Mother's Tears"; they admonished "Mother Is Your Best Friend" and "A Mother You Must Obey." The most famous song of them all was "Yiddishe Mama," a hit for Sophie Tucker in 1925 and a validation for Rose Hatkin in 1938.

Ikh vil bay aykh a kasha fregn:
Zogt mir ver es ken,

Mit velkhe taeyer farmegers
Bentsch Got alemen . . .

A yiddishe mama,
Es gibt nit besser in der velt;
A yiddishe mama,
Oy vey, vi biter ven zi felt
Vi sheyn un likhtik iz in hoyz
Ven di mama is do . . .

Nit haltn ir tayer,
Dos is gevis di gresta zind.

I want to ask you a question
And tell me the answer, whoever can
With which treasure
Does God bless everyone? . . .

A Jewish mother
There's nothing better in the world
A Jewish mother
Oh, woe, how bitter when she is missing
How pretty and bright it is in the house
When the mother is here . . .

Not cherishing her
Is certainly the greatest sin.

In just a few nights, on the Friday evening of February
4, the McKinley Square would open its newest produc-

tion, a musical comedy called *Rachel Becomes A Bride*. With her eldest daughter almost fourteen, Rose could soon entertain just such hopeful fantasies.

Two weeks into February and the new semester, Elmer E. Bogart brought his craggy frame to the stage of the Morris High School auditorium to address a convocation of the elite, past and future. For twenty years the principal of Morris, Bogart was a New Englander who had graduated from Cornell in 1894 and grown into a scholar of Greek and Latin, a world traveler who once attended the installation of a pope. With his stiff, high-collared shirts and pince-nez spectacles, he exuded the aura of a former century. The immigrant parents of Morrisania applauded or even bowed as he strode into school each morning from his motorcar.

Into the curving rows of wooden seats before Bogart settled the object of those parents' hopes and his own, the finest 150 students in a school of 3,000, Eleanor Hatkin among them. This select number had earned admission to the Goodwin School, the honors program named for Morris's first principal. Virtually all of them, including Eleanor, had skipped one grade in elementary school and combined three years of junior high into two in the program known as Rapid Advance. The juniors and seniors in the auditorium already knew about Elmer Bogart and the Goodwin School. The incoming sophomores, brainy and naive all at once, were about to find out.

The Goodwin School required the study of two foreign languages and an accelerated course of mathematics and science. It mandated a semester of economics, a subject Eleanor and her classmates had barely heard of until this day. The course in "physical training" included a unit of fencing. A student in the Goodwin School could amass fifteen or twenty college credits while at Morris. But academic excellence was not all the Goodwin School demanded. Each student in it received a kind of membership booklet, which listed the "ennobling principles" and "vital characteristics" of the program's namesake, from "fair play" to "immaculate cleanliness." "I pledge myself," the Goodwin students stated, "to sympathetic understanding, personal responsibility, courage, and truth." And also punctuality: Mr. Bogart stood outside Morris's front door each morning with his watch.

For Eleanor and the rest, the setting magnified the gravitas. The Morris auditorium was a grand and serious place, with stained glass windows, arched stone ceiling, and a pipe organ the width of the stage. Murals hung on both the east and west walls—scenes of Bronx history, which had been donated by the Municipal Art Society—and above the proscenium stretched a tableau honoring the Morris faculty and students who had fought in the Great War. It showed the charred ruins of a French village and on the horizon, where the sky was clearing, an American flag being raised.

The ceremony this morning marked a transition that was more than simply generational. Like their principal, many of the Morris teachers were old-stock Americans, Protestants raised in North Dakota or St. Louis, educated at Dartmouth or Columbia. They were, at the same time, a worldly sort, cosmopolitans who had ascended the Alps, explored the Andes on horseback, committed *Paradise Lost* to memory. And they held to their own ancestral notions of propriety. Morris maintained separate gyms and cafeterias for the genders. Only recently had the dean of girls, Charlotte Knox, ceased her morning ritual of monitoring skirt lengths and inspecting fingernails for offending polish.

The Goodwin pupils, even more than the student body as a whole, were Jews. Eleanor's sophomore class was the roster of an Ellis Island manifest: Fleischman, Fisherson, Solomon, Gantz, Goodman, Sokolsky, Hirsch, Hirschman, Kraft, Kreisman, Koval, Kolander. Even the Negro boy in the program, a violin prodigy named Levi Bough, belonged to a congregation of Black Hebrews. Few had ever met a Presbyterian or Methodist; few had traveled much farther than the Grand Concourse. They experienced the wider world mostly through the distorting lens of the movies and the siren call of big band radio shows, so they craved Clark Gable, Deanna Durbin, and the jitterbug, all of it vapidity to their elders. The previous year, an elevator operator at Morris had knocked the harmonica out of the mouth of a boy playing dance tunes.

What these students offered their teachers was the ferocious aspiration fed of penury. The Goodwin School promised the way out of walkups and sweatshops, out of watching your mother faint because she hadn't eaten in two days and your father trudge home from the relief office with boots and a shovel for his job clearing snow. An 85 average essentially guaranteed a boy entrance to City College, "the poor man's Harvard." A girl could aim for Hunter College, also a public institution free for the qualified, and train to become a teacher, the finest occupation available for a Jewish woman.

Eleanor felt such appetites; she bore them the way, in a different family, a firstborn son might. For all Rose Hatkin didn't understand or care to understand about America, she always had insisted that Eleanor take the academic track in school. Rose did not know that Morris consigned the girls in its commercial curriculum (typing, steno, bookkeeping) to a dingy annex until senior year. She did not know that other girls in the Goodwin School—Ruth Liebowitz, Bea Flesichman—had parents who told them, "You'll get a job and you'll go to work." Rose simply had absorbed in some blunt, visceral way the realization that her eldest child, who had entered kindergarten speaking only Yiddish, was brilliant. She had been hearing it from teachers at least as far back as Miss Clancy in second grade. All those awards in the china chest proved it. Much as Eleanor resisted the messenger, she accepted the message. Besides, she had a model of her own. Across the courtyard from her apartment, in the connected building of 1459 Boston Road, lived a paternal cousin named Leonard Hatkin, the closest thing in her life to an older brother. Leonard was attending City College right now, majoring in physics, picking up Russian and French, going to the fifty-cent classical concerts at Lewisohn Stadium. To hear his stories of college when the families shared a meal, just to see him walking to the streetcar with his briefcase, was to glimpse a future.

For now, Eleanor started every day in official class (that is, homeroom) 3–21, alongside Marion Herzog, her oldest friend. The girls had met in Mrs. Krim's kindergarten in the autumn of 1929, and although they attended different junior high schools, they had stayed close as cohorts in the Union Avenue Gang. Of all Eleanor's girlfriends, Marion was the one who most shared her intellectual bent, the one who also frequented the Morrisania Library, the one with whom she could talk about books like a grown-up. If anything, Marion took the life of the mind even more seriously than did Eleanor. By age five, she had resolved to become a lawyer; two years later, she commenced piano studies with the goal of Carnegie Hall. Her own grandmother called her *alter kup,* old head.

Despite all the affinity between the girls, or maybe because of it, currents of envy and competition coursed through their friendship. Marion's mother, Florence, cut a figure of assimilation and style, precisely the traits Rose Hatkin lacked. Although she had immigrated from Rumania at age six, Florence spoke flawless, unaccented English, and worked as a saleslady at Levine and Smith, one of the fancier stores on the Lower East Side. With her hazel eyes, statuesque figure, and a complexion out of Titian, she was often taken to be Marion's sister. The Herzogs, mother and daughter, lived in a first-floor railroad flat just off Boston Road on Minford Place, but into it Florence brought such treats as a plastic pumpkin from Schrafft's filled with candies for Halloween and a volume of Walt Whitman from the book department at Macy's. She relaxed her ironclad rule against buying on credit to purchase a set of the Encyclopedia Brittanica and a Baldwin Studio piano.

Marion wasn't so impressed with Morris High and the Goodwin School. She had wanted to go to Evander Childs with her junior high school pals, or to Christopher Columbus, the brand-new high school in the middle-class neighborhood lining Pelham Parkway. Marion viewed Morris as a dilapidated brickpile, and, in fact, it was awaiting nearly $20,000 in repairs to its radiators, floors, plumbing, and wiring. In that supposedly glorious auditorium, she gashed her right foot on a rusty nail.

For all that, Marion coveted what Eleanor had, two parents at home. Marion's own father had died when she was five. Her mother's only day off from Levine and Smith was Friday, and those weekends alone in the railroad flat were crushingly quiet. In the Hatkin household, so stifling to Eleanor, Marion found the chatter, the aromas, the attention it was often impossible for her own widowed, working mother to provide. Rose and Sol, in turn, treated Marion with doting tenderness. And Marion, unlike Eleanor, drank it in.

The Goodwin School, though, could remind Eleanor just how parochial she was. The skinny, black-haired boy in most of her classes, Bernie Solomon, had grown up in a Socialist family, being jounced as a toddler on Norman Thomas's lap. His mother's cousin, Maxim Litvinov, served as the Soviet ambassador to the United States. Then there was Mel Goodman, another sophomore, who had been introduced to *Das Kapital* by his bar mitzvah tutor and gave occasional streetcorner speeches for the American League for Peace and Democracy, a Popular Front outfit.

To Eleanor, it was pure revelation. Her parents' political vista stopped at the Jackson Democratic Club. Rose and Sol, and all the children, were oblivious to the radical orators inveigling from atop vegetable crates outside the El stop at 174th Street. They knew so little of the roiling factions of the Left that Rose once sent Eleanor to Hashomer Hatzair for Jewish education without the slightest inkling the Zionist group was pretty much Communist. Many of the shoe factories where Sol worked had sweetheart unions, if any union at all, cutting the family off from even a breadbasket sort of class consciousness. Their plight seemed to them merely their plight, same as everybody else's in the neighborhood. Bernie Solomon and Mel Goodman, talking so passionately in the Morris hallways about fascism and capitalism and the Spanish Civil War, perceived the larger design.

The more formal instruction was just as exhilarating. Helen Hunter Smith, one of the history teachers, posted a sign on her classroom wall with one passage from the Gospel of John—"What Is Truth?"—and it was not hyperbolic to think of the Goodwin curriculum as an elaboration on that theme. One of Eleanor's first English teachers, Hedwig Hilker, belied her starchy, pinched appearance by having her students write about family members as if they were literary characters. Edward Kolevczon taught math not as rote memorization but the quest for proofs, encouraging his students to discover them. Latin class with Edward Coyle began with translating the children's book *Ferdinand the Bull* and culminated in reading Caesar's *Gallic Wars* and Plutarch's *Lives*.

For teachers and students alike, high culture represented a liberating force. To master great books or fine art was to prove that a scruffy Jewish kid from the tenements was worthy. Goodwin students plunged into *King Lear, Ivanhoe,* and George Eliot's *Mill on the Floss*. Morris sent its chorus to perform on Walter Damrosch's radio program; its orchestra entertained when Chiang Kai-shek appeared at the Hotel Astor to raise money for Chinese war relief. In May of 1938, toward the end of Eleanor's first semester, the school's Shakespeare Fellowship presented *Twelfth Night*.

It was all part of Elmer Bogart's scheme of enlightened social engineering, or what he called, in a favorite phrase, "achievement to capacity." The process had its moments of friction, of course, especially the gratings of creed. Marion used to overhear Edwin Tracey, the goateed orchestra director, muttering about how America under Roosevelt was becoming the "Jew-nited States." Sarah Bogart, Bernie Solomon's Latin teacher, confronted the Jewish pupils who had missed school for the High Holy Days. "What were you doing out?" she said, trawling up and down the desk rows. "You weren't in there praying. You were playing stickball." She gave up only when, to her astonishment, black Levi Bough informed her that, yes, he was Jewish and had been in *shul.*

As the summer of 1938 passed and fall returned, as winter arrived and with it 1939 and Eleanor's junior year, she was palpably blossoming. She ran for and won a seat representing the junior class in the Morris Organization, the student government, and got her name in the *Bronx Home News,* the borough's daily newspaper. She joined the Morris newspaper, the *Piper,* receiving a license for inquiry and a stickler's instruction in grammar from Arthur Strom, a faculty advisor who enjoyed referring to the staff as "my slaves." Despite his authority, the writers were always trying to slip in double entendres just to show how sophisticated they were; one issue of the *Piper* mysteriously dropped the first letter of a comely girl's name and identified her as "harlotte."

Irreverence was part of confidence. Eleanor wore saddle shoes, making certain they were scuffed in keeping with the current vogue, and "sharpie socks" with horizontal stripes in bright colors. In economics class, she and Marion drove Mr. Kammiter half mad by jingling tiny bells they had lashed to their laces. They called him Dick Tracy behind his back, because his nose was as sharp as the comic strip detective's, and lampooned Mr. Coyle, who had a speech defect, as "Mr.

Curl." Some afternoons, when the girls walked north toward home on Boston Road, Eleanor would just rear back her head and bray like a donkey.

She stuck out; there was no question. Her visibility was not just a matter of racking up As, but the effortless way she seemed to do it. The Goodwin School, after all, could be a fierce arena, where final grades were calibrated to the hundredth of a point to determine class rank, where Bernie Solomon and Mel Goodman once got into a fistfight arguing about Plato. Eleanor floated above the tumult, seemingly sweatless. Not even her sister Fannie, who shared the same room and daybed, ever saw Eleanor study very much. She relied on an eidetic memory, the file cabinet for all those equations and conjugations and formulas. She used Latin to unlock French. She learned to write by being a voracious reader. And like a star athlete who has experienced victory so often as to expect it in every contest, she admitted neither hesitation nor doubt.

Still, none of that quite explained Eleanor's ease to her classmates. Bernie Solomon stopped trying to best her and settled for admiring what he thought of as her modesty. Joe Lempert marveled at her generosity in explaining assignments, as if she were above the pettiness of competition. But Marion Herzog, cramming and grinding and always finishing second, except in the 75-yard dash, could not help being exasperated. How could Eleanor treat her own talent with such casual disregard? Didn't she know what it was worth? How proud it could make a mother? Mel Goodman looked at Eleanor even more skeptically. Yes, she mastered all the material, as if by osmosis, but to what end? She was a brain without an intellect, accomplishment without purpose, a rudderless boat.

None of them, perhaps, recognized the achievement that counted most to Eleanor. Back in late June of 1938, the last day of her first term at Morris, she had been called in by her French teacher, Madame Celia L. K. Moers. The room was empty except for them. Improbable as it seemed, given her high marks all semester long, Eleanor steeled herself for a dressing-down and a C+.

"Tell me what you eat," Madame Moers commanded.

Eleanor only stared in return.

"You Americans," the teacher sighed in derision. "You are too fat. A pretty girl like you. Who can tell?"

Those words pierced the vulnerable underbelly, quite literally, of Eleanor's academic prowess. She began to sob, and between spasms, she asked, "What can I do?"

At Madame Moers's behest, she delineated her diet— bread and cheese, peanut butter by the jar, milk from the icebox at home and in the school cafeteria for two cents a glass.

"Two quarts of milk a day?" Madame Moers said. "Impossible. That would feed three French children for a week. Shame on your mother."

Now here was the sort of criticism Eleanor could welcome, more evidence of Rose's inadequacy. Here was someone, a petite, chic, and continental someone at that, who knew exactly why no boys were calling Kopelov's candy store looking for Eleanor. Over the summer, she cut down to one glass of milk and took to the tennis courts of Crotona Park and shed all Rose's fretting with feigned concern over the starving children in Europe. The pounds melted off, and with them the fear of size 18.

With two months' worth of babysitting money, Eleanor ventured to Alexander's to buy herself an outfit: pleated, polka-dot dress, a pair of wedgies, stockings, two faux pearl bracelets. In the final days before classes resumed at Morris, she tried it all on, and went to the tar roof of 1461 to pose for Fannie's camera. Eleanor tried to affect a dreamy, middle-distance gaze, but her hands betrayed her insecurity. She was tugging at her own fingers as if trying to yank loose from a pair of Chinese handcuffs.

On opening day at Morris in September 1939, she was walking down the maelstrom of a hallway between periods, carrying her books across her chest, as usual, when she detected hands patting her. They started at her waist, newly trim, and worked their way up her back, toward her brassiere. By the time Eleanor turned, the groper was gone. Someone had just made a pass at her. A pass, right in the middle of school. And far from being offended, she felt triumphant. This crude compliment was harder-earned, and so more valuable, than all those columns of As on her report card.

When Sol Hatkin trudged through the door of Apartment 24 at day's end, his shoulders were invariably slumped in defeat. Hunched over, he appeared even shorter than the five-foot-five he measured, and his clothes hung awkwardly on his frame, the belt riding just under his rib cage, the pants cuffs several inches above his worn shoes. As Sol turned forty-three in January 1939, he was losing his hair and coloring what was left to hide its gray. He hoped the dye might give him the appearance of youthful vigor, and so help him to find a job. Mostly, though, the stuff advertised its falsity with its harsh odor and shoe polish gleam. Getting regular work would take more than that.

Rose greeted him in the kitchen with a desultory peck, and then he sat heavily and sighed. Even when he had a job, he frustrated the bosses with his slow pace, repeatedly getting laid off. "They're pushing me, they're pushing me," he would tell Rose in a feeble bid for sympathy. "I give you a *knip*," she'd reply, pinching and twisting his nipple. Then she would grumble, *"A grayser ferdiner"* a big earner. Sol could only answer, *"Vus villstoo foon mir"* what do you want from me? In the tiny apartment, Eleanor, Fannie, and Seymour heard it all.

The last year had been especially harsh. Sol had worked almost half of 1937 for I. Miller & Sons, an elite shoe company with its own store on Fifth Avenue and franchises around the country, making more than $1,300. Early in 1938, Miller had let him go, and since then he had found only sporadic work at La Valle, a lesser outfit. His entire income for 1938 had come to $682.99—just $180 more than his family's annual rent,

$150 less than the federal minimum wage of forty cents an hour for a forty-hour week, barely one-third the amount economists deemed necessary for a comfortable standard of living. In the last two months of the year, always a slack time in the shoe industry, Sol had not earned one cent.

No matter what Rose believed, the fault was bigger than Sol's own. America was sliding into what the New Deal's critics dubbed the "Roosevelt Recession." By mid-1938, there were ten million unemployed, 19 percent of the workforce; the stock market had dropped by one-third and corporate profits by four-fifths during the preceding year. The Works Progress Administration's rolls were passing three million, double the figure in November 1937. Chastened by a Congress that had defeated his plan to expand the Supreme Court and was roiling with isolationist sentiment besides, Franklin Roosevelt did not even offer new economic or social legislation for the 1939 session.

Sol teetered on the brink of losing everything he had cobbled together during a quarter-century in America. He had immigrated in 1913 to escape deprivation, the deprivation of a fatherless boy who had started working at age eight. Even in the shoe factories of his native Latvia, he had been smacked across the face for slowness, and he reached Ellis Island so destitute the authorities marked him "LPC"—likely to become a public charge. Fortunately, Sol's three older brothers had landed six years earlier and already gained a foothold in New York—especially Sam, who had abandoned the rabbinate for the security of printing.

The one skill Sol possessed happened to be a skill in demand, at least initially. While the shoemaking industry was centered in New England mill towns like Lowell, Massachusetts, small and midsized operations dotted New York and made copious use of Jewish immigrants. "No boy of native American stock will learn the shoe trade," a state inspector put it in 1918. "The men in the fitting rooms are practically all Hebrews. Their racial power of endurance seems to enable them to stand the strain of power operating."

As a stitcher, Sol bent by the hour over a sewing machine, one in a row of ten or twenty atop a metal work table stretching the length of the room. In parallel rows other men and women performed other tasks. There might be 300 separate operations in manufacturing a shoe and Sol executed no more than several of them, with numbing monotony. Before getting to him, the leather had been sorted, cut, skived, and pounded; he, in turn, joined the loose pieces of collar or upper or tongue in a seam; during the next stages, soles would be fastened and then the whole piece fitted onto a model called a last.

The stitching room was the noisiest and most furious section of almost any shoe factory. Around Sol belts and wheels whined, and needles clacked in relentless staccato. The stale air smelled of tanned hides. The floor was littered with leather, thread, and used bobbins. Sol's job required skills—choosing bobbins, oiling the machine, determining the proper number of stitches per inch—but the skill it required most was speed. The boss demanded speed and, in a different way, so did Sol's wife and children. Even in union shops, he got paid by the piece, not the hour.

During the booming 1920s, Sol had worked and earned steadily. He moved his family to the Bronx, of course. He contributed money to Rose's family abroad. At her insistence, he even loaned $200 to a cousin's husband, an aspiring physiotherapist named Morris Osder. Rose worshipfully called Morris "the doctor," even if his specialties actually ran to spinal manipula-tion, ultraviolet radiation, and a water enema known as a high colonic. Quackery or not, the practice had situated Morris's family on Eastern Parkway, the fanciest boulevard in Jewish Brooklyn.

Lately, when Sol could scrounge up the five-cent sub-way fare, he traveled out there in pursuit of the decade-old debt. What could $200 mean to a rich man? To Sol, it meant food and rent for several months. So he skulked through the Osder apartment, staring at the radio or the grandfather clock, gathering the gumption to say, "If you got the money for that. . . ." Morris just waved him off and said they were gifts from his pa-tients. At best, Sol got a free meal before the long jour-ney home.

"You're not good for anything," Rose told him. When he lingered at the table after dinner for just a moment's peace, she ordered him away. Sol's relatives across the courtyard in 1459 avoided his home rather than watch him be humiliated. He started so many sentences *"Rosie hut gezugt"*—Rosie says—that finally his older brother Sam shot back, "I don't care what Rosie thinks. I want to know what *you* think."

He did have thoughts. Unlike his wife, he exuded passion for America. He had begun the process of gaining citizenship only three years after arriving. He had gone to night school to learn English fluently. In graceful script, he wrote in Eleanor's autograph book, "My sincere wishes to you. Lots of luck & good health & and happiness in your future life." When Seymour asked once about prejudice against Jews, Sol answered, "You're in America. If you can't get into one entrance, there's another entrance. This is a beautiful country."

Mostly, though, Sol protected himself by staying outside the house. He had a whole life in the neighborhood, a life that Rose ignored and the children barely perceived. There was his friend Oscar the barber. There was an Italian guy whom Sol had met on the boat to America; the man now owned a shoestore in the East Bronx and let Sol make some money doing on-the-spot repairs every Sunday. On summer evenings, lacking any better plan, Sol sank into a bench alongside Crotona Park and snoozed, dreaming his private dreams.

His favorite destination by far was the Jackson Democratic Club. There he had value; there he had purpose. Sol Hatkin occupied the bottom rung of a ladder that climbed all the way to Franklin Roosevelt. He reported to an election-district captain who reported to the club's executive directors, Harry Cook and Mildred McCaffrey, who reported to the chairman of the Bronx

County Democratic Party, Edward Flynn. And Ed Flynn, "Boss" Flynn, was an intimate of FDR's, hand-picked to oversee the Democratic National Committee. Flynn had broken years earlier with Tammany Hall, but he was no starry-eyed reformer. As he wrote later in his career, "You can't have government without elections, elections without organizations, organizations without a spoils system."

Sol eagerly apprenticed himself to that system. On Monday and Thursday evenings, the club convened in its offices above the Tower Theater. Anybody in the neighborhood with a problem—a landlord who cut off the heat, trouble signing up for Social Security, a boy getting out of jail and needing a job—lined up to ask for help. McCaffrey noted each request on an index card, and delegated a dozen girls (women, actually) to follow up on them. Each favor supplied was fidelity earned. Sol himself may have first entered the club as a supplicant, trying to smooth the path to citizenship for Rose in 1936.

So in 1461 and a few adjacent tenements, Sol played the loyal minion. He collected signatures on nominating petitions. He went door-to-door for candidates. He passed out sample ballots, as well as palm cards with this instruction: "PULL DOWN ALL LEVERS ON LINE 1. You are urgently requested to vote with your family and friends for the DEMOCRATIC PARTY." On the dates of the primary and general elections, Sol occasionally served as a polling inspector, a paying job that didn't depend on piecework. One lawyer in the club gave Sol hand-me-downs for the children.

Sol's greater reward was proximity to power. Not that Sol wanted power for himself, only the sensation of importance that nearness to it imparted. The Jackson Democratic Club included judges, commissioners, court clerks, and a state assemblyman, Isidore Dollinger, who lived in a luxurious building beside Crotona Park. The Jackson Club packed the auditorium at Morris High when Herbert Lehman spoke there in the waning days of the 1938 gubernatorial race. And because Lehman beat Thomas Dewey by just 70,000 votes in the most important election in the nation that fall, and because he took the Bronx by 200,000 votes, and because he carried 80 percent of the vote in the Jackson Club's territory, then couldn't Sol Hatkin take an iota of credit, regardless of what *Rosie hut gezugt?*

From literally the day of Eleanor's birth, she had been one of their marital battlegrounds. Sol wanted to name her Sylvia, while Rose favored Eleanor. Sol pretended to concede and then, being the parent capable of writing English, entered the name Sylvia on the birth certificate. Only when Eleanor entered kindergarten five years later did she—and Rose—discover that wasn't her legal name. Still, Sol had other ways of winning. He brought Eleanor strips of ornate leather—silver braiding for a slipper, the strap for an evening pump—that she turned into bracelets. He taught her to sew her own blouses and skirts. When she went to buy shoes, he hovered over the salesman, inspecting the handiwork, especially the seams. "Always remember your dear old Mother & Dad," he had written in her autograph book when she graduated from junior high. Remember them she did, and for diametrically different reasons.

Toward the end of June 1939, Eleanor flipped through the pages of graduating seniors in Morris's yearbook. She stopped midway through the Ks, and moved her gaze down the column to the portrait of a boy with wavy brown hair, intense eyes, and the hint of a cleft chin. His tie was puffed out between the lapels of his suit coat, as if to suggest an ascot, and a collar bar crossed beneath the knot. A line of capital letters identified the boy as Hy Keltz, but Eleanor already knew that. The information she needed appeared in the next few lines: his address.

She had mooned over him all the previous fall in Mrs. Witte's geometry class. Eleanor was the class whiz, true to form, and Hy a senior trying to complete the sophomore-level course for his diploma. He was nearly seventeen then, three years older than she, a grown man compared to her Goodwin School peers. Boys like Joe Lempert or Bernie Solomon made fine company for wisecracks or drama club rehearsals or deadline sessions on the *Piper*, but at thirteen or fourteen they were smooth-faced and shorter than most of the girls, timorous and stammering in any sally at flirtation. They were little brothers.

Five-foot-nine and 125 pounds, Hy Keltz was taut and sinewed as a whippet. He played stickball and basketball and three-wall handball; he played football with a wadded newspaper wrapped in rubber bands replacing the pigskin that was an inconceivable expense. With a bunch of his buddies, Hy formed a "cellar club," scraping together enough spare change to rent one basement room on Home Street as a hangout. A couple of neighborhood girls, friends' sisters mostly, took the club boys up to the roof with a crank-up Victrola and a stack of 78s and taught them the lindy and the fox trot. Something of that grace, that confidence in the physical self, shimmered off Hy even in geometry class.

Eleanor had strained to catch his eye as she collected homework for Mrs. Witte. When Hy didn't seem especially impressed by her acumen with a compass and a protractor, she tried playing dumb, asking in a disingenuous flutter, "Is a right-angled triangle like an isosceles?" If she dropped to his level, she reasoned, maybe he'd notice her more. Wasn't that was Rose was always telling Eleanor, that boys were jealous of her? The next time she went past Hy's desk, though, she received no more than a polite grin.

Now, an entire semester later, Hy Keltz was about to leave Morris and Eleanor's crush behind forever. No time remained for subtle charms or cunning snares. She wrote him a letter asking if he wanted to go out. Such forwardness went against all social convention. It promised only more humiliation. Between hope and dread, she didn't sleep the whole night after mailing it. But anything was better than what she imagined as her affliction: unrequited love.

Eleanor's letter found an intrigued recipient, and Hy

answered with a letter of his own. Behind his respectful exterior in geometry class, he had noticed plenty about the smart girl who'd lost all that weight last summer. He was too polite to ever say so to Eleanor, but to his buddies he might have described her as a "Grade-A product," no mere cliché for a teenager who worked part-time in a grocery store. The only thing Hy couldn't figure out was why she would possibly be interested in him. He realized that he was handsome, and a smooth dancer, and hardly a dummy, having skipped fourth grade, but he was nobody's idea of a genius, not college material. Like it said in the yearbook, the only thing it said about Hy Keltz in the yearbook, "His ambition was to say he graduated Morris." And Eleanor Hatkin had been mentioned in the *Bronx Home News* only a few weeks earlier for her "high scholastic attainment."

There were distinctions in class, too, invisible perhaps to outsiders amid the sweeping privation of the Depression, but real in all their microscopic increments to the Morris students. Who was on relief and who wasn't? Who had trolley fare and who didn't? The grade of poverty ran with the grade of the land, with the school building itself at dead center. Heading north from Morris, Boston Road followed a ridge line gently upward to the shopping district on Tremont Avenue; heading south, a hill sloped down toward the foundries, rail yards, and marshes along the East River. The Hatkins, poor as they were, lived on the ridge; Hy Keltz, whose father had died a year earlier, lived down the hill. He had been working every weekend since becoming a bar mitzvah, delivering groceries for an uncle's store near Yankee Stadium. Sometimes he was lucky enough to fill an order for Red Ruffing or Tony Lazzeri, one of the ballclub's stars, but mostly it was toil and tedium. For nineteen hours on Saturday and eight on Sunday, he made four bucks. Half of that went right to his mother.

Finished with high school now, he took a full-time delivery job, starting at $8 a week. It was enough money to launch a courtship. One day he rented a bike, a dime for an hour, and cycled up Boston Road to call on Eleanor. She had fixed her hair with curlers the previous night so that it fell to her shoulders like dark water passing over smooth stones, leaving one insouciant twist on her forehead. On the way to answering the door, she consulted the mirror to curl her eyelashes. That eyelash curler, Eleanor's girlfriends liked to joke, was getting to be her trademark.

There was, perhaps, never a more thrilling summer to start dating. The New York World's Fair had opened on the final day of April 1939, with Franklin Roosevelt's train stopping in the Bronx to pick up Boss Flynn for the occasion. Like any other sensate teenager, Eleanor had been tantalized for years ahead as a twelve-hundred-acre ash heap was transformed into the World of Tomorrow, so much steel and stucco and gypsum board shaped into the clean modern lines of Art Deco and Bauhaus. But it was a dear miracle at 75¢ admission, $7 by the time a typical family had eaten a meal, and some Bronxites walked miles across the new

Whitestone Bridge and into Queens because they couldn't afford subway tokens on top of the expenses at the fair. They patched together lunch from free miniature loaves of Wonder Bread at Continental Baking Company's exhibit, complimentary ketchup at the Heinz Dome. Hy Keltz, a working man, could pay for both himself and his girl Ellie.

Her arm on his, and he proud to have it there, they strolled from the IRT station down the Avenue of the Patriots, passing its golden-hued pavilions on the way to the Trylon and Perisphere. A 700-foot spear, a globe 200 feet in circumference, the only structures in the entire grounds painted pure white, they were the epicenter of the fair and its fantasy. The Perisphere contained a diorama of "Democracity," an efficient and unblemished metropolis of the future. Much of the rest of the fair offered Hy and Eleanor variations on the theme. Of course, there were pure amusements like the Aquacade show starring Johnny Weissmuller of *Tarzan* fame and the "Railroads on Parade" pageant with a score by Kurt Weill. There were, for two teenagers who had rarely if ever set foot in Queens, dozens of pavilions from around the planet. South Rhodesia boasted a replica of Victoria Falls, nearly two hundred feet tall; Britain displayed the original Magna Carta; the Soviet Union's new socialist man, rendered with rippling muscles in stainless steel, thrust a red star skyward. As if to remind Hy and Eleanor just how straitened was their native ground in comparison, the Old New York pavilion included what was bluntly called a "ghetto restaurant," an unmistakably Jewish joint whose running joke had waiters shouting orders back to the kitchen in nasal Yiddish accents.

What was most alluring, perhaps, to two children of poverty from the Bronx were those visions of a comfortable present hovering barely beyond reach— gleaming Buicks and LaSalles at the General Motors pavilion, the AT&T building with curving glass booths for transcontinental calls, Carrier Company's mock igloo cooled by air conditioning, General Electric's ranks of washing machines. If you didn't even own a bike, if you took your calls at Kopelov's candy store, if you slept on a blanket in Crotona Park on stifling nights, and if your mother Rose did the laundry with a rub-board and a block of Octagon soap, then what could have been more beguiling? Well, maybe holding hands with your first boyfriend when the fireworks and colored fountains rose from the Lagoon of Nations into a summer night's sky.

Most often, Hy took Ellie to the movies, and not simply to the movies but to the Loew's Paradise, a theater as magical in its way as the World's Fair. Erected on the Grand Concourse in the last flush years of the Roaring Twenties, the Paradise of a decade later exuded escape from hard times. One dollar transported Hy and Eleanor into a realm of tapestries and mahogany panels and a marble fountain, which replenished the water for a pool of live goldfish. The bathrooms even had attendants in uniform. Hy and

Eleanor ascended, like most dating couples, to the balcony, and there beheld the most renowned of the Paradise's accoutrements, a ceiling painted with clouds and lit with twinkling stars.

The movies that summer enhanced the romance. Hy and Eleanor clutched their way through *Wuthering Heights* and *The Wizard of Oz* and the double-feature of *Café Society* and *St. Louis Blues*. They caught up belatedly with the newest pairing of Nelson Eddy and Jeannette McDonald, cast as bickering Broadway stars in the musical comedy *Sweethearts*. In their adolescent way, Hy and Eleanor thought of themselves as such a couple, with the same kind of crackling chemistry between body and mind, the attraction of opposites. He was rugged and robust like Eddy, she as witty and independent as McDonald, and thanks to her eyelash curler at least attempting the same dewy, upswept gaze. No matter that in real life Eddy was the former journalist with operatic training while McDonald had begun as a teenaged chorine; no matter that all her repartee in the movie flowed from the pen of Dorothy Parker. All that mattered was the way their eyes locked and voices entwined in the duet of "Sweetheart Waltz."

> Been waiting all my life
> To waltz with you, love of my life
> I'm floating on your charms,
> I'm holding heaven in my arms.

The balcony of the Paradise, nearly touching the faux firmament, was the right place for a first kiss. It was an acceptable place for a male hand to slip suggestively across a shoulder in the dark, even to slide inside a blouse and bra. Both Hy and Eleanor understood the physicality could proceed no further; the proper consummation of a Paradise date was a walk across the Concourse after the picture for a chocolate frappe at Krum's, two straws please. The fellas in Hy's cellar club drew a divide between nice girls and the other kind, one for marriage and the other for practice. Eleanor already had seen the consequences of blurring that line in the form of a neighborhood girl nicknamed Pedgie, who'd gotten knocked up early in her teens. She'd had to marry her boyfriend, some guy a few years older who shot pool, and move in with her parents. Eleanor had only the vaguest sense of precisely how Pedgie had become pregnant, but she didn't have to know the details to know the rules. Nice girls didn't do it. Whatever *it* exactly was. Pedgie had transgressed, and now her life was as good as over.

Meanwhile, the world refused to stop turning in deference to the self-absorption of first love. "Sweetheart Waltz" notwithstanding, Eleanor thought of "Over the Rainbow" from *The Wizard of Oz* as her song, hers and Hy's. *"Some day I'll wish upon a star / And wake up where the clouds are far / Behind me."* This was all of Eleanor's longing set to music. But the week after the movie opened in mid-August, as Judy Garland was doing promotional appearances and advertisements were declaring that "The Whole Town Is Oz-ified," Nazi Germany and the Soviet Union signed a nonaggression pact.

On the Bronx side of the Atlantic, the Jewish year 5700 dawned in glorious fashion. As the Hatkin family gathered for a portrait on the Thursday morning of September 14, 1939, the first day of Rosh Hashanah, the sun was warming the late-summer air well into the seventies and the faintest breeze drifted dryly from the northwest. Sol and Rose and their children assembled in Crotona Park, standing on a dirt patch that the WPA was turning into a baseball diamond. They wore their only finery—Sol in a double-breasted coat, Fannie modest in a dark skirt and white blouse buttoned to the neck, Seymour stretching a suit that he had plainly outgrown to the button-popping point. Rose and Eleanor stood beside one another, their expressions as polar as the masks of Comedy and Tragedy outside the McKinley Square Theater. Eleanor smiled so broadly the camera caught her teeth glistening; Rose, her lips flat, stared somewhere thousands of miles beyond the photographer.

For the last year or two, the High Holy Days had supplied yet another frontier in the conflict between mother and daughter. Rose Hatkin kept a kosher home, and Sol regularly attended services. Although the family could not afford a synagogue membership, and affiliation was a fairly loose affair among poorer

Jews, Sol paid for seats for Rosh Hashanah and Yom Kippur at Tifereth Israel, a sturdy brick synagogue with a red canvas canopy at its entrance. It sat on Prospect Avenue a half-block west of Boston Road and a half-block east of the entrance to Crotona Park. The location should have meant nothing but convenience, since the East Bronx's Jews promenaded through the park between morning and afternoon services, and ended Rosh Hashanah by casting the sin-laden bread of *tashlich* into Indian Lake. For Eleanor, that half-block meant liberation.

Eleanor still dressed for the occasion, and Eleanor still promenaded. Eleanor simply made a point of not going to synagogue. When the rest of her family on this holy day repaired from the park back to Tifereth Israel's pews, she met up with her girlfriends. There were Marion Herzog from Morris High and the Union Avenue Gang and Lillian Golden and Vicky Behar, her fellow Musketeers from the Fulton Avenue crowd. Marion wore a gray suit, fitted trimly to her five-foot-six frame, and the rest had dresses and handbags, with Eleanor in a red number belted at the waist and ruffled at the hem. For the other girls, spending a few hours in Crotona Park indicated no rebellion. Lillian's and Vicky's parents did not attend synagogue, and Marion always made sure to join her mother on Yom Kippur for *yizkor,* the memorial service, so she could mourn her father, dead a full decade by now. Eleanor alone flouted her family. As if her absence on Rosh Hashanah were not inflammatory enough, on Yom

Kippur she made certain to inform Rose that she'd defied the fast by eating Chinese.

She associated Judaism with superstition in the Old World and hypocrisy in the New. Here was her family, nearly broke nearly all the time, and when Rose's relatives the Gartenbergs—so observant, so *frum*—came over there'd be money thrown away on luxuries like tomato herring and Sol would put on a yarmulke as if he could fool them into thinking he wore it any other day. Besides, everyone knew that Mr. Gartenberg, a tailor, worked on Shabbos. "In the Jewish religion," Rose offered in his defense, "if you have to work on Saturday, it's alright if you need the money."

Rose's efforts to imbue Eleanor with a more secular, cultural form of Jewishness at the Arbeiter Ring only had invited more ridicule. Three times a week as younger girls she and Fannie had gone trooping up the wooden stairs of the second-floor folk-shul of Smargoner Branch Number 285, fighting back the giggles when Mr. Dorin kept combing over his bald spot, wishing she were outside in the Jennings Street market with sour pickles bobbing in the barrel and potatoes roasting over coal fires and movie posters covering the walls with their four-color blandishments. When Dorin got mad and wrote a note in Yiddish to her parents, Eleanor tossed it in the garbage as she skipped home. Years ago, as a small child, she'd sung that *eins, tzvei, drei* doggerel with the earnest desire to please, to show off; these days, she subjected it to a witheringly nasal rendition. She used the same voice to mock Rose's friend from the building, Mrs. Oguz, a busybody, yes, but still a grown-up unprepared to hear a teenager's derision. *Zi tanst arine, zi tanst arois, arois, arine, arine in hoiz.* She dances in, she dances out, in and out, and back in her house.

The friction between Eleanor and Rose this year, though, was complicated and compounded by forces far beyond them. Two weeks earlier, the German army had invaded Poland, advancing with such speed that Western journalists invented a word for it: *blitzkrieg.* As of Rosh Hashanah, Hitler himself was overseeing the troops that had encircled Warsaw. Other German forces had reached within twenty miles of Bialystok, a city with more than 60,000 Jews, including most of Rose Hatkin's family. Some nights these past weeks, as Seymour pretended to sleep in the bedroom he shared with his parents, he heard Rose weeping.

Eleanor first had brushed up against the consequences of Nazism a few months earlier with her Fulton Avenue friends, when two teenaged boys named Brenner materialized on the benches along Crotona Park. Jewish refugees from Austria, they had taken the streetcar over from Manhattan that day in search of a friend whom they'd heard had escaped. The friend, Rudy Friedlander, happened to be renting a room on Fulton Avenue and in search of companionship often hung out on the park benches across the street from the YMHA, the same spot where Vicky and Lillian and Eleanor spent so many warm evenings. Through Rudy, the Brenner brothers became part of the crowd.

It was obvious by their accents, of course, they were newcomers from Europe. They possessed, too, a kind of sophistication and chivalry that impressed the girls. Irving, at eighteen the older brother by two years, often arrived with a bag of candy for his hosts. When he started dating a Fulton Avenue girl named Fannie Povodator, a freshman at Hunter College, he took her to hear *Tosca* at the Met. After a few months of staying with relatives in Washington Heights, a neighborhood so filled with German Jewish refugees it was called the "Fourth Reich," the Brenner brothers rented their own furnished room in the West Nineties, inviting Eleanor and the rest for dripped Viennese coffee.

What the Brenners never did was to explain exactly how and why they had fled Austria, the cautionary tale that might have encouraged Eleanor to comprehend her mother's fears about the German advance on Bialystok. Privately, the Brenners thought these American kids didn't want to hear. And they did see them as kids, all caught up with movies and ice-cream sodas. For their own part, though, the Brenners threw their efforts into building lives in America rather than recounting the ones they had left behind. The sons of a wastrel father and a mother supporting the household as a peddler, they knew all about the imperative of survival. Already they had changed their names from Ignaz and Bruno to Irving and Bernie, a couple of nice Jewish boys, and found jobs at a clothing store in Brooklyn.

So on the benches along Crotona Park nobody ever

asked about and nobody ever told the story. The Brenners were from Graz, a university town that prided itself in the 1930s on being the center of National
Socialism in Austria. No sooner had Hitler marched
into Vienna on March 14, 1938, in the German annex-
ation known as *Anschluss* than Graz declared itself the
"Capital of the Insurrection" and set about becoming
the first Austrian city to be *Judenrein,* cleansed of Jews.
During Kristallnacht in November 1938, local Nazis
destroyed the main synagogue. Soon after, Ignaz and
three hundred other local Jews were sent to Dachau.
Released three weeks later, possibly thanks to a bribe or
the surrender of family property, Ignaz went with
Bruno to Vienna and managed to obtain one of the
emergency visas President Roosevelt had authorized for
German and Austrian Jews. A cousin of their mother's,
who ran a hotel in the Hudson River town of Haver-
straw, sponsored the brothers for immigration. Their
ship docked in Hoboken on March 5, 1939, and that
spring they appeared like welcome apparitions to Rudy
Friedlander on the Fulton Avenue benches. Only years
later, when Irving was married to Fannie Povodator, did
he reveal his lasting image of Graz—the synagogue
burning to the ground.

If these two refugee brothers seemed so relaxed, so
happy-go-lucky, then Eleanor and her girlfriends had
less reason to foresee doom in Eastern Europe. Life in
the summer leading to Rosh Hashanah 5700 was renting bikes in Central Park, picnicking beside Tibbetts
Brook up in Yonkers, sunning and swimming at Or-

chard Beach; it was the World's Fair and the Loew's Paradise and being in love with Hy Keltz. Sure, Eleanor hissed Hitler when he goose-stepped across the screen in Movie-Tone News; everybody knew he was a villain. But it all felt so distant, part of her parents' world. Lillian and Vicky and Marion thought pretty much the same way. Of all Eleanor's friends, only Bernie Solomon, with his preternatural sense of politics, could see. He was the one who railed about Mussolini and fascism outside the Italian pavilion at the World's Fair; he was the one who joined the Committee to Defend the Allies and pinned a tiny replica of the Union Jack on his shirt. His mother had begun washing floors to make extra money to send to relatives in Bialystok, a cause Rose Hatkin surely endorsed.

Rose's distress spanned hemispheres and continents; it inscribed a triangular path on the globe, from the Bronx to Bialystok to Montevideo. Her favorite sister Ester Dina remained in Bialystok, of course, hapless and destitute and burdened with three young children. So did Rose's four other siblings. She had not heard from them in nearly a year, since a postcard dated September 11, 1938, a cameo portrait of her sister Menuchi with the usual inscription on the back: "Forever remembering." There had been no apparent sense of urgency among the Markiewicz family, or for that matter most of Bialystok's Jews, during the intervening months, even as Hitler had gobbled up Austria and the Sudetenland and the Danzig corridor. They went shopping on Siemkiewicz Street and strolled in the City Garden and danced at the traditional party called a *hudyiowka* held one hundred days before graduating from gymnasium. A Jewish-owned company, Sektor Films, even had produced a travelogue meant to entice American Jews to vacation in Bialystok. It culminated in a shot of a pretty young woman invitingly smiling as the narrator intoned, "Come visit Bialystok. You will not regret it."

The only ones coming now were thousands of Jews from the cities and towns of central Poland, straggling into Bialystok barely ahead of the German tanks. Within the city gates, Jews locked their doors and shuttered their businesses; fearful of being conscripted on the spot, men hid as their women lined up for bread. Rose followed the war coverage in the *Forverts*. NAZI BOMBS FALL ON JEWISH CITIES, read one headline on September 2. The next day it was, NAZI FLIERS SHOOT REFUGEES FROM BOMBED TRAINS. And on September 3, THE BLOODY HISTORICAL RECORD OF GERMAN ANTI-SEMITISM. In his annual Rosh Hashanah editorial, the *Forverts'* editor, Abraham Cahan, wrote words that scored Rose in her helplessness:

> Millions of Jews are now in Europe in the fire of war. They are in an unending hail of bullets and bombs. Thousands of them, young and old, are being extinguished, wounded and crippled; thousands are being ruined, are losing their homes, everything they own, and are running down unknown, horrific roads looking for rescue for themselves and their families. . . .

Our American safety and security does not continue, so long as we know and remember that there, across the sea, the blood of our brethren who continue to live under the dark shadow of death is being spilled. Here, we can't even for a minute forget their pain, for the simple reason that we are tied, woven together by thousands of threads, for the truth is we are as much a part of them as they are of us.

At the other compass point of Rose Hatkin's world, her brother-in-law Alter David Kaczkowicz and her niece and nephew Judis and Julius were renting one room from a Jewish family named Rybka in the Villa Munoz district of Montevideo. Except for Uruguay's Spanish language and January summer, they might have been down on Hester Street on the Lower East Side. From wrought-iron balconies, the immigrant mothers of Villa Munoz called across the teeming streets in Yiddish; on Friday afternoons, the air smelled of gefilte fish boiling in broth. Alter David plied the barrio as a *cuentenik*, *cuente* referring to the account book he carried as a door-to-door peddler, selling mattresses and umbrellas on credit. Like her aunt Rose, Judis worked a hairdresser, not so surprising since Bialystok was renowned for its beautiful women. Julius, who had started supporting his mother at age twelve in a chocolate factory, took two jobs in the effort to raise enough money to reunite the family, selling *chorizo* at soccer matches and assembling bed springs in a factory.

By September 1939, Uruguay's was one of the last

doors ajar for Jewish refugees in the Western hemisphere. Argentina and Brazil had halted immigration years earlier. Cuba had recently closed its ports, forcing the ocean liner St. Louis to beg futilely for landing rights in the U.S. before turning back to Europe with its 907 Jewish passengers, two-thirds of whom ultimately would perish. Uruguay admitted more than two thousand Jews in 1939, objecting at first to those without papers but almost always relenting or looking the other way in the end. The problem for Ester Dina and her youngsters was getting out of Poland. No longer was it 1934, when Judis and Julius simply had presented themselves to the Uruguayan consulate in Warsaw, proven they had neither a criminal record nor an infectious disease, and come away with visa stamps in their passports. Their ship tickets had cost Rose $75 apiece. The going rate for forged papers as Poland fell ran to $700, more money than Sol Hatkin made in an entire year.

Rose hunted for information about her relatives. She spoke with Minnie Osder, her cousin in Brooklyn, and her friend Simmy Plansky, both of them natives of Bialystok. Neither had news. She traveled down to the Lower East Side to the Bialystoker Center, the ten-story building that was the hub of émigré activity. But while leaders of the *landsmenshaften* expressed concern about events abroad, it was concern of a lower order than Rose's own. They envisioned calamities akin to those Bialystok had already endured and survived—the 1906 pogrom that killed eighty-eight, the poverty and unemployment in the ruins of World War I. The Bialystokers in America would provide money for relief, as they faithfully did in every crisis, and the *muter shtot* would persevere. The coming weeks and months held a Sukkot dance, a Hannukah Ball, a Linen and Grocery Shower, a card party, a performance of the Yiddish play *In A Jewish Grocery Store*, all of them proven fund-raisers. So David Sohn, the director of the Bialystoker Center, struck a cautiously positive note in his Rosh Hashanah message: "All the world is beginning to suffer from the Nazi monster, and we hope it will be annihilated soon. Let us, therefore, hope and believe that the coming year will bring genuine salvation to our people and a decisive, well-deserved defeat to our enemies."

Nothing in Rose's pessimistic nature allowed for any such hope and belief. All she had to do was bump into Mr. Libby, the super of 1461, to hear him crow, "Hitler's making it good." Just two weeks before the German invasion of Poland, 1,000 members of an anti-Semitic outfit called the Christian Mobilizers had rallied in the South Bronx, unveiling a "Buy Christian" campaign and denouncing Roosevelt as a "stooge of the Jews." Back in April, 1,200 would-be storm troopers from the German-American Bund had celebrated Hitler's fiftieth birthday at a South Bronx beer hall, its stage decorated with swastikas and the slogan "One People, One Bund, One Führer." On the evening of September 15, just as Rosh Hashanah was ending, the aviation hero Charles Lindbergh took his isolationist ideology to a nationwide radio audience, warning against "hurling ourselves thoughtlessly" to the Allies' defense in response to "propaganda both foreign and domestic." It was an unmistakable reference to President Roosevelt's decision to seek repeal of the arms embargo provision of the Neutrality Act so that the United States could send at least materiel to embattled Britain.

Rose did the one thing she could do. A few days after Rosh Hashanah, with Bialystok having fallen to the Germans, she counted the money she had secreted in the sack under the mattress, and folded the used clothing she had *handeled* for on Bathgate Avenue, and packed it all together and told Sol to mail it to Ester Dina.

"Rachel," he said, serious enough to use her Hebrew name, "I'm not bringing this. They're not going to get it."

"Send it," she replied.

He returned some time later, still holding the package.

"Hitler has Poland," he said. "It's not going anywhere. They told me at the post office."

"Send it," she commanded.

He trudged out the door to comply.

Late one night in January 1940, Eleanor heard uncharacteristic noise seeping out from her parents' bedroom, a rhythmic set of sighs and moans. Even at an unenlightened fifteen, she recognized something private and intimate in the sounds, and in the way they had been withheld until the Hatkin children were all presumably asleep. The next morning Sol was leaving for work in a tiny, distant place called Bangor, Maine, and no one in the family knew when he would return. As they all said their good-byes to him before school, Rose kissed him on the lips, pulled away to look him square in the face, and said, *"Zai gezunt, kum gezunt. Mach uns a sacht gelt."* Go healthy, come healthy. Make a lot of money.

Nobody in the household knew quite how Sol had found this job. Here the man could hardly get work in New York City and he was headed for a place called the Penobscot Shoe Company, hundreds of miles away, somewhere in the woods. It was one of those mysteries of Sol's life outside 1461. But maybe it was not really so inexplicable at all. Sol had first learned leatherwork in Riga, the capital of Latvia, and so had another Jewish immigrant named Max Kagan. Kagan settled in Lynn, Massachusetts, in 1918, worked for the next dozen years at a shoe factory in nearby Salem, and when cash was tight during the Depression had the foresight and *chutzpah* to ask his boss to pay him with equity in the company. He wound up a partner, with an owner's income and an owner's headaches; during the wave of labor strife after federal law enshrined the right of collective bargaining, Kagan headed away from unions into central Maine. There he encountered a Jewish cobbler who, during years of peddling amid the hamlets and country crossroads, had learned from the Penobscot Indians how to sew moccasins. Kagan seized on the idea of producing them in volume by machine, and in the fall of 1939 he opened a moccasin factory in a moribund woolen mill several miles outside Bangor in Old Town. Most of Kagan's employees there were French Canadians and he had hundreds competing for jobs. But through a loose network of Riga Jews word of Penobscot reached Sol Hatkin in the Bronx. Perhaps Kagan took special pity on a *landsman;* perhaps he put high value on Riga's quality handiwork. However it had happened, Sol set forth to Maine on his longest trip since steaming to America a quarter-century earlier.

There was nothing the least bit puzzling about why Sol grabbed at the opportunity. Throughout 1939, the Depression had further deepened in New York. In the final month of the year, 2,000 men lined up three days in advance to apply for a single street-sweeping job paying $33 a week. The WPA, the New Deal's employer of last resort, laid off more than half of its 140,000 workers in the city. A man named Cleary who lived on 166th Street, just a few blocks from the Hatkins, dropped dead of a heart attack while protesting outside Bronx WPA headquarters with a picket sign pleading, STOP ALL LAYOFFS—WE WANT JOBS. For all its ballyhoo, the World's Fair cut 500 men and women from its payroll as it sank tens of millions of dollars into debt. Even the Jackson Democratic Club moved out of its offices above the Tower Theater for cheaper rent on McKinley Square. When Sol had scoured the want ads of the *Bronx Home News*, he spotted openings only for errand boy, pin setter, bill collector (needs own car), egg salesman (commission only). The Penobscot Shoe Company was a godsend.

Sol did not make a lot of money, as Rose wished, but he made more money more steadily than he had for almost three years. Penobscot was running two, sometimes three, shifts, expanding from one factory into several. Each week an envelope from Sol reached 1461, with maybe $30, maybe $20, maybe $40, depending on the pace of his piecework. One particular envelope contained a snapshot, as well, dated March 17, 1940. It showed a Sol that Eleanor had rarely if ever seen—shoulders thrown wide, posture erect, cheeks full. In fedora, plaid muffler, and frayed pea coat, he stood before the granite pediment of a statue of three lumberjacks. This Sol had purpose and plenty to eat.

To his surprise, Bangor proved not so alien a place at all. More than 1,000 Jews filled a neighborhood of frame houses rising up a hillside from the railroad depot where many had arrived as greenhorns. They were shopkeepers and factory workers, candy wholesalers and dealers in cattle and lumber. They maintained a burial society and a Zionist lodge. They had enough synagogues and kosher butchers to provoke feuds over who was doing which rituals wrong. From the second floor of the old woolen mill in Old Town, where the stitching department was located, Sol could look out on a landscape far more pleasing than the

Lower East Side—rushing river, timbered shoreline, even an occasional moose. For a moment in time, until Rose scoffed out her veto, Sol considered moving the whole family to Bangor.

Back in the Bronx, Eleanor missed him fiercely. She missed his presence at the dinner table, facing the window, a glass of water beside his plate. She missed him buying used books for her. She missed him telling her every cold morning, and many not-so-cold ones, "Button up your chest," even though she always let her coat flap open anyway. Sol sent money for a Sweet Sixteen party on her birthday, April 25, 1940, but even the rare spectacle of crepe paper and punch in the dreary confines of Apartment 24 did not compensate for his absence. Mel Goodman, a classmate in the Goodwin School, noticed an unusually somber quality to Eleanor that winter and spring, and finally asked Marion Herzog if something was the matter. "Her father's been away," replied Marion, who understood all too acutely the void left by a missing father.

As for Rose, she went so far as to confide to her cousin Minnie that she was worried Sol would find another woman in Bangor. The *Bintel Brief* column in the *Forverts*, after all, carried a steady flow of letters from wives abandoned by their men. It was the first time in decades Rose had thought of Sol as a catch. The pay envelopes from Maine, meanwhile, sustained her hope of rescuing Ester Dina. The Soviet Army now occupied Bialystok, having replaced the Germans by the end of September 1939 under the dictatorships' plan for dismembering Poland. Back in World War I, when Rose lived in Bialystok, it was the Kaiser's troops who had qualified as the lesser of evils, being greeted with bread and salt by Jews grateful to be rid of the czar. Rose herself often described the plight of Jews in her home city by degrees of worse: "The Poles are worse than the Germans. The Russians are worse than the Poles." Having experienced a brief sample of Hitler's sort of Germans, however, Jews like Rose's brothers and sisters had cheered the Red Army with its Jewish officers and troops as liberators. The *bourgeois* elements, the "unreliables," were packed off to Siberia, of course, but one Markiewicz brother was already a revolutionary, and prosperity was not a curse under which Ester Dina in particular suffered. Rose stuffed the dollar bills from Sol in the sack amid the box springs.

Then, abruptly, the season of comfort, or what passed for it in Apartment 24, came to an end. Sol's brother Dave died in June of 1940, and when Sol traveled home for the funeral, he stayed put. Rose wept with relief to have him back; she clutched him with a passion the children had rarely seen. Sol's last pay envelopes bought a secondhand couch and chairs for about $20, the first such furniture the family ever owned, and a $5 upright piano from a friend. Now Eleanor, who had been taking lessons at a settlement house, could practice at home. Sol also bestowed on her a pair of Penobscot moccasins, a special women's model, creamy white with brown stitching and tassels.

Eleanor took them straight out to Crotona Park to show her girlfriends. But the moccasins were not what excited her most. In the final week of school that June, the halfway point of her senior year at Morris, Eleanor was walking up Boston Road with Marion. "Come on upstairs and say hello to my father," she said. "He's home now." As Eleanor gave Sol a hug and kiss, father-less Marion looked on with envy. As if sensing her longing, Sol said, *"Nu, Marion, un du gibst mir nit a kush?"* So, Marion, aren't you going to give me a kiss? Marion savored every second of his embrace, and Eleanor savored the sight of her closest friend being compensated, at least for a fleeting moment, for eleven years without a father.

In the end, Sol had earned precisely $850 in slightly less than six months in Maine. During the remaining months of 1940, he bounced through seven different factories, making less than $400. On the day Eleanor applied for a Social Security card, she listed her father's occupation as "unemployed."

On the stage of the Morris High School auditorium, from which Elmer E. Bogart had held forth during Eleanor's first week as a Goodwin pupil, she herself now commanded the lectern. In the autumn of 1940, her final semester, she was running for president of the senior class. More than a platform, she offered a re-sume—first in class rank; Honor Society member; associate editor of the school paper; Service League selectee; participant in the literary society, drama club, yearbook staff, and infirmary squad; only girl in the calculus class; and a real looker besides. As lightly as Eleanor customarily wore academic garlands, she coveted the presidency. It bespoke the popularity she craved rather than the intelligence she took for granted. For weeks now, she had been making campaign stops in one homeroom after another.

Across the stage from Eleanor stood her opponent, Buddy Rashbaum. He seemed by no measure her equal. He had entered Morris's main building only for his senior year, having spent his first two years among the commercial and general-curriculum students at the battered old annex. None of his three older siblings even had graduated from high school. Buddy lived down the hill from Morris, down the economic ladder from subsistence to survival, and with his father out of work as a paper-hanger and the family sometimes resorting to "midnight moves" to dodge the landlord, the Rashbaum children devised their own methods of bringing in money. Abe, the middle of three brothers, fought bare-knuckle bouts in vacant lots, betting on himself to win. Buddy served as a runner for a neighborhood bookie named Sammy B.

He brought those street smarts to the campaign. He had a loyal constituency from the annex, which he'd represented in the student government as an underclassman. He was pals from shooting pool and playing craps with the tough Irish boys who starred on Morris's sports teams. All those kids, Buddy understood, resented the Goodwin program's eggheads. And the fact that Eleanor was such a beauty, and seemed to know it with the swishy way she walked, gliding like she was above it all, would turn the plainer girls against her. With his dark wavy hair and thick brows, Buddy excited their fantasies instead of their jealousies.

Heading into this day's confrontation, Buddy had gotten a professional sign painter, a friend of his sister's, to dash off flyers for the Morris hallways: VOTE FOR BUDDY, HE'S YOUR BUDDY. When he spoke, he didn't even try to volley Eleanor's list of ideas and proposals, much less her credentials. He just promised parties and dances, and then he launched his ultimate weapon, a slogan that declared, "Vote to see who the better man is." As the audience roared, Buddy slipped a glance sideways at Eleanor. She shot back a bitter smirk. The next day, when the votes were tallied, she would most uncharacteristically lose.

Out in the middle rows of the auditorium, a boy named Howard Gropper took in Eleanor's performance with appreciative eyes and a slack jaw. Like Buddy a recent arrival from the annex, Howard had spotted Eleanor occasionally in the hallways, enough to feel his teenaged sap rising. Now he found himself just as wowed by her speech. The son of a clothing salesman, albeit one relying these days on a clerk's job with the WPA, Howard placed high value on presence and persuasion and public image. He had learned an incessant, almost valiant kind of positivism from his father, who never let hard times dampen his taste for dancing, schnapps, and seven-card rummy. Because Howard carried himself with similar confidence, whether on the basketball court or behind a drum kit, few classmates guessed just how precarious his family's existence really was. Howard walked forty minutes uphill to Morris from the Clason Point neighborhood to save the nickel streetcar fare.

"You see that girl up there?" Howard whispered to the classmate beside him in the auditorium. "I'm gonna take her to the Senior Prom."

The boy snickered and said, "Where do *you* come to *her*?"

"I'm gonna get to know her," Howard said, rising to the challenge. "And I'm gonna see that she goes with me to the prom."

When the campaign speeches ended, Eleanor and Buddy left the stage, and their classmates now looked unimpeded on the auditorium's mural. As it had every moment since its unveiling in 1926, the painting portrayed shell holes, barbed wire, and gun carriages around the burned ruins of a French village. It also showed three heavenly figures descending from a clear sky. The mural was entitled, "After Conflict Comes Peace," and those words had formed the civilized world's promise after the Great War. But more with each passing day, the painting's image of wartime destruction seemed as timely as a newsreel.

Just five months earlier, near the end of the spring semester, France had surrendered to a new German invader. On the September weekend before the fall term began, the German blitz of London had killed 600 people and wounded 2,000. A week later, Congress had enacted the first peacetime conscription in American history, and hundreds of the East Bronx's young men reported to a processing center at Morris High School when registration commenced on October 16. Draft Board 95 meanwhile set up shop in P.S. 40, Eleanor's old junior high. Her Morris classmates now included a handful of Jewish refugees from France and Morocco. One's family had escaped occupied Paris, or so the school gossip had it; another had been fortunate enough to be marooned in New York on a vacation trip to the World's Fair when the Maginot Line cracked. As with the Brenner brothers on the Fulton Avenue benches, nobody asked or told very much. Hints just slipped out sometimes. On the day Paris fell in June 1940, Eleanor and Marion Herzog had been rehearsing folk songs for a presentation by Morris's French club when a refugee named Irene Violette Bellot broke into tears. The two of them walked her home along Boston Road that afternoon, and when their classmate Mel Goodman caught up and started to ask why Irene's face was so red, Marion said softly, "She's having a hard time."

Except in such rare, abbreviated moments, though, the war remained for Eleanor and her friends merely the backdrop to being a teenager. Draft age started at twenty-one, five years away from most of the precocious boys in the Goodwin program. Girls weren't eligible for much besides the "Stop Hitler Now" poster contest, sponsored by the Women's Division of the Committee to Defend America by Aiding the Allies. When Eleanor and some other Morris seniors wrote and performed satiric skits in the annual show called "Morrismania," the greatest laughter went to a sketch about conscription. It had Flo Zipkin, one of the prettiest girls in school, trying to register, being informed that "we can't take you," and replying with a coquette's sass, "Oh, never mind, but I'll take that lieutenant over there." For every gung-ho movie like *Dawn Patrol* or *U-Boat 29,* there were more confections on the order of *Down Argentine Way* with Don Ameche and Betty Grable, or Jeannette McDonald as *Girl of the Golden West.* If you were Eleanor, sixteen and a half, eyelash curler in your purse, senior cap on your head, the autumn of 1940 was a time to think about college, a time to go a little boy-crazy, a time to become who you wanted to be.

The sensation of feeling grown-up first had taken hold a few months earlier in a Manhattan nightclub called the Hurricane. With its palm fronds, thatched beach grass, and renderings of outrigger canoes, the place fancied itself as "Tahiti on Broadway," "New York's smart tropical rendezvous." Certainly, it was as close as Eleanor ever had come to inhabiting those Charles Nordhoff novels of Polynesia that she had adored in junior high, and with two decidedly welcome additions—a date and a drink.

Marion Herzog's mother had sprung for a Sweet Sixteen party for her daughter at the Hurricane, and

Eleanor was there with Hy Keltz. Fetching as Marion looked in a strapless gown, her escort was not a true beau, but an older, urbane, and obviously dutiful family friend named Bob. Never before had Eleanor partaken of this Manhattan, slinky and nocturnal. When a waiter took cocktail orders, not demonstrating the slightest interest in discerning who had reached the legal drinking age of eighteen, Eleanor asked for what sounded appropriate: a Manhattan. Somebody at the table warned her she'd hate the taste and her throat would burn, but the first sip went down warm and nearly sweet, and left behind a dizzy sort of confidence. By the time several rounds later that the Hurricane's photographer snapped a table portrait, she could offer only a glassy, if contented, gaze.

Over the next few months, Hy Keltz drifted away from Eleanor, and first love gave way to first heartbreak, which was its own sort of maturation. She was still in high school and he was more than a year out, now earning the incredible sum of $45 a week cutting shoulder pads in the garment district. Scissors in hand, Eleanor went through every snapshot of them both and methodically snipped out Hy, leaving as proof of his existence only a single disembodied hand clutching her arm in one photo. When Marion sat down at the Hatkins' piano one afternoon and started playing "Somewhere Over the Rainbow," Hy and Ellie's song, Eleanor demanded she stop.

Hy had been more than a boyfriend, he had been a type, what Eleanor in some not quite articulate way was starting to realize was her type. A rugged guy. A guy with brawny forearms and a strong jaw and smoldering eyes. Capable, handy. Quick, even smart, but not as smart as she. And sort of from the wrong side of the tracks. The archetype had been up there on the Paradise screen when she watched *Wuthering Heights*—Heathcliff the Liverpool guttersnipe, Heathcliff the brooding stableboy, Heathcliff the "gypsy beggar," Heathcliff telling highborn Cathy, "Some of that beggar's dirt is on you" and Cathy answering, "Yes, yes."

Eleanor's moping subsided as the fall went on and the social whirl of senior year gathered momentum. Having finally consented to co-ed lunchrooms, Morris held Friday afternoon dances in the gym for its seniors. Even the sallow, callow Goodwin boys were discovering the opposite sex, Joe Lempert by sneaking peeks through *Paris Night* at his uncle's newsstand. When Morris voted on senior favorites at an assembly in mid-November, Eleanor didn't repeat her mistake during the class election of trying to be accepted as both female and serious. She made her pitch to be chosen All-Around Girl while wheeling around on roller skates. It worked.

Eleanor's sister Fannie was by now a first-semester junior at Morris, an eyeful herself with a Betty Boop figure, and they become partners again in the chase for boys. Together with Fannie's friends Ruth Klekman and Hilda Saltzman, they formed a group called the Cadettes, sort of a cellar club without a cellar. "Twinkle, twinkle little star, powder and a cold cream jar," went one of the doggerels they wrote. "Eyebrow pencil, lipstick, too, might make a beauty out of you." Sometimes the Cadettes went to dances at the Fulton Avenue YMHA, music by Owen Ellington and His Harlem Dukes. Sometimes they carried a windup phonograph and an armful of 78s into Crotona Park, jitterbugging on the playground asphalt. Sometimes they received a letter like this:

October 17, 1940

To the Cadettes,

We the Amis wish the presence of your members on Saturday evening to a party at 599 Jackson Ave., apt. 3. We would like you to arrive by 8:30 o'clock at the very latest, and for once would appreciate *"promptness"!*

Then, in the first week of December, every senior received the first formal announcement of the prom. It carried the imprimatur of Mrs. Alice C. Hartley, Faculty Adviser. The prom would be held a month hence at the Hotel Astor in Manhattan, feature a live orchestra, and proceed until the hour of 1 AM. Mrs. Hartley quoted Ralph Waldo Emerson on the subject of decorum ("the power of manners is incessant") and specified the dress code ("simple evening dress" for girls, dark suit with white linen shirt and "shoes and tie in harmony with the suit" for boys). Most of the two-page missive, though, consisted of myriad warnings and worries—not to smoke or chew gum, not to request songs from the band, not to spend too much on cabs or corsages, and especially not to venture after the prom to a nightclub. "If you feel you must satisfy your craving for nourishment," the letter went on, "choose a place that may do so without emptying your pocket book or mortgaging your financial future."

Howard Gropper, reading the announcement, knew it was time to make good on his vow to take Eleanor to the prom. And doing so, he recognized, would mean violating many of those rules. He planted himself in strategic stretches of the Morris hallways between classes so as to oh-so-incidentally run into Eleanor. He walked up Boston Road after school with Eleanor and Marion, pretending it was on the way to his part-time job. Instead, once he dropped off Eleanor at 1461, he doubled back at a gallop to Sol Brooks's lingerie store on Prospect Avenue. He earned $4 a week returning damaged goods to the garment district in Manhattan, and he began setting aside a portion of his keep for the prom. Sometimes he walked into Manhattan with the delivery so he could pocket the thirty cents the boss gave him for carfare. No matter what Mrs. Alice C. Hartley, Faculty Adviser, advised, Howard intended to bring flowers, take a cab, and top off the night in a club.

First, of course, he had to get Eleanor to say yes. In the hallway shortly before Morris broke for Christmas vacation, he spotted her, waited for the crowd around her to disperse, and strode up with his salesman's moxie to say, "I'd sure love to take you to the prom." Eleanor told him she'd let him know. The demurral only intensified his competitive spirit and his crush. This wasn't just the prom anymore; he could picture himself marrying the girl. Around the neighborhood, inside Morris, he seized every chance to sidle up to Eleanor and rhapsodize about the flowers and the cab and the club, how he'd give her the kind of prom night she deserved. And, heck, he was a handsome enough guy, maybe not the coiled physical specimen that Hy Keltz was, but tall and broad-shouldered. Finally, Eleanor accepted.

On prom night, Howard walked nearly an hour from Clason Point to 1461 Boston Road; he didn't dare waste even a nickel on the trolley. He was dressed the way his father had taught him, draped in a double-breasted suit with boutonniere on the lapel and pocket square plumped up just so. He carried in a cardboard box a corsage of tea roses. When the door to Apartment 24 opened, Howard beheld Eleanor, ravishing in a pink taffeta gown. Near her sat Marion Herzog, unadorned. She had turned down her two offers for the prom—one boy had acne, the other had blackheads—in favor of helping Eleanor primp and settling again for second place. Howard walked Eleanor by the arm down the hall, through the courtyard, and onto the curb so he could hail a cab. Until this moment, she had not fully believed he was telling the truth. Who could afford a taxi all the way to Manhattan? Neither Howard nor Eleanor had ever taken one in their lives. In their wake, Marion left Apartment 24, too, to sit alone through Deanna Durbin in *Spring Parade* at the Loew's Boston Road, something ridiculous with her baking bread for Emperor Franz Joseph.

Meanwhile, Howard and Eleanor flirted and fox-trotted through the prom, which was really just the pre-amble of their night. At one o'clock, they left the Astor for the Coconut Grove nightclub, where Howard had made reservations. Between sets by the house band, the club invited guests to race across the dance floor on miniature wooden thoroughbreds, and Howard won first place and a bottle of champagne. He presented it to Eleanor, one more luxury in a night of them. Finally, toward four o'clock, they tumbled into a cab for the trip back to Boston Road. On the stoop of 1461, in the January chill, Howard kissed Eleanor—a long kiss, though not too long, because the cabbie's meter was still running. For all of prom night's costly elegance, all the saving and scheming, all the persuading and persist-ing, Howard could tell Eleanor wasn't his girl. The lyrics to a blues song ran through his head:

> I took you to a nightclub
> I bought you pink champagne
> I took you home in a taxi
> Then I caught the subway train
> That's not right. . . .

Howard gave it one last lavish try a few weeks later. He took Eleanor to the Glen Island Casino, just north of the Bronx in New Rochelle, to hear Glenn Miller. They nursed a few drinks between dances, and Howard kept checking his watch. He had calculated that he couldn't afford to buy Eleanor dinner, but the casino served a lower-priced breakfast after midnight, and he hoped bacon and eggs to a Glenn Miller soundtrack would count for something on the Boston Road stoop later on. Instead, Eleanor's goodnight kiss seemed perfunctory, passionless. Does she expect every night to be prom night? Howard wondered. Does she want a guy who's rich? Why is she always mentioning other guys? Howard dragged his confused self back to Clason Point and talked it over with his mother, who already had sized up Eleanor as a tease. "She wants a little more out of life," he conceded, "than the average fella can give her."

Not all of it, of course, involved romance. She wanted the way out of the East Bronx that her brain could provide, and that wasn't so easy for a girl. The renowed uptown campus of City College admitted men only. The downtown branch, though co-ed, was three-quarters male. Hunter College turned out women to be teachers, not Eleanor's aspiration. And even with free tuition for qualified students, how many families could afford to have a child, especially a daughter, taking up bed and board instead of helping out with a job? Eleanor's friend from the Fulton Avenue benches, Lillian Golden, had switched from the academic to the commercial curriculum, abandoning her dream of teaching math in favor of bookkeeping. Lillian's parents enlisted Eleanor to try to dissuade her, and they them-

selves vowed, "We'll eat bread and drink water." But
Lillian had seen enough during the Depression—her father wiped out in real estate and getting lead poisoning
from his fallback job as a painter; her mother crying the
day they lost their apartment; those home relief inspectors snooping through drawers and closets. She would
wear the same dress to graduation as to her first day on
the job in the garment district, keeping books for a
clothing distributor called H. H. Butler.

Materially, things weren't much better in the Hatkin
house; the relative windfall from Bangor had been spent
long ago. But at the top of her class with an average of
95.24, Eleanor qualified for a state scholarship, one of
only three hundred for the entire city. It would provide
her with $100 a year for all four years of college. She
stood a strong chance, too, of getting help from the National Youth Administration, the New Deal program
sometimes called the "junior WPA." One of its chief
goals was to democratize higher education, largely by
supplying financial aid in the form of $10 or $15 a
month for an on-campus job. The NYA was aimed at
students just like Eleanor, bright kids from families that
had never sent anyone to college. The alternative path
was Lillian Golden's, matriculating at a *schmatte* shop.

As Bernie Solomon won admission to City College
and Marion Herzog chose Hunter, Eleanor made her se-
lection in typically headstrong fashion. She would en-
roll at Brooklyn College starting in February 1941. The
campus lay two hours and several transfers by subway
from the East Bronx, but at least it was a genuine cam-

pus, newly erected on forty acres of a former golf course. Brooklyn College had a clock tower, a quadrangle, Georgian architecture, and a landscape planted with 8,000 shrubs, trees, and flowers. The surrounding neighborhood, except for the business district along Flatbush Avenue, consisted of tidy brick or stucco bungalows on shady streets. For an urban college, Brooklyn offered a passable facsimile of Jeannette McDonald's Vassar in *Rosalie*. At least it did to a girl from a Boston Road tenement.

Something beyond the physical setting recommended Brooklyn to Eleanor. Unlike her other options—Hunter with its assembly line for future teachers, City's downtown campus with its emphasis on business skills— Brooklyn College espoused a liberal arts curriculum untainted by what its president disparaged as "sloppy vocationalism." Even amid complaints by state officials about its "frills," Brooklyn offered Greek and Latin, ancient history, advanced mathematics, the very subjects that had stirred Eleanor's intellect at Morris. Brooklyn told her there was more to college than getting a secure job; there was a life of the mind.

For now, she only had to depart Morris High School in glory. Standing eleven places behind Howard Gropper and three in front of Marion Herzog, Eleanor marched into the Morris auditorium to the stiff cadences of the "Triumphal" march. Outside on the Wednesday morning of January 29, 1941, it was bitterly cold, with ten inches of slushy snow frozen hard overnight and cars skidding through intersections and into lampposts. While 480 seniors would graduate, some 235 young men from the Bronx were reporting that day to Fort Dix for basic training. Congress was heatedly debating the lend-lease bill proposed by FDR.

All the worldly distress, though, receded for the festivities. Only one Morris boy, Charles Shannon from the commercial curriculum, had enlisted in the military, and he was far from the auditorium, on a Navy base in Rhode Island. In the essays and short stories that seniors contributed to the yearbook and the *Tower* literary magazine, virtually none referred to the European war. "We must all eventually face the world and its problems," wrote a girl named Marguerite Reid. "The greatest of these problems is the securing of employment." Eleanor's contributions wryly traced the hemispheres of her person, the dueling realms of her brain and her heart. In the *Tower*, she cracked wise about grammar, recalling the English teacher who had likened an appositive to a pig that would rumble loose unless penned in by commas fore and aft.

Instead of counting sheep when I can't go to sleep, I count pigs trying to escape captivity by running down a street and leaping over a pen at the other end. When I've finally dozed off as a result of this torturing procedure, I see hogs playing at circus by jumping through loops consisting of two commas joined together at the ends. It's too late for anything to cure me of my run down condition; my teacher has done the damage and I'm doomed to a life of nightmares and troubles.

And in the yearbook, beneath the headline "Ah, How I Loved You," she unfolded a farce of schoolgirl infatuation. She depicted herself swooning over an algebra teacher given the pseudonym Mr. Milner—"tall, well-built, black wavy hair, blue sparkling eyes"—who bore a certain resemblance to the actual Mr. Kolevczon. When Mr. Milner invites Eleanor to stay after-school to discuss third-degree equations, she conceives of it as a date. When he asks her to do some typing, she interprets it as growing ardor. The story built to this conclusion:

> Then one day, "You know, Eleanor, there's something about you that I've noticed and liked for a long time." My heart stood still. Could my dreams be coming true? I began to make mental calculations. I was almost seventeen. Mr. Milner couldn't be more than twenty-seven and after all what was ten years' difference when two people really loved each other? Then he continued, "Yes, I've always liked the way you keep brushing that hair back that falls into your eye when you type. It brings a little domestic life into my business life. My wife has the same habit."

As the moment arrived for awards and diplomas, Elmer E. Bogart did not approach the podium. He had retired as principal the previous June, but the Goodwin students, above all others, ratified his insistence upon "achievement to capacity." Bernie Solomon and Marion Herzog had been voted the boy and girl Most

Likely to Succeed. Mel Goodman joined them among the twenty-eight students on the Honor Roll; their names would be painted in gold on a plaque in center hall. The morning, though, belonged to Eleanor as to no other. She won the Mathematics Medal (98.62 average), the Award of the American Association of Teachers of French (95.50 average), and the Medal for Cooperation in Government. She received pins as a member of Arista and the Service League. Most notably of all, she accepted a medal with a ribbon in the Morris colors of maroon and white and a brass pendant showing the lamp of knowledge illuminating an open book. The medal bore the inscription:

THE MORRIS H.S.
ALUMNI ASSN.
TO ELEANOR HATKIN
HIGHEST RANKING GRADUATE
JAN. 1941

When the ceremony ended, the graduates flipped their tassels, tossed their mortarboards, and marched exuberantly into the auditorium lobby. Parents struggled up the jammed aisles, searching for their children to kiss and hug and fuss over. Howard Gropper found his mother and father and introduced them to Eleanor. It wasn't so unreasonable to keep hoping, was it? Just a few days earlier, she'd been his date for his eighteenth birthday party. "Bring your folks to meet my Mom and Dad," he said. Eleanor said she didn't know where they were. "Come on, they've got to be here," Howard persisted. "Bring 'em over." Eleanor muttered some other excuse, but Howard noticed she didn't seem to be looking very hard. Then he remembered something from prom night. When he'd picked up Eleanor at 1461, she'd hustled him in and out of Apartment 24 so fast he barely had seen Sol and Rose, not even been able to say a proper hello. So eloquent and articulate, and suddenly so evasive and indifferent—Eleanor was ashamed, Howard realized, ashamed of her parents.

Moments after the Groppers drifted off, Rose made her way to Eleanor. Eleanor clutched her pins and medals in her fist. For most students, they were the most precious of keepsakes, amulets infused with memory and achievement; you might part with your senior pin only to ask a girl to go steady. Rose, of course, maintained her china cabinet shrine for just such mementos, and the Alumni Association medal would complement Eleanor's award from elementary school for "General Excellence and Character," engraved brass with an orange and black ribbon. The cabinet gave Rose status, or so she believed, with her better-off relatives, the Gartenbergs and the Osders; it gave her that parental pride known in Yiddish as *nuches*. "*Ay-lee,*" she called in her Bialystok voice to her American daughter. Eleanor shoved the medals and pins at Rose and said, "Here, take them home."

Marion Herzog and her mother Florence, standing nearby, had seen the whole showdown. Florence shook her head, bemused. Marion silently seethed. After all her early misgivings about Morris, that creaky heap of bricks, she had grown to cherish its teachers and to crave excellence by their standards. So how could Eleanor be so blasé? Here Marion had missed that French medal by a single point. How much would it have meant to Florence had she won it? Marion knew she had studied harder than Eleanor, studied with the self-discipline acquired in a decade at the piano. Eleanor, infuriatingly, was a natural.

Yet there was something other than modesty or disregard in the Eleanor Hatkin that the Herzogs had just witnessed. All the delight in her yearbook and *Tower* essays, all the wild joy when she brayed like a donkey, all the delicious mischief of tinkling bells in Mr. Kammiter's class—all that pleasure had been purged from Eleanor's flat, dismissive tone. She would give Rose the hardware but none of the *naches*.

On June 27, 1941, five days after having attacked its putative ally the Soviet Union, Nazi Germany conquered Bialystok. The next day, German troops ordered 2,000 Jews into the Great Synagogue, locked the doors, and burned it to the ground.

One sunny afternoon in September 1941, the Hatkin family climbed the six flights to the roof of 1461 Boston Road. As Sol held his Brownie box camera, Fannie and Eleanor mulled their pose. Fannie was wearing a dark skirt and white cotton sweater. Eleanor had on a waisted dress in a floral-print pattern with a low neckline trimmed in lace. She had on lipstick, earrings, and the faux pearl bracelet she had bought the summer she lost all that weight. There was a white gardenia in her hair.

Both sisters recalled a scene from *It Happened One Night*. Clark Gable is trying without any luck to hitch a ride and finally his companion, Claudette Colbert, steps onto the road to take over. Just like in the movie, Eleanor and Fannie each cocked the thumb of one hand while using the other to lift her skirt and display an alluring length of thigh. Fannie shifted uneasily into position, her grin pinched, her eyes slightly averted, as if the flourish made her self-conscious. Eleanor beamed. She was on her way somewhere.

Ruth Klekman, Hilda Saltzman, and Eleanor,
Coney Island, Summer 1943

Two
Waiting
1941–1945

HUDDLED TOGETHER under a single umbrella, lashed by a cold, slanting rain, Eleanor and Fannie Hatkin and their father Sol lurched down Boston Road and toward the dance at the Painters Union hall. They had not even wanted to go, the sisters, not on this foul night. Sol was the one who insisted. Somebody in his union had given him two tickets, and he was not somebody to squander a freebie, even if this particular mixer was being sponsored by the Young Communist League. The Russians were fighting off Hitler, after all, and how else were his daughters supposed to meet nice Jewish boys? So when they resisted, he promised to walk them down to Intervale Avenue, keep them dry, and then discreetly disappear.

Fannie and Eleanor teetered squeakily in galoshes they had pulled over their high heels. The wind swept under the cotton kerchiefs they had tied over their hairdos. It would be a miracle if they made it seven blocks to the dance looking presentable enough to be asked. Coming on nine o'clock, five hours into darkness, the streets were practically deserted, the sky ashen, the puddles black as ink. A few peddlers in stocking caps and aprons roasted chestnuts or potatoes over sputtering fires fed with slats from vegetable crates. Dim light showed from the occasional candy store or newsstand, already displaying the early edition of the Sunday papers. The *Herald Tribune* had a photo of a submarine chaser being launched in the Harlem River that morning; the *Bronx Home News* posted a banner headline, ROOSEVELT URGES HIROHITO PRESERVE PEACE. Sol would treat himself to some reading when he returned to 1461, his own Saturday night indulgence.

Eleanor and Fannie stepped out of the gale and into the union hall, which they could at least give credit for being warm and dry. The main room had been cleared of the rank-and-file's folding chairs. A couple of tables at the front held a phonograph, records, and a spread of coffee and cake. As usual, the women had withdrawn to one wall, the men to another, all of them bashful and yearning at once. At sixteen, halfway through her senior year at Morris, Fannie never had had a boyfriend, unless she counted that time Neil Rosenberg waited for her outside 1461, handed her a gift box containing an orange sweater, and ran blushing away. Now she shed her coat to reveal a green rayon dress with a shoulder bow, the only one she owned outright. Eleanor undid her kerchief, touched up her curls, and freshened her lipstick.

Among the men stood three or four from an athletic club called the Collegians. Leon Becker, the short one with the shock of black hair, was the reason they were here. He had dropped out of high school when his father died, gone to work in a ribbon shop and then a garment factory, and already been beaten up for passing out handbills for Local 65 of the Distributive Workers of America. He liked to say that was how he learned the meaning of class struggle. The tall one next to Leon, hair slicked back to reveal a pronounced widow's peak at just twenty-one, was Danny Schlomkowitz. Working days in a printing plant, going to City College at night, he was along for the ride. Any free dance was a good dance. Danny's family had spent much of the Depression on home relief and moved twelve times from concession to concession.

Danny sized up the two girls across the room as an Italian and a Puerto Rican, enticing but off-limits, though everybody said Communist girls believed in free love. It took some small talk for him to discover that these were in fact sisters and Jews, and the one he had taken to be Italian, Fannie, had a shyness that to his smitten eyes seemed like an aura of mystery. Leon set his gaze on Eleanor, older and sexier, but Eleanor was more interested in a different Collegian, Sid Cozin, a star on City's baseball team. That was a mistake. Everybody in the club knew Sid wanted to marry a rich girl, which ruled out a girl from Boston Road.

So they danced to "Deep Purple" and "I Said No" and "All The Things You Are." Eleanor went through several partners, none worth pursuing, while Fannie and Danny coupled up. He wasn't much of a dancer, she figured that out right away, more enthusiasm than elegance on the floorboards. Yet at nearly six feet and a rock-hard 190 pounds, he had a presence, a vigor you could feel right through his suit. And the way he joked and laughed and bounced to the music in his gum-sole shoes, there was an ebullience. The man Fannie knew best, the standard by default for any suitor, was her father, and Danny exuded a strength and an effortless joy that were traits alien to fragile, feckless Sol.

When the dance ended toward midnight, Danny walked Fanny and Eleanor a few blocks to McKinley Square to pick up the Boston Road streetcar. It was colder now, still overcast, but no longer pouring. At the corner of Bristow, just opposite the entrance to 1461,

Eleanor got off. Fannie and Danny continued on several more blocks to a bowling alley. By the time she tiptoed into Apartment 24 and climbed beside Eleanor into her half of the daybed, it was two hours into the Sunday of December 7, 1941.

Shortly before 12:30 the next afternoon, Eleanor grappled her way toward a seat in the Pauline Edwards auditorium of City College's downtown branch on East 23rd Street in Manhattan. Normally the room was an island of serenity amid the sour clamor of a campus that really wasn't a campus at all but an eight-story building crammed from morning to midnight with 7,000 students. Eleanor could slip into a back row to study undisturbed, or at worst have her attention flit to a theater rehearsal onstage, somebody singing Gershwin. In the late summer of 1941, after just one semester, she had abandoned Brooklyn College's quadrangle and its liberal-arts curriculum for the practicality and shorter commute of City downtown, formally known as the School of Business Administration. Even in an economy heated up by war mobilization, Sol had earned less than a thousand dollars so far in 1941, and nothing at all since October except for sixty bucks from some random shifts at a luggage factory. His shortfall was forcing Eleanor, four months shy of eighteen, into the position of breadwinner.

All around Eleanor, students dropped into seats, waiting for the radio broadcast of Franklin Roosevelt's address to a joint session of Congress. They stashed away their graph paper and capped their India ink, those staples of statistics class. With the room at its capacity of 2,500, latecomers lined the walls and jammed into the entry doors. "Dirty Japs," some guys hollered. "What's this mean to us?" others asked in muffled tones. The rest held a silence that was both somber and self-interested. Until 2:26 the previous afternoon, when an announcer named Len Sterling had broken into the Mutual Broadcasting Network's coverage of the Giants-Dodgers football game, few of downtown City's young men had even known where Pearl Harbor was. The student paper, the *Ticker,* recently had run a joke about avoiding conscription: "Izz Klein told his draft board he has a heart murmur. It keeps murmuring, 'Don't go, don't go.'" The humor column in another edition cracked, "There's one thing about working in a concentration camp—you beat such interesting people."

At the uptown campus of City College, Jewish students responded to the Depression and global turmoil by trying to remake the world; every radical sect claimed its alcove in the cafeteria. The downtown branch's Jews wanted, as their parents unceasingly put it, to "make something of yourself." With banks and insurance companies largely closed to them by anti-Semitism, 70 percent were majoring in accounting, aspiring to reach the glassed-in offices of the garment factories where their fathers cut or pressed or sewed. One of their standard quips was that the curriculum could be boiled down to one precept: Marry the boss's daughter. Much of the interventionist sentiment that did exist at downtown City derived from a dubious source, Communist sympathizers who contorted their position to suit the party line. Until Hitler abrogated the Nazi-Soviet pact, they had been the pacifists carrying placards saying, THE YANKS AREN'T COMING.

Out of family necessity, Eleanor had joined the pragmatists. She was putting in thirty hours a month at the college library for the National Youth Administration, working alternately as a salesgirl at McCreery's department store and a bookkeeper for the F&G Doll Shoe Company, and all the while taking eighteen and a half credits. And those credits were a dull billet—required classes in English Composition, Hygiene, Public Speaking, and Principles of Economics; Mathematics of Finance with three hours a week of bonds, mortgages, annuities, and interest; and an Advanced French class devoted not to Proust or Molière but to contemporary writers on business. Overwhelmed and uninspired, and perhaps expecting to coast on natural talent as she had at Morris, she was heading for a lot of Cs.

City downtown had a way of making its women in particular feel unwelcome. They were poachers, competitors, distractions to the young men learning to do men's work. The college had gone co-ed only grudgingly less than a decade before, and still required female applicants to have an 88 average, compared to 80 for males. Not surprisingly, women wound up as a minority, one-fifth of the student body, and then were blamed for being one. A dean bluntly complained that their "unnatural popularity . . . interfered with the concentration on study."

Eleanor might well have wished he were right. At least then City downtown would have supplied the semblance of a social life. She had stopped in at a few parties thrown in off-campus apartments that approximated frat houses and tried a college hangout called the 23 Room, a cabaret with cocktails for 23 cents and a lady pianist doing songs rife with double entendres, what she called "frisqué ballads." A student in his early twenties named Jack Steinglass introduced himself—an accounting major, naturally, and Orthodox besides, not exactly Eleanor's taste—but he did have a kind of suave Adolph Menjou look with his mustache. So for lack of other social options, Eleanor went with him to the movies a few times.

Otherwise, the pickings were less than slim. The elite Townsend Harris High School occupied the top two floors of the 23rd Street building, and many of its precocious graduates stayed there for college, entering at fifteen or sixteen, pale and frail as yeshiva boys. Eleanor could cast her eye around the lecture hall in her introductory courses and not see enough facial hair for a mug of shaving cream. These whiz kids were more the sort to spit out their chewing gum in the water fountain. Either that or hide at the bottom of stairwells so they could look up skirts, which was as close as any of them were going to get to s-e-x. Eager for any friend, Eleanor had talked Lillian Golden into trying City downtown this semester. Lillian already had realized, though, she couldn't manage both college and her bookkeeping job at H. H. Butler, and decided to drop out. A girl accustomed to popularity, Eleanor was a stranger to this new isolation.

Meanwhile, in the Pauline Edwards auditorium, Roosevelt's voice was to issue from the public-address system at any moment. Eleanor's older classmates were doing a new equation, calculating the odds of being able to finish a degree before being sent off to Fort Dix. A similar expectancy took form all around the city. A dozen people gathered outside the open door of a Bronx taxicab with its radio playing. Five thousand waited beneath the loudspeakers in City Hall Park. Men in Times Square removed their hats. A judge in Brooklyn halted a trial to switch on the broadcast. Like all those anonymous strangers, like the classmates in the Edwards auditorium, Eleanor heard Roosevelt call December 7 "a date which will live in infamy." She heard him speak of the Japanese attack on Pearl Harbor and of the assaults that had followed on Hong Kong, Malaya, and the Philippines. And, as if there could be any doubt remaining, she heard him say, "Hostilities exist. There is no blinking at the fact that our people, our territory, and our interests are in grave danger."

The next day, Eleanor obediently paced through downtown City's first air-raid drill. Early the following week, the college announced it would move up graduation from June 1942 to January, cancel school vacations, and impose a three-semester schedule, all of it designed to more rapidly disgorge graduates into the armed forces. Downtown students bought $1,600 worth of defense stamps in five days. All women began taking first-aid training. The starting center of City's renowned basketball team was called up for active duty. As the downtown branch's yearbook, the *Lexicon,* put it several months later: "The walls were ripped down and the college could no longer hold any pretense of its independence as an entity. . . . The ivory tower was no longer. Facing entrance into the armed forces, the student body developed an indifference toward studies and student life."

Back home in the Bronx, Eleanor found the known world similarly upheaved. There was a run on sugar in anticipation of rationing. With a quota expected on rubber, too, five-and-dimes sold out of tennis balls and Spaldeens. Nearly a hundred couples a day, quadruple the usual, applied for marriage licenses in the borough. Federal agents shut the Bronx branch of an Italian bank, while a group of boys down on 151st Street lynched a Japanese in effigy. Alexander's advertised blackout cloth for 24 cents a yard, touting the "same quality as is being used in England." Across the street from 1461, the Loew's Boston Road featured Betty Grable, pert in her peaked cap, in *A Yank in the R.A.F.* And on December 10, three days after Pearl Harbor, it was confirmed that a fireman's son named Edward Cashman had died in the attack, making him the first son of the Bronx killed in action.

Eleanor felt some relief that the two males in her own

household were safe. Sol had passed the maximum draft age of forty-four, while Seymour was eleven, nine years from being eligible. He played war with a second-hand set of plastic soldiers given him by Mr. Libby the super and his wife, an odd bit of kindness to a Jewish boy from a couple so admiring of Hitler they had moved back to Germany a few months earlier. Nearly every boy Eleanor knew from Morris, though, would soon be old enough for conscription—her first boyfriend Hy Keltz, her prom date Howard Gropper, Bernie Solomon and Joe Lempert from the Goodwin program, even her antagonist from the senior class election, Buddy Rashbaum. Danny Schlomkowitz, Fannie's new beau, was already twenty-one. Bernie Murowitz, one of the Amis cellar club, had been trying to enlist underage in Canada. Jack Steinglass, the one City classmate Eleanor had dated, went into the army eight weeks after Pearl Harbor, having secured her promise to write to him.

Partly to distract herself, and partly in a moment of compassion for her parents, especially for Rose, now three years without word from Bialystok, Eleanor treated them to the first motion picture of their lives. It was *The Chocolate Soldier*, a tuneful little frippery, insubstantial as meringue, with her favorite Nelson Eddy playing dual roles as husband and would-be suitor of the same woman. "Thank the Lord the war is over," went one of the songs. If only vanquishing Hitler and Hirohito were so simple. One weekend day that first month of the war, Sol took Seymour for a walk through

Crotona Park, and there they spotted a group of soldiers in uniform, perhaps on a final home leave before shipping out. Sol looked at them, considered the duty ahead, and said to his son in a pitying tone, "They're babies."

One Monday evening early in the new, war-torn year of 1942, Sol Hatkin presented himself at Morris High School to learn to defend his country. He enrolled in the series of five classes that trained air-raid wardens. And on February 19, having attended lectures covering gas warfare, incendiary bombs, fire control, and even public relations, he received the rank of post warden in the Air Warden Service of the United States Citizens Defense Corps. He was assigned to the territory of Sector 3, Zone A in the 46th Precinct, otherwise known as 1461 Boston Road and two or three adjacent buildings.

Sol could not afford the uniform of khaki shirt and olive-drab pants that wardens were expected to purchase. But in the rudimentary garb of steel helmet and felt armband, equipped with flashlight, police whistle, and gas mask, he rose to duty every time the local siren spewed out the five-five-five sequence. He checked the roofs, the fire escapes, the alleys; he poked through corridors, courtyards, and stairwells. "Everybody put your lights out," he called up to every unshaded window. "Lights out! Lights out!" There was ample reason to think the Bronx would be a target with its shipyards and foundries, its armories and coastline. Should an attack start, Sol knew the nearest call-box to summon the firemen or police. Should rescue be required of him, he knew where in the precinct house to find the crowbar, shovel, axe, and pick. The cops even kept a fleet of carrier pigeons in case the telephone lines were knocked out by the Luftwaffe.

Every drill gave Sol that rare, coveted sensation of capability. Like electioneering for the Jackson Democratic Club, like stitching moccasins at Penobscot, patrolling behind the beam of his flashlight compensated for all those times Rose belittled him with complaints and a *knip*. She looked on with actual pride when he strode out of Apartment 24 to enforce the blackout, perhaps because Bialystok's war was now America's as well. Sol took Seymour with him to the civil-defense office on Wilkins Avenue. It was a storefront filled with men like himself, men with Yiddish accents and patched coats, too gimpy and gray for combat, yet eager to participate in the great common cause, to show loyalty, indeed love, for the nation that had delivered them from Cossacks and pogroms. In the old land, some had cut off a finger or blinded an eye to avoid conscription; here they volunteered for the home guard.

Sol and his cohorts notwithstanding, it had taken the Bronx some time to fully fathom being at war. During the first air raid, two days after Pearl Harbor, grown-ups chatted on the steps of the county building, pointing skyward for enemy planes as innocently as birdwatchers. Children dispatched from schools for the presumed safety of home instead picked up their sidewalk games of immies and ringalevio. A civil-defense zone commander on Bathgate Avenue got fired for smooching it up with female wardens at a rooftop New Year's Eve party. And for those young women, the most patriotic way to dodge an unwanted date was to gravely explain, "I'm a watcher tonight."

By this time, deep in the winter of 1942, even the cut-ups took civil defense seriously. The war, no matter how headlines and newsreels and censorship tried to shape it into cause for optimism, was going almost catastrophically. The Japanese had captured Manila on the second day of the new year, conquered Singapore the next month, and by early March reached almost to Australia and halfway across the Pacific toward California. Rommel's troops were driving through North Africa and into Egypt. Although the Russian winter had stalled the German army short of Moscow in December 1941, its U-boats had penetrated to America's Atlantic seaboard, sinking allied vessels carrying hundreds of thousands of tons of supplies. With New York slow to comply with blackout regulations, a German U-boat easily spotted and destroyed eight ships just offshore one January night. So there was nothing hyperbolic when Mayor Fiorello La Guardia, who was also the national chairman of the Office of Civil Defense, warned in an address that "the war will come right to our streets and residential districts."

In Apartment 24, the war was pervasive and yet elusive, there and not there. Sol continued to guard Section 3, Zone A against German bombers that did not appear. In junior high school, Seymour crouched under his desk during air-raid drills and received an identification tag for purposes of evacuation and family reunification. The plan called for Bronx schoolchildren to be shipped to the Catskills, which didn't sound half-bad if your family had never had the money for a vacation. Danny Schlomkowitz bought Seymour a bombardier game, made of cardboard instead of the metal needed for real planes, calculating that winning over the family was part of winning Fannie's heart. The Cadettes started publishing a newsletter entitled *Ah-Men!*, which included this account of the couple's second date:

> After a careful survey of all the different shows playing at various theaters, they ended up in the Paradise. There they saw "Nothing But Truth" with Bob Hope and another picture. She found him very entertaining, as usual. After that, Danny wanted to go to eat Chinks. Since Fannie doesn't like Chinks, they went into an Automat, where she had a good time with the waiters. When he took her home, he asked when he could see her again and they decided on their next date. He forced her into a 'good-night kiss.' However, Fannie promised she would never do it again, as it disgusted her.

Several months later, in May 1942, the Hatkins trooped over to Morris High School to receive their first ration books, pages of perforated coupons with the insignia of a battleship or cannon or tank. Sugar already had been rationed for a month by then, coffee and gas would be added by the end of the year, and both canned and fresh meat included in early 1943. Tea, cutlery, razor blades, toothpaste tubes, electric toasters—all ultimately fell under quotas. "If you don't need it," read the slogan on the Hatkins's rationing books, "DON'T BUY IT."

Rose and her household required no such admonition. Without even the remotest hope of a car, they were unaffected by the limits on tires and fuel. They had no electric appliances to repair or replace, just the icebox and washboard. They rarely had bought meat during the Depression, so they were hardly going to indulge when wartime shortages pushed chicken above $1.00 a pound. Rose could dicker informally with neighbors to get the extra sugar she needed for baking, and she didn't need a ration coupon to paw through the discarded vegetables at the Jennings Street market. Indeed, long before scrap drives became a national crusade, the Hatkins were well-practiced in scavenging. Now it qualified as patriotic for Rose to collect fat and grease, for Seymour to strip the silver paper from cigarette packs and fish tin cans from vacant lots. As for "Mr. Black"—the black market—that was something Rose and Sol had neither the desire nor the cunning to explore. It took those consummate survivors, Irving and Bernie Brenner, the Austrian Jewish refugees in the Fulton Avenue crowd, to start a lucrative traffic in bootleg nylons.

For Eleanor, the shortage that mattered most was a familiar one, the shortage in Sol's pocket on payday.

Having closed out 1941 almost constantly unemployed, he managed to earn barely two hundred dollars in the first quarter of 1942, here a few days in a belt factory, there a couple of weeks stitching slipcovers, then a few shifts doing camera cases. Even in shops plumped by military contracts for tents and boots, Sol did not last long.

More and more, the pressures and responsibilities descended on Eleanor, and at the same time she had troubles of her own. McCreery's had laid her off after the Christmas rush. Bookkeeping jobs were fitful because she had to wedge them in around fifteen or twenty hours of class. Congress had cut the National Youth Administration's funding for 1942 by two-thirds, ending Eleanor's job in the college library. Those $15 a month were a large part of what paid for her textbooks and supplies, the rare lunchtime splurge of cream cheese on raisin bread at Chock Full o' Nuts.

But what exactly was she killing herself for, anyway? If the point of a degree from City downtown was to go to work, then she might as well go to work. If her father couldn't support the family, somebody had to. Besides, her grades were already suffering from her juggling act. She had taken five Cs in eight classes in the fall term of 1941, more Cs than in her entire academic career, and racked up two more among her five courses in the spring semester of 1942. None of her friends from Morris would have believed it, the valedictorian just another face in the pack, the All-Around Girl outshone by those twerps from Townsend Harris. Luckily, most of Eleanor's friends simply assumed she was bound for *cum laude,* if not Phi Beta Kappa. It let her save face, keep up appearances. The private truth, of course, was a lot more humbling. Eleanor's friend Marion Herzog, the perennial also-ran at Morris, was nearly halfway through Hunter College on an accelerated schedule and aspiring to Columbia Law School.

As the term ended in June 1942, Eleanor made her decision. She was going to look for a full-time job, cut back her studies, and transfer into City downtown's night school, which was just like the dreary day program, only more so. The next semester, she took only three classes, all of them requirements for a degree in business administration, the utilitarian major for someone who loved French and Latin and journalism. The choice brought with it one more humiliation: Now that Eleanor was no longer a full-time student, the state revoked her scholarship. It was not just $100 a year she lost but the prestige and prowess it connoted, the memory of her excellence at Morris. When Fannie's friend Clare Abramowitz heard what happened, she pulled Eleanor aside, incredulous. "How can you give it up?" she asked. "The whole world is out there." Eleanor didn't want to hear it; she had already amputated the limb. "I want to see that my family has money," she simply answered. "If I work, they have money."

Most weekends the summer of 1942, Eleanor went to Orchard Beach. She hopped the Fordham Road bus, its open windows a respite on stifling days, and she wore a two-piece swimsuit beneath her sundress. That way she could save the cost of the bathhouse and have enough change to take the bus back home instead of hitching. At eighteen now, a college girl, she was more confident than ever showing off her figure, seeing how that shapely flesh registered in the mirror of a boy's eyes. Besides, the government was telling girls to shorten those hems and sleeves, to prune the pleats and ruffles off skirts, because all the fabric was needed for military uniforms. Eleanor couldn't have wished for a more felicitous coincidence of nationalism and narcissism.

People called Orchard Beach the "Bronx Riviera," one part resort and one part city, a place as magical in its way as the Loew's Paradise. Less than ten years earlier, it had been a spit of land with cottages reserved for Tammany Hall insiders. For the rest of the Bronx, there was a single municipal pool, in Crotona Park, and piers dropping into the filthy water off Hunts Point or Throgs Neck. Now, after Robert Moses and the WPA, Orchard Beach was a mile-long crescent of sand, not the pebbled, mucky stuff naturally found there along Pelham Bay but a fine-grained variety hauled in from the Atlantic coast. There was a stone promenade and a colonnaded pavilion. And the place belonged to everyone—the families swigging down Dr. Brown's Cel-Ray, the kids having splash fights in the shallow water at high tide, the young men sneaking off into the bushes to change and sometimes getting arrested for public nudity in the process.

A different mood suffused the beach in this summer,

not overtly changing anything, not dulling anyone's good time, and yet steadily rumbling beneath the giddy surface. No longer did mothers smear butter on children's sunburned shoulders; it couldn't be wasted when domestic supplies had been cut to steer dairy products to the armed forces. No longer did lifeguards scan the horizon only for swimmers in trouble; just a few weeks before, a U-boat had attacked several freighters off a busy Virginia beach. The hit songs floating on the shore breeze from portable radios were war songs—"Der Fuehrer's Face," "Don't Sit Under the Apple Tree," "Praise the Lord and Pass the Ammunition." All the flirtation and sexual horseplay—the co-ed chicken fights, the ice cube slipped down a buxom neckline—had a slightly desperate tinge. Nobody knew when these boys were shipping out, and nobody knew if they were coming back.

Eleanor went to the beach with Vicky Behar, because they were both unattached. Their third musketeer from Fulton Avenue, Lillian Golden, had fallen in love with a man four years her senior named Ralph Betstadt, and was trying to fend off her parents' pleas to break it off because he was too old and too sickly, a 4-F in the draft. Newly graduated from Morris High, Fannie was busy with secretarial school and Danny Schlomkowitz. Marion Herzog, self-disciplined as ever, was attending summer school at Hunter, working part-time at Gimbels department store, and volunteering as a Junior Hostess in the servicemen's canteen operated by Temple Emanuel, the German Jewish institution of Fifth Avenue.

With Vicky around, Eleanor had no worries about attracting male company. Of all her friends, Vicky was the firecracker, with a mound of red hair and lipstick to match, the object of crushes from Crotona Park to Pearl Harbor, where one of her unrequited admirers from the old neighborhood had survived the Japanese attack. Plus, Vicky had a couple of cousins, named Lou and Murray Glass, and those cousins had a bunch of friends from their neighborhood in East Harlem. Somebody would bring a radio, somebody would bring a blanket, somebody would bring a basket of peanut butter sandwiches, and they would stake out their little stamp of sand, seven or eight people among the hundred thousand at Orchard Beach on a scorcher. And that was how, one of those weekends in July 1942, Eleanor first met Charlie Greco.

He was a couple of months past twenty, with a wide, ruddy face and dark eyes topped by coarse, untamed hair. Stripped to his bathing trunks, he revealed etched muscles on his torso, shoulders, and legs. "Rugged, not pretty," Vicky Behar said to Eleanor. Charlie worked doing deliveries for a company in Manhattan that made sewing machine parts, mostly attachments for particular buttonholes or seams. Charlie imagined designing the pieces himself someday, maybe even becoming an engineer. But those aspirations, most of his serious self, lay hidden below a jocular exterior, jokes and hugs and a ready laugh. In his high school yearbook, when everyone else was proclaiming ambitions for the law or medicine or at least the police force, Charlie cracked that his goal was to dig ditches for the WPA. He had memorized Borsht Belt routines, and could entertain a whole party doing *shtick* with Murray Glass. In fact, and this was the thing about Charlie Greco, for an Italian guy he seemed mighty Jewish.

"You will learn from the Jews," his mother had told him so many times growing up in East Harlem. The Greco family's walk-up happened to be on Lexington Avenue and 114th Street, one of the Jewish pockets in a mostly Italian neighborhood. And Mary Greco had followed her own advice. Having left school after eighth grade, married at sixteen, and borne the first of five children two years later, she willed herself into a life of political engagement. She had helped the garment workers' union organize the factory where she sewed, canvassed for the Republican Party because it was the party of Fiorello La Guardia, and admired Congressman Vito Marcantonio of the left-wing American Labor Party. Rather than sending her children to Catholic school, the common choice in her heavily Italian neighborhood, she enrolled them in public school and headed the PTA. In all these enterprises—the labor union, reform politics, public education—Mary immersed herself among Jews. She bought *challah* on Fridays; she bargained in Yiddish with the pushcart peddlers.

So Charlie, the mama's boy of a different kind of mama, spent much of his childhood around the Harlem Hebrew Institute, a combination of settlement house and synagogue. There he made his closest friends, all of them Jews—Lou and Murray Glass, Abe Kronenfeld, Dick Gumerov, Bernie Dunetz, Bill Rosenhoch. He more or less joined their Zionist boys' club, the *Agudath Naarei Israel*, Gathering of the Children of Israel, and not just to be the *goy* ringer on the baseball team. At the Harlem Hebrew Institute, Charlie learned how to fox-trot, debate, and harmonize in a chorus. He picked up the right New York Jewish intonation to ask for a *"mawl-ted"* at Iffy Feiner's candy store. Every Saturday noon, he met Bill and Bernie outside the synagogue doors, and often they went down Fifth Avenue, itself another world, to the Metropolitan Museum of Art. Mary Greco was right about which kids were going places: Bernie and Bill were both admitted to Stuyvesant High, pinnacle of New York's public school system. Their example helped convince Charlie to take the academic curriculum at Benjamin Franklin, the neighborhood high school. Even after the Grecos moved into the Bronx during Charlie's sophomore year, he kept returning to those couple of Jewish streets in East Harlem.

It wasn't exactly or entirely that Charlie wanted to be Jewish; it was more that he associated Jewishness with intelligence, striving, and upward mobility. Most of all, in crossing the line, in stepping beyond the parochial bounds of Italian Catholicism, he was becoming an American. Marie Greco saw it at the dinner table. She might put hours into preparing a savory peasant stew, the whole apartment fragrant with escarole and peppers and figs, and Charlie would rather have white bread, diced carrots, and a chop, each carefully situated in a separate region of his plate. "My American eater," Mary would sigh in surrender.

For all that, Eleanor recognized well enough the rules, rules that were more like laws. Most of her friends wouldn't even consider dating a non-Jew. Just recently at the Temple Emanuel canteen Marion Herzog had turned away the interest of a handsome sailor from Chicago, who happened to have mentioned he was Italian. Why lose your heart on someone you couldn't possibly marry? Why lose your own family in the process? Everybody heard about the Jewish parents who cut off children who married out, who pronounced them dead and sat *shiva,* who spurned all appeals to sentiment or reason and spat back, "So you'll give me a *goldeneh matsayvah,*" a golden headstone. Eleanor understood all that. But wasn't she a line-crosser herself? And she wasn't really dating Charlie Greco. She wasn't going steady or anything. They were just sort of, golly gosh, hanging around.

Sometimes they hung around with the whole crowd at Orchard Beach. Sometimes they strolled alone in Crotona Park, an easy spot for Eleanor to slip into from 1461. Sometimes they met after work in the city, since the sewing machine shop where Charlie worked was only two blocks from the fur supplies business for which Eleanor was keeping books. Eventually they went out in the evenings, dancing at Starlight Park, catching a band at Glen Island Casino. In those settings, Eleanor discovered another part of Charlie, a romantic. He was a

graceful dancer, thanks to those lessons at the Harlem
Hebrew Institute. He sang in a confident baritone and
had a weakness for ballads, torchy numbers like "Have
You Met Miss Jones?" He even took the occasional
crack at writing lyrics of his own, filled with rhymes
about the stars and the moon and arms and charms. His
favorite refrain went, "It's love, baby."

The more Eleanor got to know Charlie, the more
clear it became he was exactly her type. A Nelson Eddy
type. A Hy Keltz type. A Heathcliff type. Again: robust
and earthy, at home in his skin. Again: deft with his
hands, good around machinery, but not really an intellectual match. Again: from the wrong side of the tracks.
In Eleanor, Charlie saw one more facet of his affinity
for things Jewish. In Charlie, Eleanor saw the thrillingly
inappropriate Other, the *shaygetz* guaranteed to break
her mother's heart.

Inevitably, Charlie presented himself at the threshold
of Apartment 24 and received the scrutiny of Rose
Hatkin. At first, clueless, she welcomed and fed him.
Charlie obligingly ate her chopped-vegetable patties, and
he solicitously asked Seymour what kind of toys he had,
recognizing just like Danny Schlomkowitz the strategy
of gaining little brother as an ally. Ultimately, though,
Rose pulled aside Eleanor to ask, *"Er iz a Yid?"* Is he a
Jew? And Eleanor answered with the truth. Many more
times as the summer of 1942 ended and the months
passed and the war, at least America's part in it, entered
its second year, Rose and Eleanor exchanged words.
They exchanged them to the point of ritual.

"Stop it, Ellie. He's not Jewish."

"Ma, we're just friends."

The last week of March 1943, dressed in her job-hunting best, Eleanor stood before a brick factory building on Bruckner Boulevard, an industrial strip that ran along the Bronx shore of the Harlem River. Above the entry door hung a banner proclaiming MORE PLANES SHIPS TANK MONTH. The company inside, Burndy Engineering, manufactured none of those things, but it made the electrical connectors they all needed to join wire to wire, cable to cable, and thus to fly, run, cruise, bomb, and shoot. Eleanor was there to join what President Roosevelt had christened "the Army of Production." She was there, more prosaically, because Vicky Behar, who was already working in the Production Control department, had told Eleanor the place was hiring.

That news was welcome, if hardly surprising. All over the Bronx, factories and businesses that had limped through a dozen years of Depression were gorging on defense contracts. A shipyard on City Island built landing craft; the furniture stores of the Hub provisioned Fort Dix; even a covert slot machine manufacturer in Hunts Point had gone legit, cranking out machine guns. Burndy itself was in the process of more than doubling its prewar workforce from 300 to 680. There were defense industry jobs for 200,000 Bronxites, and they were opening up, of course, when there were fewer and fewer men around to take them.

All the boys Eleanor knew well—all except, to her relief, Charlie Greco—had gone to war. Hy Keltz had enlisted in the Navy the previous November, Howard
Gropper in the Army Airs Corps the same month. Jack
Steinglass from City downtown was already in Panama,
ordered to protect the canal. Joe Lempert and Danny
Schlomkowitz were both at Fort Dix, though Fannie
was praying that Danny would be discharged because
of high blood pressure. On the uptown campus of City
College, Bernie Solomon was marching with ROTC,
waiting for his call-up to fight fascism, the struggle he'd
been wanting to join since the Spanish Civil War. Just
one month earlier, in March 1943, City downtown had
thrown a farewell party for 325 students being moved
onto active duty from the Enlisted Reserve Corps. The
incoming freshman class was the first in the college's
history to have a female majority.

So Eleanor was part of something much larger, seven
million women newly entering the labor force during
the war, when she went to see Bernard Pacter in the
Cost Accounting department. Fleshy and genial, Bernie
understood the difficult necessity of paying for night
school with day work. He had spent ten years getting
through City downtown, forgoing his lifelong ambition
of law for the practicality of accounting. Along the way,
he'd married the classmate who first explained to him
the difference between credit and debit. Ten days after
being hired at Burndy in 1938, he'd been charged with
creating a Cost Accounting department, which now
meant finding women who knew numbers. What a

stroke of luck when Eleanor Hatkin, she of the Mathematics Medal from Morris High, appeared.

They talked at Bernie's desk, the only wooden one in the department, a sign of rank. The floor vibrated from the heavy machinery in the foundry below, and whenever the door opened into the adjoining machine shop, conversation competed against the whine of drilling, threading, grinding. Nothing waited in Burndy, not now. The factory was running three shifts and had just rented ten thousand square feet from the Roman Catholic Orphan Asylum. There were ensigns showing up every day to deliver new specs and hurry old orders. Burndy connectors, as the company literature boasted, went into the Flying Fortress, the Liberator, the Coronado, the Catalina, the Mitchell, the Lightning, the Avenger, and the Hellcat; into battleships, cruisers, destroyers, patrol craft, tank-landing barges, and submarines.

Bernie explained what Eleanor would be expected to do. Every different part Burndy made traveled through the production process with a record called a shop ticket, a list of all the time and material used in the various stages of manufacture. With a desktop contraption called a Comptometer, a sort of typewriter with numerals instead of letters on its keyboard, Eleanor had to calculate the value of the item, so it could then be marked up to an appropriate profit. There was only one problem: the Comptometer didn't do multiplication. But if Eleanor messed up occasionally, Bernie would try to catch it before the comptroller did. "All you need," he told Eleanor, "is an eraser on the pencil."

She rarely did. Bernie appreciated the poise and professionalism in Eleanor. Although she was nine years his junior, Bernie treated her more like an equal, certainly a cut above the other four or five girls in the department, the giggly ones. When it was just the two of them left working late, he sought out her advice, calling her "my psychology advisor." Most of the questions were about tensions in the department, but Bernie trusted Eleanor, too, to hear about his best friend's marital problems. The guy, she advised, was paying too much attention to his mother and not enough to his wife. Eleanor knew something about Jewish mothers.

Burndy was more than just another factory, the sum of its power presses and bench lathes and plating tanks. It was the expression of its idiosyncratic founder, Bern Dibner. A Jewish immigrant from the Ukraine, Dibner had risen from the Lower East Side to an honors degree in electrical engineering and an assignment in his twenties to design the electrification of Cuba. He also had the good fortune, quite literally, to have a rich and inobtrusive brother-in-law to bankroll the nascent Burndy. As much scholar as businessman, Dibner took a sabbatical from his own business in 1936 to study Leonardo de Vinci at the University of Zurich, and began collecting artifacts and manuscripts related to the history of science. His personal collection, which someday would enhance the Smithsonian Institution, resided in a bank of metal cabinets in the Burndy office. The president himself was, at the moment, serving as an

Army major and filing dispatches about the war to Burndy's house organ, which he had given the impossibly cornball title *Howdy!* Even in Dibner's absence, the company exuded his influence—the way it paid workers their hourly wage for time spent donating blood; the way it raised money to buy an ambulance for civil defense; the way it percolated with ideas from the drafting tables of the Engineering Department.

For Eleanor, Burndy offered the antidote to the tedium of night school at City downtown. Burndy was her classroom, her campus, her sorority. It made her knowledge feel both valued and valuable in a way it rarely had in the two years since her illustrious exit from Morris. It let her share in the epic cause of the war, a war being fought by Burndy men. She was earning $30 a week, more with the frequent overtime, as much money as Sol could during the sporadic times when he even had work. The salary established her, still in her teens, as the breadwinner of the Hatkin household, and more than that the *de facto* parent.

Fannie Hatkin soon joined Eleanor and Vicky Behar at Burndy. Then Bernie hired his cousin Ruth Pacter. Ruth wound up sitting next to Eleanor in Cost Accounting, and they chatted during lunch or night shifts or just when their eyes and fingers needed a break from the Comptometer. Ruth was the middle of three children, with a kid sister named Estelle in high school and an older brother, Sam, doing war cartography in Washington. She had gone through school on the Rapid Advance track, started college at City downtown, then

dropped out for all the reasons Eleanor readily fath-
omed. She had a boyfriend in the Navy named Al Taylor, whom she'd met the previous summer, when he was
head waiter and she a counselor at the same summer
camp. Such a roughneck, that Al Taylor, a real Lower
East Side boy, already put in the brig once for mouthing
off to an officer. A long-legged eighteen-year-old with
cherubic cheeks and thick black hair, Ruth touched the
other side of his emotional nature, the part that showed
up at her apartment clutching a bouquet.

The friendship between Ruth and Eleanor unfolded
over the succeeding months. They played tennis in their
winter coats on a blustery day at Crotona Park. They
roasted hot dogs, strictly one apiece under rationing, on
a picnic at Tibbett's Brook, and Ruth just about cried
when hers fell off its stick into the coals. They took Estelle with them to see *Oklahoma,* acting out their favorite parts on the subway back to the Bronx, dancing
amid the straphangers. They howled together about the
sailor on shore leave they bumped into who was aston-
ished to discover that Jews, at least these girl Jews,
didn't have horns. When Ruth went a few weeks without a letter from Al, Eleanor said she had dreamed one
would come the next day, and so it did. In a return letter to Al, Ruth recalled another instance of similar tenderness:

> Yesterday Eleanor, her sister Fannie and I went
> down to the blood bank. If you're under 21, you need
> a consent slip from your parents. Although my mother

has given blood three times, which is something for a woman her age, she insists that I shouldn't go again. And so this time I decided not to tell her . . .

I went upstairs for registration and everything was going smoothly. . . . but my previous consent slips told the truth. I couldn't worm my way out. . . . Honestly, my heart just fell. You just don't know what a rotten feeling it is, first to be caught doing that but most of all to have to leave without doing what you came for.

And then I thought of those luscious raisin cookies that I love and their delicious coffee that I wouldn't have. And then I smiled even though I felt like crying for all those silly thoughts that run through one's head. Eleanor knew how I loved those cookies. . . . And as I sat down at the table at which Eleanor & her sister were sitting, she guiltily opened her bag, pulled out the little raisin cookie I knew she'd bring out for me.

The most significant outings for Eleanor were visits to Ruth's family, kitchen conversations over tuna fish and cottage cheese. Ruth lived about a mile from 1461, just off the gardens and baseball diamonds of Bronx Park, in a parallel universe. Her father, Noach, was a Communist, and her mother, Fannie, was either sympathetic or long-suffering enough to fellow-travel. Her most fervent support went toward Planned Parenthood, radicals of another sort. The Pacters raised their three children in a Tudor apartment complex run and populated by party members and called the Workers Cooperative Colony, or, more colloquially, the Coops. Its entry portal bore a bas relief of the hammer and sickle. The comrades of the Coops—and *chaver,* Yiddish for "comrade," was the word they used—imbued the young generation with what they perceived as "higher values." Only in part did that mean Rodin sculpture, Martha Graham dance, and the Metropolitan Opera broadcast on Saturday afternoon. Kids skipped school to march in the May Day parade, wearing the red neckerchiefs of the Young Pioneers and chanting about "fighting for the working class against the bourgeoisie." Their version of a cellar club was the Teivos, "Soviet" in reverse. At Passover, families told the story not of Exodus but the Haymarket massacre.

Noach Pacter barely spoke to his brother Harriss, Bernie's father, who had committed the capitalist atrocity of owning a garment factory. Noach managed to maintain his own ideological purity despite being a rather successful tradesman, tailoring custom suits for big-band musicians and gangsters. (His specialty was leaving extra room in the waistband for a gun.) He had even weathered his wife's private opposition to the Nazi-Soviet pact. In any case, by the time Eleanor started coming around, Stalin was Uncle Joe, on the Americans' side, and the mothers of the Coops were busily knitting scarves for soldiers.

Ruth herself was the least political member of her family. She had grown up as the neighborhood tomboy, the champ at jacks, the quickest up the monkey bars. Until the war and Burndy intervened, she had intended to become a teacher. But even the most moderate child of the Coops was more politically engaged than anyone in Eleanor's wartime circle. Living there meant being entertained by Paul Robeson and Woody Guthrie. It meant rallying on behalf of the Scottsboro Boys and the Abraham Lincoln Brigade. It meant reading the *Freiheit,* the Communist daily in Yiddish, while sneaking the *Daily News* for the funnies. And in the more intimate aspects of experience, it meant seeing divides of religion or race as part of capitalism's grand scheme for oppressing the proletariat. In the Coops, Jews married gentiles, whites married blacks, and some couples didn't marry at all. Just a few months earlier, the brother of Ruth Pacter's best friend in the Coops had wed an Irish Catholic girl. "Leave the key on your way out," said the bride's mother in banishment. The Jewish mother in the Coops, meanwhile, told her Christian daughter-in-law, "Come, you'll live with us."

For Eleanor, this was revelation. As far back as high school with Bernie Solomon and Mel Goodman, she had been groping for some way of making sense of the world, some way of explaining all the longings and resentments she felt, some instrument for battering her way out of Apartment 24 and its Old World constraints. Without intending to serve as political tutor—far from it, in fact—Ruth Pacter was exposing Eleanor to nothing less than a critique of society. In the person of Ruth, that critique wasn't orthodox Marxist but secular progressive, not rigid and severe but liberating, life-affirming, fun. For the first time, Eleanor could understand her battles with her mother, over eating Chinese food on Yom Kippur or dating an Italian Catholic, as more than visceral rebellion, her own personal and lonely mutiny. In Ruth Pacter's family, in the Coops, the old boundaries no longer applied. They were objects of ridicule and scorn. And for Eleanor to defy them, perhaps with Charlie Greco, was to join the struggle of the enlightened future against the benighted past.

On the hazy Saturday morning of June 19, 1943, spring according to the calendar but summer by the sheen of sweat already on him, Seymour Hatkin buttoned up a starched white shirt and reached into the closet for his bar mitzvah suit. The blue wool pricked and scratched in the airless heat of Apartment 24, the trouser legs bunched at his feet, and the double-breasted coat hung nearly down to his knees. Thin and dark with deep-set eyes, Seymour seemed to disappear into the fabric. But at least the suit was new. For weeks ahead of the ceremony, Rose had insisted that Sol buy a secondhand one at the Salvation Army. When Sol tried to at least get his son a hat, and on a markdown from the store run by his cousin Harry Schneer, Rose ordered it returned. "Hats are expensive," she lectured. "Two dollars is a hat." It was Eleanor's income from Burndy that finally allowed for a suit from S. Klein's, on the condition it be large enough for Seymour to wear for several more years.

Eleanor was accustomed to playing the parental role with her younger brother. Not that Seymour wasn't a pest, of course, especially when his sisters had company.

He would hide under the table to eavesdrop or spy from the other room while Fannie and Danny necked. His efforts at affection, stroking his sisters' hair, mostly irritated them. Still, Eleanor had a patience and an empathy for the *nudnik* that her sister couldn't summon. Or maybe it was more like pity for any child being raised by Rose and Sol. Eleanor took Seymour to museums in Manhattan, even performances by the Negro American Theater in Harlem. She gave him an allowance from her pay. She taught him how to slowdance to Frank Sinatra. In Seymour's autograph book, where Fannie inscribed an entry to "my most annoying brother," Eleanor offered optimism and praise and a signature phrase from her old principal, Elmer Bogart:

> To my Romeo brother—
> I know that someday you'll make me proud of you. I know you've got what it takes. Just don't make the mistake of not using your abilities. Always make sure you're working to capacity & things will always go your way.

She had reason to worry. Seymour wasn't in the Rapid Advance classes, and Rose was steering him toward vocational school. On the eve of Jewish manhood, he was still sleeping in his parents' bedroom. Sol was a doting father but a weak man, someone to duck confrontation and submit when conflict couldn't dodged, the last father on earth able to teach a son how to take care of himself on the street. And in the near decade between

Eleanor's childhood and Seymour's, Boston Road had become a tougher, tenser place with an influx of Negro and Puerto Rican families drawn by wartime jobs. One of the Schneer daughters had been beaten by some Negro girls recently after calling one a nigger. Seymour was just finishing his first year of junior high school in a class that was largely black, and he had been strong-armed for spare change on a daily basis. The intimidation only ended when Seymour instead offered his lunch, one of Rose's spinach pancakes on day-old bread. The bully took a few bites, blurted, "Man, that shit is dry," and moved on to more promising targets.

Seymour approached this morning's duties, though, with uncommon confidence. Hebrew had come easily to him. He often accompanied Sol to Sabbath services and had been studying for the past two years with a group of bar mitzvah candidates. Nothing about the setting would be intimidating. The Hatkins attended formidable Tifereth Israel with its raised *bimah* and stained-glass windows only for the High Holy Days; Tifereth Israel cost money. The rest of the time they picked their way among the pushcarts to a storefront near the El and climbed the wooden stairs to a second-floor sanctuary simply known as the Jennings Street Synagogue. The place was presided over by the elfin figure of Rabbi Donner, he of the bald dome and big ears. Instead of stained glass, the window frames of his *shtibel* held wire mesh to ward off burglars and black-out curtains to hide from Nazi bombers.

The questions Seymour had about Judaism were of a

larger scope than how to chant his Torah portion. At the very beginning of bar mitzvah lessons, Rabbi Donner had told the class, "Boys, do you know how jealous the *goyim* are of our Torah?" Seymour said that was hard to believe, since he'd never met a Christian who seemed the slightest bit interested. Gentile hate, not gentile envy, had set the world on fire. Then, one afternoon a few weeks ago, Seymour had been sitting on the fire escape outside the bedroom window when Sol entered the apartment and walked over to talk. The subject turned to God.

"Daddy," Seymour asked, "do you believe?"

Sol sighed.

"Not all the time," he replied delicately. He waited, as if debating whether to continue. The courtyard below was silent, or perhaps Seymour did not notice the noise. "How can I believe all the time? Look what happened to Mama's family."

By now, almost four years since the Nazis had invaded Poland and two since they had driven the Russians out of Bialystok, Rose and Sol grasped the larger picture of tragedy, if not yet the full, hideous detail. Reports had been leaking out of Poland about the Nazi campaign against the Jews: deportation, ghettos, starvation, disease, mass executions, poison gas. In late 1942, the Allies formally confirmed the Nazis' bestial policy of cold-blooded extermination." These disclosures were not given much prominence in the American press, and in many quarters they were disregarded as propaganda or exaggerations, just another version of the Huns bayoneting babies in World War I. But the dispatches were there, with one-column headlines on inside pages, for the interested reader, and a portion of American Jewry began to rouse itself. In early March of 1943, as Seymour's bar mitzvah ceremony neared, Madison Square Garden held both a mass rally to "stop Hitler's decimation of the Jews" and a performance of Ben Hecht's pageant *We Will Never Die* with its call for America to rescue European Jews. Through late April and early May, the Warsaw Ghetto uprising flared before being crushed. There was going to be a memorial service to the slain heroes this very night at Carnegie Hall.

"I'll never see my sisters again," Rose cried often, her voice keening, her arms outstretched. They might have died on "Red Friday" in June 1941, when the Nazis burned alive 2,000 Jews in the Great Synagogue. They might have died on the "Black Sabbath" of July 12, 1941, when the Germans tortured and executed 5,000 just outside the city. They might have died in February 1943, when 12,000 Jews were shipped off from Bialystok to Treblinka. They might have died almost any other day. Few details of Bialystok's tortures had yet trickled out, though, and in some way the blackout allowed Rose the possibility of hope. So until Rose knew for a fact her family was dead, she persisted in desperate belief. She called on her cousin Minnie Osder and friend Simmy Plansky, both Bialystokers, to ask if anyone had word. She dragged herself in her lumpy dresses and clomping shoes to Temple Eden on the Grand Concourse, where the Bialystoker League of the Bronx met, or down to the Bialystoker *landsmenshaften* on the Lower East Side. She scratched out letters in Yiddish and assembled parcels of used clothing for her relatives in Uruguay—her brother-in-law Alter David Kaczkowicz, her niece Judis, her nephew Julius. They were as close as Rose could get to her favorite sister, Ester Dina.

At night in the lamplight, Rose squinted into the pages of the *Forverts,* poring over the appeals placed by European Jews who had escaped and were seeking American relatives. *"Israel Danziger, lived on Norfolk Street, searched for by his brother Solomon."* *"Schwartz, Arthur & Emil, lived once on 71st St. in New York City, are being searched by their sister, Mrs. Mathilda Weiswasser."* *"Doner, Jacob Sholem, from Brooklyn, is being searched for by his sister-in-law, Golde Rukhl Lak, from Russia."*

But no relative ever reached through the columns of the *Forverts* to find Rose. Minnie and Simmy knew nothing. In February 1943, the Bialystoker association published one eyewitness account of Red Friday, slave labor, and ghetto conditions, but otherwise remained almost willfully disengaged. After all the paeans to the *muter shtot,* all the lamentations about exile in New York, the war reversed allegiances, stirring the émigrés to embrace America rather than plead on behalf of Bialystok. Their newspaper, the *Bialystoker Stimme,* urged readers to buy war bonds and ran pages of photos of Jewish GIs, "Our Boys in the Service—God Bless Them." Amid existential threat, the language of crisis applied only to institutional needs. When the newspaper wrote in April 1943 that "it has indeed been difficult for us to usher in the Passover holiday," the anguish referred not to the war, not to the genocide, but to the shortfall in fund-raising for the Bialystoker old-age home on East Broadway. If Rose had expected some modest portion of advocacy and comfort, especially in the absence of hard information, then she must have trudged home abject.

In their rented room in the Villa Munoz district of Montevideo, meanwhile, Alter David Kaczkowicz and his two children remained just as bereft. Mail from Poland had stopped arriving in late 1941. The last Jewish refugees reached Uruguay the same year, only 138, almost all from Germany. So there was no longer any point in Julius haunting the port as the boats disgorged, dashing from one vagabond to the next, piping out his pleas for news of Bialystok. The three Kaczkowiczes could do only what the rest of Uruguay's Jews did— tune in the BBC if they understood English and read the Yiddish papers *Folksblat* and *Unzer Fraint*. More to keep from feeling helpless than to anticipate success, many bought classified ads, something like this:

Ruth Hausner is looking for any information about her niece Ana, born in 1920 in Volcovsic, from parents Zalman and Malka. She left for Warsaw last August, and since then there is no news. Please contact. . . .

So maybe there was something appropriate about a bar

mitzvah ceremony in a sanctuary darkened by blackout curtains, about ascending to Jewish manhood against a backdrop of Jewish death. It was the same reason the groom smashes a glass after his wedding vows, to remember the destruction of the Temple even in a moment of greatest joy. Seymour read his Torah portion without error that stifling morning, and then he carried the scroll down the narrow aisle of creaky planks so the congregation could touch it with their prayer books or *tzitzit*. Behind Seymour walked Rabbi Donner, holding aloft a portrait of FDR. This particular bit of ritual had been Rose's idea, more like her demand, and no one laughed. If anyone was going to save Ester Dina, and so absolve Rose of all the guilt and failure she felt for a sister stranded on the other side, it would be Roosevelt. He was as close to divine as anyone on Rose Hatkin's earth.

After the ceremony, the several dozen guests ate honey cake and chicken soup. Sol took a nip from a bottle of Canadian Club. Seymour accepted cards with two or three dollars apiece, and when Rose saw him throwing out the envelopes, she scuttled to him in panic, thinking he was tossing out the cash. Then the day ended and Seymour stashed away the money and read the morning paper so he could keep charting the progress of the American army on his map. The Yanks had just captured two small islands off Sicily, the preparation for invading Italy.

For all her worship of Roosevelt, Rose did not place her faith wholly in liberation. A few weeks after the bar

mitzvah, on the second anniversary of Red Friday in Bialystok, she asked Sol to go to the Jennings Street *shul*
to say *kaddish,* the memorial prayer. Then, alone at the
kitchen table of a threadbare apartment, twenty years
since reaching America with the obligation to bring
over her family, she lit a *yahrzeit* candle for Ester Dina.

In the summer of 1943, for the first time in her nine-
teen-year-old life, Eleanor Hatkin went on vacation.
She went as far as the subway could take her, out to the
beach of Coney Island. There she pooled together fifteen dollars with four other girls to rent a one-bedroom
flat for the season from Mrs. Levy. Ruth Klekman and
Hilda Saltzman shared one bed, Clare Abramowitz and
Florence Brodsky the other, and Eleanor took a cot in
the kitchen. That turned out to be lucky. A few hours
into their first overnight, Hilda and Ruth, the two neat-
niks of the whole bunch, scratched themselves awake,
their mattress infested with bedbugs. After neither Flit
nor burning candles finished off the insects, the pair
shuffled off to boardwalk benches to sleep.

However miserable the prelude, this was a summer
of unprecedented independence, autonomy made possible by the war. Like Eleanor at Burndy, the other girls
were holding office jobs and earning adult money—
Ruth as a legal secretary, Clare as a purchasing agent.
The money paid for new freedoms, new freedoms that
stretched old rules. Clare's mother had sputtered out
disbelief at the first word of this summer rental.
"You're going with girls?" she cried. "To a place in

Coney Island? A step from the gutter. Who's going to marry you?" To which Clare had replied, with an iron certainty Eleanor could appreciate, "I'm working now. I'm going."

So they posed on the front steps of the Levy house in their swimsuits and pumps, Eleanor as always with a gardenia. They played the radio loud and sang along to the loopy novelty hit with all the nonsense words, "Mairzy Doats." They chattered and snickered and annoyed the neighbors. They rode bikes side by side down the boardwalk. They sunbathed until they burned, even Eleanor with her dark olive skin, and the housewife in the next unit, fed up with the girls' noise, informed them the cure was a nice hot shower. After taking the bait, Eleanor wound up at the hospital with a diagnosis of sun poisoning and orders to slather on the Unguentine.

Clare's mother had the right worry for the wrong reason. The problem with finding a husband wasn't a bad reputation; the problem was a shortage of prospects. Well over 100,000 men from the Bronx had entered the military by the summer of 1943. Every month, Burndy added more names to its roster of servicemen, as the company went from having nine female employees to two hundred sixty, nearly half its workforce. City downtown had seen so many men enlist or be drafted that rumors arose that the entire campus would be shut down. As for Coney Island, a family place even during peacetime, it rattled with the racket of mothers and children.

Sometimes Eleanor and the others rose early enough to watch the Coast Guard sailors, who were being garrisoned a few blocks away at the Half Moon Hotel, high-step down the boardwalk through their morning march. The girls curled their hair and wore their flowered shifts, showing lots of leg for the occasion, but their motives were muddled. They didn't want to have just a fling, to swoon for the uniform like some trashy little V-girl. They didn't really know if they wanted to marry either, if it meant you could be a widowed by any bullet. They wanted what wartime didn't provide, a steady guy sure to stay alive. The song the girls heard so often on the *Lucky Strike Hit Parade* told them what they already knew about social life on the homefront:

> They're either too young, or too old
> They're either too gray or too grassy green
> The pickings are poor and the crop is lean.
> What's good is in the army,
> What's left will never harm me.

Eleanor's sister Fannie was the fortunate one. Her boyfriend Danny had been discharged due to high blood pressure after just three months of basic training, sent back to the Bronx with his army overcoat and a pair of combat boots two sizes too big. He and Fannie had their own summer plans as a couple, and then he would resume college at City uptown. Eleanor was writing to Jack Steinglass in Panama, true to her word, even as she spent time with Charlie Greco. Jack was not the only one without a clue about Charlie. Eleanor kept him at a distance from any friends whom she suspected would disapprove—Marion Herzog, for instance, had never even met him—and at first the presumed doubters included everyone in the Coney Island apartment.

As the summer passed, though, Eleanor grew close to Clare Abramowitz. Clare was originally Fannie's friend, and Eleanor had always assumed that meant she shared Fannie's moderate and conventional ways. It turned out Clare more resembled Ruth Pacter. She wasn't a Red-diaper baby, but her father often voted for the left-wing American Labor Party and was that rare male unabashed in his admiration for Eleanor Roosevelt. During the week, Eleanor and Clare sometimes met after work to hear the radical orators in Washington Square Park, nibbling their sandwiches as some firebrand on a step stool stemwound about antilynching legislation. Clare introduced Eleanor to the newspaper *PM,* a progressive tabloid that spunkily declared it was "against people who push other people around." On more familial matters, Clare confided that one of her cousins was dating a Catholic. Here, like Ruth and Vicky, was an ally for Eleanor.

Charlie accepted a dinner invitation to Coney Island one weekend that August. As if to deflect the controversial sense of himself and Eleanor as a pair, he brought along a buddy named Pat, also an Italian Catholic. Eleanor and the rest tried to oblige ethnicity by preparing a spaghetti dinner, a culinary first for them all, and they boiled the pasta for the half hour duration they were accustomed to with matzoh balls or *kreplach*. Pat being a good sport and Charlie a diligent suitor, they gummed their way through the glutinous mess, cheeks stuffed, too polite to object. Before long, the lousy meal became the inside joke of the evening. And when Charlie laughed, with his teeth pearly as a row of Chiclets and those dark smudges of eyebrows lifting and a chunk of that coarse hair flopping onto his forehead, Eleanor beamed in return.

There was, however, one competitor for Charlie's attentions on which Eleanor had not reckoned. On September 15, 1943, he presented himself at the Navy recruiting station in Lower Manhattan to enlist. One week later, he reported to a training base called Sampson in upstate New York. Charlie had not talked much to friends or family about his impending decision, but it should not have come as a total surprise. By this point in the war, waiting around to get inducted meant being assigned to the Army; enlisting offered the chance to choose your branch of the service. Charlie's friend from East Harlem, Bill Rosenhoch, had already signed up for the Army Signal Corps, and Bernie Dunetz kept trying to enlist for the air corps, even though his high blood pressure continued to keep him out.

As for Eleanor, she was suddenly the girl left behind. There was a song making the rounds about a girl bucking rivets in an aircraft factory while her boyfriend fights the war. Norman Rockwell had even painted his version of her for the cover of the *Saturday Evening Post*, a shipyard welder with mask and coveralls.

"Rosie's got a boyfriend, Charlie," went the song, "Charlie, he's a Marine." True, Charlie Greco wasn't a Marine, just a "boot," Navy slang for a trainee. And Eleanor, totting up numbers on the Comptometer, wasn't exactly assembling bombers or destroyers. Still, those lines jumped out, every time she heard them. The song said Rosie the Riveter was "red, white, and blue," protecting her guy by working overtime. Eleanor knew there was more than one way to be blue.

About the same time Charlie departed, the Hatkins moved out of 1461 Boston Road. There was nothing nostalgic about leaving the old neighborhood, that dark apartment with its piles of dirty laundry, those blocks with their weedy lots and peddlers. The place had always been poor, and ever since the Schneer cousin got attacked it felt dangerous, too. Besides, the goal of every Jew in the East Bronx was to move to the West Bronx, if not into the Art Deco buildings with elevators and doormen on the Grand Concourse then at least to a roomy walk-up on a respectable side street. With Eleanor bringing home more than $100 a month from Burndy and Sol finally secure in a luggage factory, the family could at last realize the fantasy.

Sol and Seymour had ridden the trolley across the Concourse many times during the summer, prowling for apartments with FOR RENT signs, suddenly rare with the Depression ended by the war-production boom. They finally found one in a five-story brick building at 2101 Harrison Avenue in a neighborhood evenly divided among Irish and Jews. Sixty dollars a month rented the Hatkins the inconceivable expanse of five rooms, most of them sunlit, and the grace note of French doors. Although Fannie and Eleanor still had to share a daybed, and Rose insisted on stringing a clothesline inside, Seymour finally acquired his own bedroom, a place to hang his battlefield maps and Susan Hayward pinups. In deference to his idea of modern style, Sol had Danny Schlomkowitz saw the legs off the family's china cabinet.

Down the street from 2101, delicatessens and bakeries thrived along Burnside Avenue, along with dry cleaners, bookstores, and a lingerie shop, businesses that bespoke a middle-class clientele. Around the corner stretched a park following the route of the old Croton Aqueduct, a pleasant route for an evening stroll. The uptown campus of New York University, with its neoclassical Hall of Fame, commanded a nearby bluff above the Harlem River. (It was so famous a place that *The Wizard of Oz* slipped in a wisecrack that everybody at the Loew's Paradise must have appreciated. After a tornado drops Dorothy's house on the Wicked Witch of the East, killing her, the Munchkins chant in gratitude, "You'll be a bust, you'll be a bust, you'll be a bust in the Hall of Fame.") Soon after moving onto Harrison Avenue, the Hatkins donned their dresses and suits to stand for a portrait outside the hall, proof of their escape from Boston Road, much of it paid for by Eleanor.

All the hours at Burndy, all the night shifts, all the

time and a half purchased comforts Eleanor had rarely known, even if in wartime they felt like guilty pleasures. She bought jodhpurs to go horseback riding at a Westchester stable with Marion Herzog. She hiked through Palisades Park with Vicky Behar and Lillian Golden, posing together with jutting hips beside a road sign saying WARNING CURVE. Lillian sent the snapshot to her boyfriend Ralph Betstadt, who had been upgraded from 4-F to 1-A and shipped to the Italian campaign. With Ruth Pacter, Eleanor traveled by train to Washington, D.C., the farthest either had ever been from home. They found the capital geared less to tourism than self-defense, with a bomb shelter beneath the White House lawn and anti-aircraft batteries atop Congressional offices; Ruth's brother Sam, the girls' host, was busy diagramming Kwajalien in preparation for the Navy's assault. Still, Eleanor and Ruth cut swank figures in fitted coats, pearl necklaces, high heels, and clutch purses as they visited the Capitol, the Supreme Court, and the Lincoln Memorial. Over dinner, Sam Pacter talked to Eleanor all about cartography, saying a math whiz like her ought to take some drafting classes. They could sure break up the monotony of business administration.

When the weather cooled that autumn, Eleanor treated herself to one more piece of fashion. She bought a waist-length fur jacket, the style called a "chubby." Hers was made of cheaper pelts, probably muskrat or rabbit, but dyed to the coffee shade of mink. Like her eyelash curler in high school, like the gardenia in her hair at the beach, the chubby became a trademark, the symbol of unapologetic vanity. Hilda Saltzman, one of the girls from Coney Island, simply called it The Coat.

Eleanor slipped her arms into its sleeves exactly one week before Christmas Day, when Burndy threw its largest holiday party ever. Closing out a year of record production, the company took over the grand ball-room of Manhattan's Commodore Hotel for a night of willful optimism and slightly forced cheer. There were gags about rationing and songs about war brides and a mural of Santa wearing Uncle Sam's tophat. Only the flag draping the podium admitted to the sobering reality of war; it was emblazoned with the blue star of military service and the numeral 97 for Burndy's employees in the armed forces. As Burndy reveled, American troops were battering at the Germans along the Gustav line in southern Italy and bombing the Japanese defenses on New Britain. The war was a long way from over.

Through the whole merry evening, Eleanor chatted with Bernie Pacter and her Burndy girlfriends—Vicky, Ruth, Fannie—and accepted the occasional dance. Some chemistry was palpably missing, though, some crackle of flirtation, some come-on line, some soul-kiss under the mistletoe. With those ninety-seven guys gone, virtually their entire generation at Burndy, the party resembled a father-daughter social, plunging neckline beside receding hairline. Nights like this suffused Eleanor with a certain kind of aloneness. Even when surrounded by friends and colleagues, especially then, she was inhabiting a world without men.

Maybe that explained why she was so thrilled to hear Jack Steinglass was back home on furlough. After seventeen months and two cases of malaria on a strategic jungle hilltop in Panama, he had a few weeks in New York in January 1944 before being transferred to a base in Georgia to train inductees on anti-aircraft guns. He had plenty of money saved from his military pay of $21 a month (less laundry and insurance) and a set of miniature bongos that he'd bought for Eleanor at a wood-frame PX. She'd done nothing more than watch movies and share sundaes with Jack when they knew each other at City downtown, but now he was the only alternative to just pining for Charlie, four months gone and thousands of miles away. So Jack lined up his buddy Artie Bernfeld, home on leave from the same unit, and Eleanor got Marion Herzog to round out the double date.

Flush with army cash, Jack sprung for tickets to *Oklahoma*, and they made a whole day of it in Manhattan, strolling through the bare trees and frozen ground of Central Park, peeking into the lobby of Radio City, catching the show, dining over cocktails at Child's. At one point, they prevailed on a passing Frenchman to shoot some photos. The men formed a mismatched pair, Artie portly and pale, Jack so dark from the tropical sun and an antimalaria drug called atabrine that his nickname in the unit was "Black Joe." When he stood beside Eleanor in his army coat, leaning just a bit into her, she kept her hands tucked in the pockets of her chubby, as if not to give him any ideas. Then the two girls posed, and they were a ravishing sight for a couple of GIs, Marion in a trim blue suit and fur wrap, Eleanor in her chubby with a white cashmere scarf looped under her chin and around her dark hair like a corona. "Shall I cut off ze leks," the Frenchman said, backpedaling on the sidewalk to frame the shot. "No, zey are too beeyootiful." Eleanor mimicked him for the rest of the date.

At the end of the night, Jack escorted her to the front door of 2101 Harrison, deposited a chaste kiss on her lips, and turned to leave. "Is that all?" Eleanor asked. "You're just gonna kiss me goodnight?" He couldn't even begin to form an answer. She had held herself so noticeably apart the rest of the day. And what exactly was it she wanted? To be held? To be fondled? Where? How much?

Jack heard the voice of his brother sending him off on a date with the admonition, "Behave," the voice of his mother warning him, "You go out with a girl, be a *mensch*. Don't do anything hanky-panky." Outside the family, he had learned the same moral code in his school years at the Yeshiva Israel Salantner, and even on the East Bronx streets. Jack was not such a prude, especially after all those celibate months in the jungle, but he respected the boundaries. If you wanted to get laid, there was a neighborhood chippie who'd do it for a Chinese dinner, or so everybody said. To kiss a nice girl was one thing, to feel her up was even alright. But once the buttons started coming undone, once that hand slid down inside her panties, once you'd touched *that,* how on earth would you put the brakes on? And if you didn't, if you went all the way, then your nice girl wasn't so nice anymore, and why would you want to be with her?

Famished for a man's caress, aching to confirm her allure, Eleanor was straining against the very rules Jack honored. She was nearly twenty now, with an office job, for all practical purposes the head of her household, an adult in every way save one. Single girls her age, the daring kind, anyway, found their way to Havelock Ellis books, or to that rare gynecologist willing to prescribe an unmarried patient a diaphragm. Had Eleanor taken those steps? Not that she had told anyone. How far did she want Jack Steinglass to go? She probably didn't know herself. Just somewhere beyond proper, somewhere beyond polite, somewhere Heathcliff lurked.

They saw each other a few more times before Jack left for Camp Gordon in Georgia. Even after Artie Bernfeld tutored him on how to be more forward, even after Marion Herzog tipped him off that Eleanor might like it, Jack just couldn't make his hands and tongue comply. He settled for asking her to keep writing, enough to stave off isolation, enough keep alive his dream of a correct marriage someday. Write she did, however passionlessly. It would have been unpatriotic to refuse.

* * *

On June 18, 1944, the aircraft carrier U.S.S. Nehenta Bay cruised out of the naval port in San Diego, carrying among its crew Aviation Machinist's Mate 2nd Class Herman David Keltz of the Bronx. By that day, Hy had been in the Navy for slightly more than fourteen months, since enlisting on a Friday the 13th. His luck actually had proven more than adequate up to this point. After finishing training on bases in Illinois and Oregon and being assigned to the Nehenta Bay, he mostly had done the wartime equivalent of commuter runs, carrying planes, mail, and provisions from the West Coast to Pearl Harbor, returning to America with damaged aircraft and wounded soldiers. In his diary, he recorded the more prosaic parts of naval service—"the worst case of seasickness I ever had," the ship's dance with "enough beer on the deck to give all the sailors in the South Pacific at least one bottle," the round-the-clock labor when the ship docked. "Seems like it never will stop," he wrote in one entry. "Load, unload & then clean, clean, clean." Even the Nehenta Bay's one journey to the Marshall Islands occurred a month after American forces had secured them. On shore leave, Hy chowed down with the Seabees and went swimming.

Now his distance from the battle line was narrowing. In a convoy of sixteen ships and about 10,000 troops, the Nehenta Bay was headed for Eniwotek in the Marshall Islands, the staging area for the invasions of Saipan, Guam, and the rest of the Mairanas, halfway point to the Philippines and base for bomber runs against Japan itself. Hy had been promoted to plane captain, the man responsible for upkeep and repairs to an NM-2 antisub fighter. "This is it!" he wrote in his diary as the ship cruised west into the Pacific. On June 27, arriving at Eniwotek, he started the entry with the exclamation, "Waiting!" Five days later, in the waters off Saipan, the waiting ended. "Did patrol duty while planes from other carriers bombed the island," he recorded. July 6: "Our planes went on strafing missions." Which meant that Hy spent day and night soldering, patching, tuning up, whatever a plane needed, grabbing a meal of fried Spam at two in the morning. July 9: "The conquest of Saipan was completed. We did our <u>bit</u>. That's all!"

True enough, Hy and the crew of the Nehenta Bay had been spared the hand-to-hand fighting up the mountain slopes of Saipan, the human waves of Japanese soldiers hurling themselves against American lines, the mass suicides the enemy preferred to surrender. But he had gotten close enough to combat, danger, and death to start to long for the life back home. Since breaking up with Ellie Hatkin, he hadn't really coupled up with another girl, despite his sister Mildred's best efforts to play *shadchen*. Mail reached the Nehenta Bay so sporadically, sometimes fifty or sixty days between deliveries, that every crewman craved a letter from a girlfriend, the evidence there might be life after war. So that summer, amid the battles for Guam and Tinian, Hy decided to write to Ellie. Between military censorship and his own stoic nature, he did not share the things he told his diary: "Ensign Fischer lost today"; "Now we're hunting for survivors." More than three years since he and Ellie had parted, he couldn't very plausibly send hugs and kisses, either. It had been so long he didn't even know she'd moved off Boston Road. He courted instead with wit, like a holiday card drawn by his buddy Max Diamond, showing a sailor in his dinghy being circled by sharks.

From (CENSORED) port
On (DELETED) day
The ship (A SECRET)
Sailed (where I can't say)

We've been to (RESTRICTED)
(CONFIDENTIAL) and such
The censor will read this
So I cannot say much

But he cannot stop me
From wishing you good cheer
A very Merry Christmas
And a Happy New Year

The letters found their way to Eleanor on Harrison Avenue, and she received them with a mixture of intrigue and trepidation. She had plenty of snapshots from the summer, especially her week's vacation at a labor union resort in the Poconos called Tamiment. As if to tease and tantalize, and in so doing shield herself from rejection, she chose several of the most enticing scenes—

playing tennis in just her bathing suit and saddle shoes, languorously spread across a wooden love seat, perched mischievously in the lifeguard's tower. "Tell me how the boys react to this one," she inscribed a shot by the lakeshore. Besides the batch from Tamiment, she sent a photo of herself, Lillian Golden, and Vicky Behar goofily entwined near the NYU Hall of Fame. "We three are still together," Eleanor wrote on the back, conjuring a past that had included Hy. From that same day on the campus, there was also a picture of her poised on a tree branch, head thrown back, tomboy and temptress all at once. "No shoes," she noted on the back. "Not because of rationing—just cause the grass feels better without it." She signed every snapshot simply as Ellie, no Xs or Os, no declaration of affection, much less love. But she kept answering Hy's letters, and, unlike Jack Steinglass's, answering out of something other than duty. Then again, she had one more correspondent, as well, trawling through the Pacific on the U.S.S. Carter Hall: Machinist's Mate 3rd Class Charles Greco.

Eleanor ended the year 1944 the way she had spent so much of it, in the company of girlfriends. With New Year's Eve falling on a Sunday night, she decided to spend the weekend at Bear Mountain, a state park about fifty miles up the Hudson from Manhattan. Eleanor had discovered the place over the summer on a Burndy outing, but it was even better suited for winter sports, with a lodge and ski slopes and a rink. For company, there were Vicky Behar and Ruth Pacter, as well as Ruth's sister Estelle and a close friend from the Coops, Shirley Binenstock.

They took a bus up after work on Friday night the 29th and threw themselves into motion the next morning, ice-skating, riding toboggans, forming a gymnasts' pyramid in the snow. They had enough money even to rent skis, and went schuss-booming down the hill, enthused and untutored, shouting to the unfortunates in their path, "Get outta the way." When the sun set in the late afternoon, they trooped to the lodge fireplace, stripping off the sodden coats and boots, casting their eyes around the room for some available, unattached men. There was, to be precise, one sailor.

Materially, Eleanor had never been better off. With her last paycheck of the year, she had earned more than $2,100 in 1944, almost $700 of it in a frenetic autumn of overtime. Sol had made $3,000 for the year, meaning that the Hatkin family had quintupled its annual income since the onset of war. Eleanor legitimately could feel part of the quest for victory when she saw a rear admiral present Burndy a commendation for manufacturing parts for the landing craft deployed on D-Day, when she read a headline in *Howdy!* that boasted about the B-29 assaults on Japanese naval bases and steel mills: BURNDY CONNECTORS IN JAP RAIDS. Compared to Burndy, with its salary and its mission, City downtown had just about vanished from her life. She had dropped classes each of the last two semesters, picking up a total of just five credits, and wasn't even registering for the spring term of 1945. Four years after graduating high school, she was barely two-thirds of the way to a college degree. Marion Herzog, meanwhile, was already enrolled in Columbia University's law school. As for Sam Pacter's brainstorm that Eleanor take drafting courses, she had managed only Cs in two of them.

Whether as a career girl or a college girl, she was a single girl, and seemed fated to stay that way for a while. The German offensive in the Ardennes forest of Belgium over the past two weeks, though blunted in the last few days, had shocked Americans on the home front out of their hopes for a rapid conclusion to the war and the return of their boys. Although Eleanor didn't know it yet, Jack Steinglass had been transferred from Camp Gordon into an infantry unit dispatched to the Battle of the Bulge; he had caught shrapnel in his thigh and seen enough carnage among his comrades to count himself lucky. On their separate ships in the Pacific, Hy Keltz and Charlie Greco were both taking part in the bloody invasion of the Philippines, the Carter Hall supplying landing craft in the final battles on Leyte, the Nehenta Bay fueling up Task Force 38 for the imminent assault on Luzon.

So on that Saturday night around the fire in the Bear Mountain lodge, Eleanor and Vicky and Ruth and the rest were living out the lyrics of Frank Sinatra's new song:

Saturday night is the loneliest night of the week
Cause that's the night that my sweetie and I
Used to dance cheek to cheek.

I don't mind Sunday night at all
'Cause that's the night friends come to call
And Monday to Friday go fast
And another week is past . . .

Until I hear you at my door
Until you're in my arms once more
Saturday night is the loneliest night of the week.

Early on the Sunday evening of December 31, Eleanor and the others hopped the bus back into Manhattan so they could be in Times Square for New Year's Eve. Skates slung over their shoulders, suitcases in hand, they threaded through the multitude that had gathered, 250,000 of them by 8:30 and growing by more than 100,000 an hour, undaunted by pouring rain. For the first time since 1942, when dimout regulations had been imposed and Mayor La Guardia personally pleaded for quiet, Times Square flashed all its neon and blew all its horns. The Copa, El Morocco, all the hottest nightclubs had been sold out for weeks. A replica of Miss Liberty sixty feet tall towered over the crowd occupying every inch of pavement in the gorge formed by Broadway crossing Seventh Avenue, a crowd flecked with soldiers from America, England, and France, raucous on the timeliest shore leave imaginable.

New Year's Eve felt like New Year's Eve again, except that really it didn't. Nearly all the spare whiskey in America had been diverted to the military, newly liberated France hadn't resumed exporting champagne, and with the shortage of tin there wasn't a can of beer to be found. The Stork Club, despite all its cachet still beholden to rationing, ran out of beef and butter. In the midst of blaring plastic trumpets, twirling clickers, and tossing sixteen tons of shredded paper, some revelers pressed their ears to battery radios, struggling to catch news bulletins about the Bulge. For the first time since Prohibition, not one New Yorker drank himself to death in the celebration, though a Coast Guard sailor would be picked up by the police wandering naked through Times Square at 5:00 the next morning.

Eleanor and her friends did not stay to see the ball drop at the stroke of midnight. The rain, the mob—it was all too hard to negotiate laden with luggage and skates. Instead they wormed down into the subway and rode north to the Bronx. Far from the din of Times Square, beyond earshot even of the nightclubs along Jerome Avenue, Eleanor made her way up the slight incline of Harrison Avenue. By this time, the rain had given way to fog, and it muffled the stray lights from this kitchen window or that street lamp, softened the hiss of the occasional car rolling over wet streets. Rose and Sol sat awake in the living room, she reading the *Forverts,* he the *Daily News.* They were waiting up for Seymour, who had taken a teenaged cousin of Danny Schlomkowitz's out to an ice-cream parlor. Sol knew better than to try and monitor Eleanor's comings and goings, and Rose belatedly was learning how to choose her battles.

* * *

168

On the Saturday evening of February 3, 1945, three years and two months after another Saturday night in another world, Fannie Hatkin stepped beneath a *chuppa* laced with white roses to wed Danny Schlomkowitz. Since they first had locked eyes across the floorboards of the Painters Union hall, almost an entire war had been waged, from the Japanese attack on Pearl Harbor to the last days' reports of the Americans recapturing Manila and the Red Army smashing across Poland and toward Germany. War shadowed the ceremony in various ways, some merely inconvenient, others grave. Zernowitz and Perelmar, the caterers, had been scrambling until the last minute to locate enough chickens for the reception dinner, and Danny himself had scoured the city for whiskey, finally coming up with a few bottles of Imperial rye, rotgut stuff but better than sobriety. More seriously, he decided not to include ushers in the bridal party, because too many of his closest friends were gone. Leon Becker, his pal from the Collegians club, was fighting somewhere in France. Harry Ceitlin, another member of the group, had died in Normandy on D-Day plus four, Harry Ceitlin who had insisted on enlisting despite his crummy eyesight.

Still, with war's end within reach, the wedding offered its own promise for the future. Danny already had graduated from City College with a degree in statistics and landed a job doing market research for a firm in Rockefeller Center. In the convoluted way of such things, he had discovered that most precious of wartime commodities, an apartment for rent, through a friend's sister-in-law's downstairs neighbor and sealed the deal with $25 in key money for the super. There would be no bunking with the in-laws for Fannie and Danny. Which meant, among other things, that as she neared age twenty-one, Eleanor finally would have a bed, to say nothing of a bedroom, of her own.

As the moment to exchange vows neared, Eleanor stood nearby Fannie as maid of honor, clutching a bouquet and a lit taper. If she felt the slightest twinge of envy watching Fannie marry on a night she didn't even have a date, Eleanor did not betray it. She had been a bridesmaid once already, for her friend Lillian Golden, who had married Ralph Betstadt during a week-long furlough the previous June—proposal on Wednesday, ceremony on Sunday, a reception with sandwiches and Marion Herzog at the piano. They wanted such different things out of life, the Hatkin sisters, one loyal and one insurgent, one content and one desirous. And if Fannie and Eleanor never had shared a certain kind of closeness, at least not since their girlhood days gardening together in Crotona Park, then they had been spared the corrosive effects of competition. So Eleanor delighted in Fannie's delight. She paged through fashion magazines, sketching out examples of bridal gowns. She bought a set of serving dishes, elaborately decorated in a floral design of turquoise and cream, for a wedding present. When Danny's sister Betty threatened to boycott the ceremony because she hadn't been included as a bridesmaid, Eleanor played diplomat, persuading and assuaging until Betty consented to attend.

Elsewhere under the *chuppa,* Sol wore a top hat and tails with white vest and bowtie, the same ensemble as Danny and his father. Sol's back was straight, his gaze direct, a slight smile on his face; he had not looked this serenely confident since his months in Bangor back before the war. Only Rose took in the proceedings with a dour expression, lips flat, eyes ringed dark.

She objected to the whole principle of a younger daughter marrying before an elder. In the Old World cosmology to which she subscribed, this violation of the supernatural order could only bring bad luck for Eleanor. Rose harbored such shame and fear about it that she hid news of Fannie's betrothal from Simmy Plansky and Minnie Osder until the invitations were practically in the mail. As if in propitiation, Rose went into the apartment Fannie and Danny had rented and placed in the corner of a cupboard small dishes of sugar and salt and a candle. Then there was the matter of the engagement ring, a gold setting fitted with a diamond pried loose from a tie pin. "Faygela, I looking at the ring with a magnifying glass," Rose had said on first inspecting it, improbably using her endearment for Fannie. "Vere is the diamond?" She was still smarting about it on the wedding day.

One other reason, the most personal of all, underlay Rose's morose spirits at what should have been a joyous time. Her family in Bialystok almost certainly had perished. When the Soviet army had liberated the city six months earlier, it found only a few dozen Jews alive in the city, home to 70,000 before the war. Forty thousand had been sent to Treblinka after a ghetto rebellion in the late summer of 1943, the Jewish survivors told their Russian rescuers, and 1,200 children had been separated specially for delivery to Auschwitz.

On the night before the wedding, Rose performed her single act of maternal obligation, presenting Fannie with an embroidered white sheet for the marital bed. The custom derived from several verses in Deuteronomy, telling the story of a husband who claims his bride is not a virgin. *In such a case,* the Torah instructed, *the girl's father and mother shall produce the evidence of the girl's virginity before the elders of the town at the gate, And they shall spread out the cloth before the elders of the town.* If the sheet is bloody, the accusing husband is to be flogged and fined; if the sheet is clean, the wife is to be stoned to death. After her wedding night with Danny, Fannie simply laundered the sheet and folded it with the rest of the linens. Rose never asked for it, much less displayed it at the brick portal to 2101 Harrison. On matters of virtue, she had no doubts about at least one of her daughters.

Carrying his sea bag and a hula outfit he had bought on liberty in Honolulu, Hy Keltz stepped stiff-legged off the three-day sleeper that had carried him from the West Coast to Grand Central Terminal. He had a twenty-day leave, and almost a third of it would be used up by the cross-country trains. That left him barely two weeks to visit with his mother and his sister, take out Eleanor Hatkin on a few dates, and put the war far out of his mind. He didn't want to talk about the Japanese plane that was bearing down on the Nehenta Bay until the Donnelly brothers nailed it. He didn't want to talk about the typhoon that knocked off 15 feet of the flight deck. Most of all, he didn't want to talk about the day Ensign Fischer died, catching his left wing on the ship's catwalk trying to land and running out of fuel while circling for another chance. "Get out, get out," Hy had been screaming, as Fischer popped open the cockpit, beat his hand against the metal skin, then stopped moving. No, if anybody asked any questions about the war, all Hy planned to say was that he was serving in the South Pacific and change the subject.

New York was cooperating in his desire to escape. As Hy arrived on March 16, 1945, officially the last week of winter, the balm of spring soothed the city, temperatures rising into the seventies, the crocuses already opening. Defying presidential orders for a continuing midnight curfew, Mayor La Guardia was urging nightclubs to stay open until one, neighborhood taverns until four. Even as the war bond sales and scrap drives proceeded, even as the newspapers printed lengthy daily lists of the dead and wounded and imprisoned, people dared at last to talk about what would come after—expressways, housing projects, modular furniture, silk stockings.

On one of those glorious warm days, Hy took Ellie with him to Poe Park, a band of greenery and benches alongside the Grand Concourse. It was the first time they had seen one another in four years. Hy was, if anything, more handsome than before the war, his skin leathery from the months of salt air, his torso taut after all those calisthenics on the flight deck, curls of chest hair pushing up from the neck of his uniform. Eleanor wore a pleated skirt and matching coat, and in the afternoon sun she shed it for a short-sleeve blouse. By then, Hy had his arm around her shoulder and she was resting hers on his thigh. They held hands while leaning against a parked sedan, locked elbows like a couple of square dancers in mid-swing.

Over the next week or so, they spent more time together. Hy introduced Ellie to his mother and his sister, a declaration of sorts that they were a couple with serious prospects. Like old times, they had ice cream at Krum's and saw a picture at the Paradise. How perfect that it was *Meet Me in St. Louis,* starring Judy Garland, because they had watched her all those years ago in *The Wizard of Oz.* Back then, Ellie had thought of "Over the Rainbow" as their song, a song of escape. This new movie, though, was all about the pleasures of home, about dreams that could be fulfilled right on your own block. There was one song in particular that made all the couples in the Paradise balcony snuggle, a ballad called "The Boy Next Door."

For one final fling before leave was over, Hy treated Ellie to the 400 Club, a cabaret and nightspot on Fifth Avenue. It was a relatively new place, not famous like Jack Dempsey's or the Diamond Horseshoe, but the owner was a war veteran always glad to have GIs in the house, partly because they had so much money to spend in so little time. So Hy and Ellie caught the floor show, a singer named Rita Angel who was married to a boxing champ, and they had drinks and then some more drinks, Manhattans for Eleanor, just like the ones she'd first tried with Hy years ago at Marion Herzog's Sweet Sixteen party. No matter what La Guardia said, they left by midnight, because there were rumors the Navy had the shore patrol checking on bars and they were plenty tipsy already.

When Hy brought Ellie back to 2101 Harrison, the Hatkin apartment was unaccountably empty and usefully dark, and they grabbed for each other with latent longing. They necked and they fondled and they tugged at zippers and clasps. And then Ellie pulled Hy down onto a couch and he realized with a start that she was naked. He stood up. He drew back a few steps. It had to be the booze. There was no other way a nice girl would be so bold. After all his shore leaves in the Navy, Hy had little naiveté left, and he surely felt the attraction of that shapely flesh begging for him. But this wouldn't be seduction; it wouldn't even be conquest; it would be taking advantage, and he'd been raised better than that. What kind of hangover would they both have after this kind of a nightcap? No, when he went all the way with Ellie, he wanted her to know what she was doing. And he wanted it to be more than one impulsive night. For now, he lowered her onto her bed to pass out, and walked alone to the Jerome Avenue El.

Several days later, on March 31, Hy met two Navy buddies in Grand Central for the long trip back to the war. In the fifteen minutes before the train left, Hy knocked back three shots of bourbon, and after a few clattering miles of track he threw up. When he reached the West Coast on April 2, he wrote in his diary, "Came back today. Why oh why!"

In the months to come, as the Nehenta Bay carried Hy to Pearl Harbor, then Guam, then Ulithi, then Okinawa, mail from Eleanor followed. These were not the kind of notes she had written before his visit, flirtatious and yet guarded; these were professions of love, promises of a shared future. And at the same time, she also wrote to Charlie Greco, telling him she was breaking off. When he came home soon afterward on an emergency leave to visit his severely ill mother, he did not even try to see Eleanor. After a Dear John letter in the middle of a world war, he told friends, he was too pissed off to go begging for another chance.

Eleanor sent Hy a photo of herself wearing the hula outfit, dancing in grass skirt and leis on the tar beach of 2101 Harrison's roof. She sent him a photo from their night at the 400 Club, with the inscription on the back, "To the end of the war & the beginning of our real fun & living." She sent him a photo of herself modeling a dress with a jungle-leaf print: "To my darling, my love for you isn't camouflaged." She sent him a photo of herself beside a picnic table at Orchard Beach: "A sunny day, the seashore, a potato pancake in one hand, a tuna sandwich in the other—what more could I ask for except you!" And she sent him a photo, taken that same day in April 1945, not long after Hy had reported

back to the Navy with the single goal of surviving, of
herself standing barefoot at the water's edge.

> Think if I wait by
> the sea long enough,
> I'll be seeing the U.S.S.
> Nehenta Bay pulling in
> —for good??

> Love—
Ellie

Charlie and Eleanor, Bear Mountain, 1947

Three
Loving
1945–1948

AFTER TWO YEARS, eleven months, and twelve days in the possession of the United States Navy, after 180,000 nautical miles in the Pacific theater of war, Hy Keltz presented himself with dropped pants, bared chest, and gaping jaw for his discharge physical at a personnel separation center in the Long Island town of Lido Beach. He was nearly twenty-four years old and a trained aviation machinist, a long way from the East Bronx urchin who'd played stickball with the Acmes, a long way even from the Morris High graduate cutting shoulder pads in a factory loft and feeling grateful for the paychecks. "Is there anything you want fixed?" the medical officer asked Hy. Hy answered, "Just send me home."

Soon after, he stepped out into the cool, drizzly Sunday afternoon of October 14, 1945, precisely two months after V-J Day. At the moment the Japanese surrendered, Hy had been steaming on the U.S.S. Nehenta Bay toward an assignment to bomb Wake Island, where an enemy garrison was holding out. Everyone onboard expected then to be hurled into the invasion of Japan itself, and it was a campaign they dreaded more than ever after having endured a kamikaze attack off Okinawa back in June. So when the announcement echoed over the ship's loudspeaker of war's end, Hy wrote in his diary, "Happy day!"

Wearing his dress blues and sporting the eagle pin jokingly known as the "ruptured duck," he now took his last journey at Naval expense, boarding the Long Island Railroad for an hourlong trip to Penn Station. Of course, he had missed all the glorious hubbub back home in the Bronx on that August night—people dragging pianos into the street, kids pelting trolleys with confetti, tables of beer and cold cuts spreading across apartment courtyards, flags rippling from fire escapes and clotheslines, banners mocking "Hirohito's Last Stand," a mob of dancing and kissing and hugging and crying at the junction where Fordham Road crossed the Grand Concourse, what folks called the "Times Square of the Bronx." No, that first burst of euphoria had spent itself while Hy was starting on his excruciatingly indirect path home, via Alaska, Japan, Pearl Harbor, and San Francisco. By now, Piser's department store down on 149th Street was already selling military-surplus jeeps.

But Hy had arrived with plans, the most romantic of them represented by a gift for Eleanor Hatkin, carefully wrapped inside his duffel bag. It was a shining, silvery bracelet in the shape of two separate hearts joining together to form a third. Hy had commissioned it from his buddy Wallace Berry after reporting back to the Nehenta Bay seven months earlier in the wake of his leave and his furious pursuit of Eleanor. A machinist second class, Berry was the de facto jeweler of the Nehenta Bay; he'd already crafted Hy a man's bracelet from three braided strands of welding rod. For Eleanor, he dipped into the ship's ample supply of aluminum, which was used for patching planes. Nobody would ever miss the amount needed to wrap around a slender female wrist, and Berry buffed the strip till it gleamed. Then, during four days in San Francisco waiting for the troop train east, Hy brought both items to a Woolworth's store to be inscribed. For his own bracelet, he instructed the engraver to list every port and battle he had encountered. For Eleanor's, Hy specified that the inside be etched in cursive script "All My Love, Hy to Ellie," and the outside, across the three hearts, "Forever Yours."

Hy had no way yet to tell Ellie he was back, since the Hatkins still didn't have a phone of their own. But for months now, she had been watching the servicemen stream back to New York, 500 a day at the latest count, and thousands more passing through the city on their way to wherever home was. They were reclaiming their jobs at Burndy and adjusting to sharing the shop floor and front office with women, one of the vets explaining almost apologetically, "I have to forget my Marine lingo." They were enrolling on the GI Bill at City downtown, seventy-five vets in the fall's incoming class, scornful of the beanies and pep songs and hazing, and wary beyond their years, with more than half in a survey by the college newspaper predicting another world war within a generation. They were horsing around with Eleanor and Vicky Behar during the summer at the Castle Hill pool, making human pyramids on the grass near the handball courts, and they were treating themselves to special mud packs from Hilda Saltzman's barber uncle. They were marrying, too, in record-breaking numbers. The first wedding in the postwar Bronx had taken place just a few blocks from the Hatkin apartment in the Burnside Avenue catering hall run by an enterprising cantor named Samuel Flaum, who charged for both vows and victuals.

As Eleanor waited for her war veteran, for Hy, the

newspapers and magazines only magnified the longing. "Your hero's home!" exulted Macy's in the pages of the *Herald Tribune* on the very morning he was arriving. "You're together again!" In the current issue of *LIFE,* an advertisement for Trushay hand lotion depicted a young woman, lips parted and eyes closed, caressing her officer beau in a tableau of reunion. "This is what he dreams of," the ad promised, "the heavenly nearness of you." With life returning to normal in so many other ways—Meatless Tuesdays just had been canceled, gas rationing was over, Campbell's soup and Johnnie Walker scotch were back on the shelves—why couldn't she resume a normal love life as well?

From Penn Station, meanwhile, Hy telephoned his mother, home on her day off from the sales floor of Alexander's, and then he boarded the subway for the final leg of his odyssey. He was practically a stranger to his own address after all these years, uncertain of the closest stop to the apartment on Valentine Avenue, even though his Navy pay had helped rent it. The Keltzes had been living on Jackson Avenue in the East Bronx when he enlisted, and by now Jackson Avenue was having its troubles with juvenile delinquents, some kid named Santana having just been shot dead by a fourteen-year-old with a revolver. It was all part of the life that had gone on without Hy, part of the life he wanted to catch up on now. There was no big celebration waiting when Hy beheld his mother through the open door. She was just quietly, tearfully thankful, with one son safely home, and one more and a son-in-law still to be demobilized. The time hadn't come yet for her to take down all the blue stars. Hy squired her to dinner at Cantonese Gardens on the Concourse, the first Chinese food she had eaten in her life. As a gesture toward keeping kosher, even though the whole kitchen was lousy with shrimp and pork, he ordered vegetable chop suey.

Then Hy turned his attentions to Ellie. He had brought home not only the love bracelet but $341.48 in discharge pay. They went out for nights, maybe to hear Sinatra at the Paramount or Gene Krupa's band at the Capitol, catching two or three shows from each. Walking Ellie through Times Square, Hy basked in the lights, the theater marquees all ablaze with *Carousel* and *On the Town,* the movie palaces flourishing *Anchors Aweigh* and *A Bell for Adano,* warfare already milled into entertainment. In some weird way, he even enjoyed watching the pickpockets at work, bumping and darting among the greenhorns, many of them GIs fresh off the troop ships on the West Side docks. Bright, noisy, a little bit larcenous, this was the city that Hy remembered, and now he strode through it not just with a girl on his arm, but very likely a wife. Eleanor didn't need to tantalize him now, play the pinup girl in those skimpy jumpers; she dressed like a woman, a flesh-and-blood version of "Debby Dean, Career Girl" from the funnies, with the puffed sleeves and swirling skirts coming into style, now that fabric restrictions were in the past. Manhattan with Hy Keltz made good on the promise from that Vaughan Monroe song Ellie had heard so many times during the war:

When the lights go on all over the world
And the boys are home again all over the world
And rain or snow is all that may fall from the skies
above
A kiss won't mean "goodbye" but "Hello to love."

Still, Hy was a man governed by realism as much as romance. With his mother long widowed, his sister married, and his younger brother planning to attend college after the service, he had no intention of proposing to Eleanor until he settled into a job worthy of a family man. "Somebody's gotta make a buck," he kept telling himself. He already had forsaken one dream, the idea of moving to California after his discharge to find work in the aviation industry. Instead of luxuriating as a member of the "52-20 Club"—the postwar benefit of $20 a week for an entire year to which every veteran was entitled—he set about immediately searching for prospects around New York. There were twelve million men and women in the military as of V-J Day; where were there going to be twelve million jobs for them on the home front? Hy thought again of aviation, but La-Guardia Airport was glutted with demobilized pilots, machinists, and engineers. Everybody in town from longshoremen to elevator operators to truck drivers seemed to be going on strike. So when Hy got an offer from a print shop, he grabbed it, and when he heard three weeks later about a grocery for sale, he listened closely.

The tip came from an uncle and aunt in the Borough

Park section of Brooklyn. An elderly couple wanted to sell their store, partly because A&P just had opened a supermarket a couple of blocks away. They wanted $3,000 for the whole place, including stock and fixtures. It wasn't going to be easy; Hy realized that right away. He knew from having delivered for his uncle's store as a kid that in a Mom-and-Pop grocery your hours went seven to seven, six days a week. There were all kinds of headaches, new to Hy, from the rationing restrictions that remained in effect. You had to pay extra for your tub of butter from a black market middleman who drove out to Wisconsin every week with fifty grand to bribe the dairy farmers; to get scouring powder and toilet paper, the products customers needed, you had to take some of the canned vegetables that would rust before they sold. "One stiff, one good," the wholesaler would gloat as he counted out Hy's order.

As it happened, though, Hy's maternal grandfather had died during the war and left him exactly $3,000. So he bought the place in Borough Park and hung up the sign for HY'S SUPERETTE. For the first month, he tried to run the store himself, but that was impossible; every time he needed to use the bathroom, he had to lock up and post a window sign, BACK IN TEN MINUTES. Then Hy brought in his Brooklyn uncle to help, until he discovered the guy sneaking his thumb onto the scale when he weighed out cheese. Out went the uncle and again Hy was alone. He understood the business. He didn't have a *goyische kup,* a gentile's brain. He painted the store.

He installed freezers. He even got written up in *Grocer Graphic* magazine. But all the efforts were costing him a social life, a life with Eleanor. He slept five nights a week in an apartment behind the store, and by 7:00 on Saturday evening, when he was finally free until Monday morning, he couldn't muster much enthusiasm for the two-hour subway trip to the Bronx. Sundays had to be divided between his mother and his girlfriend, and it couldn't be drinks and dancing at the 400 Club on a grocer's precarious profits.

In the late winter of 1946, Hy decided how he could resolve his personal and vocational problems in a single stroke. On one of those Sundays in the Bronx, he took Eleanor out walking, maybe to their favorite spot in Poe Park, getting some privacy in public, away from both her mother and his.

"I've gotta have someone who can help me," he started.

Eleanor said nothing, and so he spoke again.

"And we've been going together for awhile."

And that was it, a marriage proposal, evidently. Hy Keltz was asking for her hand in holy matrimony and in stocking the shelves, sweeping the floors, handling the cash registers. She had visited the grocery once, seen enough of it not to make a return trip. Nothing was wrong with the place. It was what it was, a storefront with a counter and scale and a proprietor in an apron, sharing a city block with a butcher, a candy store, and some three-story apartments. Even in this moment of thudding pragmatism, though, Hy was more than anyone the incarnation of Eleanor's romantic spirit—the handsome boy she'd passed a note to in geometry class at Morris, the first one to kiss her lips and break her heart, the sinewy sailor who had swept back into her life on leave, the gentleman who hadn't taken advantage the night she had too many Manhattans. She asked Hy, pleaded nearly, if she could give him money from her Burndy salary to hire an assistant. He could have the help he needed; she could keep the job she enjoyed and the prospect of a college diploma. When Hy said no, she slid down into a heap and began to cry.

For years, Eleanor had granted her heart primacy over her mind. She had sought love and cultivated allure and fallen for men unequal to her intellect. As much as she coveted attention for her figure she tried to duck it for her academic prowess, as if excelling was a performance executed solely for the benefit of others. "I want to be a person," she often told her friend Clare Abramowitz, "not just a brain." Still, now she faced the choice between her warring halves, ardor versus ambition. In her memory, she could hear her mother's reproach about so many of the boys she'd dated: "For this, you have to be the smartest girl in class?" After muddling through four years at City downtown, Eleanor had finally struck upon a career choice with some appeal, switching her concentration to public relations and advertising. This semester, she was learning to design ads and plot campaigns, timely skills in a nation with one hundred forty billion dollars saved up for vacuum cleaners, Studebakers, washing machines, nylons, and everything else that had been embargoed during the war. At Burndy, business was jumping, with a new plant under construction in the Bronx and plans for expansion into Canada; the electrical connectors that had served fighters and landing craft so ably were now selling in vast numbers to the power plants, commuter trains, and radio stations of the suddenly growing suburbs. The future, so prosperous, was swirling all around Eleanor.

Saying yes to Hy, at least under the circumstances, meant saying something about herself. The whole reason Eleanor had admired Mel Goodman and Bernie Solomon in high school, the whole reason she had befriended Clare Abramowitz and Ruth Pacter during the war years, was because they taught her by example to see the world in a critical way, to resist its ordinariness. In the last few months, Eleanor had been buying and reading novels by Upton Sinclair and Howard Fast, not exactly great literature or incisive social commentary, more like Popular Front potboilers. They were stories about thrusting yourself into the great battles of the time, whether in Fast's fictional retelling of the American Revolution or Sinclair's adventures set in World War II Europe, stories about the thrill of the struggle. Nothing seemed so ridiculous about Sinclair's cloak-and-dagger hero Lanny Budd clinking glasses with Stalin, "Uncle Joe" to him, when President Truman himself recently had put up the Soviet Foreign Minister at the White House and the United Nations was convening on Hunter College's Bronx campus, not so far from the Hatkins' apartment. It wasn't that Eleanor wanted a Red, or a radical, in a husband; her own politics were naïve, impulsive. But down to her marrow, she despised the idea of being conventional. She could not chose the life her sister Fannie had chosen, or that her friend Lillian Golden had welcomed, marrying your first sweetheart, living in the old neighborhood. "Somewhere Over the Rainbow" had been Eleanor's song with Hy. Aboard the Nehenta Bay, he'd traveled more than far enough from home to appreciate the balm of the familiar and the mundane. For Eleanor, though, what kind of rainbow ended in Borough Park?

"There's nothing there," Eleanor told Clare a few days after the encounter with Hy. "He wants a store and he wants me to work in the store."

Since Hy Keltz had not given her an engagement ring, Eleanor had no ring to return. As she had after their breakup in high school, she purged her photo album of every snapshot of him. With all the tumult, she managed only Cs in her advertising classes. Hy never tried again to persuade Eleanor. Her refusal had pierced straight to the self-doubt he had harbored for seven years, the secret fear that he wasn't smart enough for her. A few months later, he went into partnership with his brother-in-law, Stanley Feldman, who had been discharged. Eleanor did keep the aluminum bracelet from Hy among her favorite pieces of jewelry, however, even as she placed a call to Mary Greco to find out whether her son Charlie had come home from the war.

* * *

In the early spring of 1946, the new issue of the *Bialystoker Stimme* supplied what Rose Hatkin had been searching for ever since the city's liberation eighteen months earlier: a roster of survivors. With the arrival of the Soviet army in August 1944, and the German surrender the following May, her spirits had dared to rise. No longer was she stuck with repeating the same futile efforts—asking Simmy Plansky and Minnie Osder, writing to her relatives in Uruguay, visiting the Bialystok *landsmenshaften* in Manhattan—simply to feel she was doing something. At her behest, Sol wrote letters in his night-school English to the organizations that were sorting through seven million displaced persons in postwar Europe, including the 250,000 Polish Jews to have outlasted the Final Solution. Between the Red Cross and the Joint Distribution Committee and the Hebrew Immigrant Aid Society, somebody had to have a list from Bialystok, somebody had to know.

Meanwhile, from the woodlands where they had fought as partisans, from the attics and barns where Poles had hidden them, from the Russian territory where they had taken refuge, the remnants of Bialystok Jewry were limping back to the city, wraiths in a landscape of ruins. The Germans had eradicated nearly every trace of Jewish existence by the time they liquidated the ghetto in August 1943. Only a heap of warped, blackened beams remained of the Great Synagogue. Janchum's fish market was reduced to bare earth, the Neuvelt *beit midrash* to a scorched, roofless shell, the Artisans School to a single stone wall. Corpses rotted in ditches and garbage heaps, prayerbooks lay scattered amid rubble, and a Yiddish message carved into the walls of the Nazi prison cried out, "Their fate should be worse than what they did to us Jews."

Now, at least, now, at last, there was an accounting. Two officials from the New York *landsmenshaften* had traveled to Bialystok in late 1945 and conducted a census of the returned Jews. From several dozen in the days after liberation, the number had grown to 470—470 out of 70,000 before the war. Rose had been trying to convince herself of a way her relatives could be among them. A cousin of Sol's had turned up alive in Latvia, after all, and made it to Argentina. Marion Herzog's mother had located her eldest sister in Rumania through the Red Cross.

Through all the months of waiting and hoping, Rose sometimes had stood in the kitchen talking to herself, putting wishes into words. What if Avram, her brother the revolutionary, had retreated with the Communists into the Soviet Union when the Germans invaded? What if Shifra, whose husband owned the beauty parlor, had been able to bribe her way to safety? Then again, how could Menuchi, so fearful of every sudden noise or dark alley, possibly have endured the Nazis? Ester Dina, her favorite, with three little children and no husband, was the most defenseless of them all.

Rose squinted at the small Yiddish characters in the *Bialystoker Stimme* list. The survivors were arrayed by surname, though not in alphabetical order. She had to find the separate clusters that began with *mem* and with *kupf,* each bunch of names like a household. There was a Majzler, Sara, and a Madlinski, Wolf, but not a single Markiewicz; there was a Kac, Josef, and a Kaplan, Hersz, and a Kanan, Avrom, but not a single Kaczkowicz. No Nissan or Avram. No Shifra or Menuchi. No Ester Dina.

Even then, Rose refused to concede. Not knowing they were alive was not the same as knowing they were dead. And if it provided any tiny consolation to her vigil, her American children now understood that all her terrors had been justified. They weren't just an obsession with the Old World, a love for family on the other side at the expense of love for family right here. Even Eleanor, the most dismissive and the most disengaged, had come to comprehend a hatred vaster and more virulent than her mother's most overwrought imaginings.

Eleanor's education had begun with the graphic newspaper reports of Nazi atrocities that were being uncovered as the Red Army marched toward Berlin— from the Babi Yar killing ground, from the Madjanek death camp, from Auschwitz. In Eleanor's own circle, the genocide was experienced intimately. Ruth Klekman's boyfriend, Bernie Murowitz, witnessed the ovens, most with bodies still inside, after American troops liberated Buchenwald. At the Allerton Coops, where Ruth Pacter's family lived, people sobbed as they sang Yiddish odes to the martyred partisans. Burndy's president, Bern Dibner, went as an army major into the Normandy village of Oradour, and wrote in the company newsletter of the massacre there, what he called "one of the cruelest acts in the history of a very cruel mankind." While this attack had been executed in retribution against the French resistance, Dibner must have reacted to it partly as a European-born Jew, and its method brought to mind Red Friday in Bialystok:

> It seems that about 200 troops descended on the town in accordance with a thoroughly prepared plan in which all roads and intervening fields were patrolled. At first all the men and boys were shot in the nearest garages in groups of several dozens. The women and children were herded into the fine old church. Then methodically grenades and incendiary bombs were thrown into every building in the entire town so that not a single one of the houses remained. The hundreds of women and children in the church were machine-gunned, sprayed with gasoline and ignited. . . .

Then, in the last week of April 1946, as New York's moviehouses were featuring the latest larks from Sonja Henie and Ginger Rogers, the first newsreel was released documenting German genocide. It was entitled "Nazi Murder Mills," and the advertisement in the *Herald Tribune* declared it, "A Film You Must See To Believe." That was more than a catchy slogan, for General Dwight Eisenhower himself had urged the production of such newsreels, as well as visits to the death camps by politicians and journalists, to shock his nation into recognition. Military censorship had spared Americans on the home front much of the carnage of war—photographs of the Pearl Harbor attack, for instance, were not published until 1943—and accounts of Nazi genocide had been commonly deprecated as propaganda designed to serve the Allied effort or even Jewish and Soviet designs. In its four minutes, "Nazi Murder Mills" proved those reports had been, if anything, unduly restrained. The camera peered into mass graves and crematoria packed with skeletons; it lingered over cadavers with open eyes, tattooed forearms, crusted blood. "Don't turn away—look," the narrator, Ed Herlihy, commanded at one point. "Burned alive. Horror unbelievable. Yet true."

Marion Herzog's mother happened to go to the movies one of the first nights the newsreel showed, when it took the audience largely unawares. She came home shaken, telling Marion how the spectators around her had shrieked, vomited, fainted away. Eleanor and Ruth Pacter probably watched "Nazi Murder Mills," too, because when Ruth wrote to her boyfriend Al in the spring of 1945, she recounted a "heated discussion" at Burndy about German atrocities, so heated that she, her cousin Bernie, and Eleanor "went into a conference room so we wouldn't disturb everyone." Ruth's words surely conveyed Eleanor's emotions as well:

> I never thought that I could say I hate anyone with all possible hate in me as I hate these Germans. With the end of the war in Germany in sight, the problem of

dealing with a nation of psychopathic cases becomes something of an important nature. . . . I don't think for a minute, though, that those b———s deserve any thought on our part. . . . What's to be done with them? Extermination or a chance at re-education? . . . It's rather pitiful that we can still think of giving them a chance after all the unbelievable crimes they've committed. And so I'm all for extermination, even though I know it won't be done.

Sometime in the latter months of 1946, Rose Hatkin received a letter from her niece Judis, the relative in Uruguay with whom she most regularly corresponded. Judis and her brother Julius had been peppering every survivor reaching Montevideo with questions. Who was from Bialystok? Who knew a family named Kaczkowicz? Anyone remember a mother named Ester Dina, a dark-haired woman, and her three children, who would've been in their teens during the war? Finally, someone answered yes. This survivor told Julius he had seen the four being marched out of their house by the Nazis. Then he had seen them again in Treblinka, herded toward the gas chambers. This could have been in February 1943, during the first stage of the ghetto liquidation, or else the final, larger one in August of that year. As for what had happened in Treblinka, the *Forverts* had been publishing an escapee's firsthand account:

> The motor in the new gas chamber didn't work well so death took longer and was very painful. They were

able to gas 20,000 in one day. There were 15 to 20 suicides a day by workers. . . . The best looking women
were grabbed by Ukrainian militiamen and dragged to
their barracks to be raped before they were delivered
to the gas chambers. . . . Crematoria got underway
when orders came from Himmler to destroy all evidence of mass killing. Women burned easier than men
so they were used as kindling. Rivalry between work
gangs ensued as to who could burn a greater number
of bodies. . . . The Germans drank toasts of choice
liquors, caroused and enjoyed themselves near the
warm fires in celebration.

Not that such details finally mattered, of course. February or August, gassed or burned, raped or not, death
was death. What mattered for Rose was the knowledge
that her beloved sister was gone. And that knowledge
mocked her for having been fool enough to entertain
the fantasy, the delusion, the idiocy of hope. She had
been right all along to have Sol saying *kaddish,* to be
kindling *yahrzeit* candles. *"Forever remembering,"* her
siblings always signed their postcards. Here was forever
remembering, indeed.

In Uruguay, Judis and Julius tried to assemble their
lives. A motherless bride, Judis married a chairmaker
named Jaime Prusky; *Dona* Rybko, with whose family
the Kaczkowiczes lived, helped her with the trousseau.
Julius adopted the more familiar name of Julio and was
courting his future wife, Rebeca Kaganas, during his
breaks from traveling through the Uruguayan country-

side, selling bed frames for a wholesaler. Rose still sent Judis used clothing to sell, as well as wigs, a sought-after item. And she included snapshots, Fannie and Danny kneeling on the boardwalk at Brighton Beach, Eleanor and Seymour in winter coats outside the NYU Hall of Fame.

This lifeline, this strand of family from the Bronx to Montevideo, could hardly compensate, however, for all the other deaths. Rose howled and keened at her failure to bring her family to America, the single task entrusted to her a quarter-century ago. She hissed resentment about Sol's cousin the survivor, who was now writing from Buenos Aires. "Don't answer," she insisted. "They want money. And you'll give it to them." Mostly, Rose's wrath found a different target. She did not blame only the Nazis. She did not blame only the Germans. *"Die goyim hubben oysegeharget mein gantze mishpocheh,"* she said again and again: The goys killed my whole family.

On January 11, 1946, three months behind Hy Keltz, Charlie Greco passed through the same Navy separation center at Lido Beach and made the same trip to the Bronx. He was carrying $172 in discharge pay, including a buck and a quarter for the train and subway fares, and wearing five battle stars, one ribbon, and the Victory Medal. WELCOME HOME, read the banner strung from his family's fourth-floor apartment off the Grand Concourse. Inside his mother Mary had laid out platters of roast chicken and ravioli and bottle after bottle

of homemade wine. With Charlie and his older brother
Sam both back, she was waiting only for her daughter
Marie's fiancé, Frank Connor, making his last long
journey from the Burma Road.

Despite all the joy and relief Charlie felt, he also
smarted from an acute sense of time having passed. His
father Carmine had died shortly before Charlie enlisted.
His older sister Ruth was married and the mother of a
little boy. One of his best friends from the Harlem Hebrew Institute, Bernie Dunetz, had returned from the
Pacific the previous June and within the month wed his
neighborhood sweetheart Anita Rosenhoch; by this
time, he was already keeping books for a sweater shop.
Another of the East Harlem crowd, Anita's brother Bill
Rosenhoch, was finishing his stint in the Army Signal
Corps and already engaged to his girl, Naomi Gruder. It
was as if they'd all gone from chucklehead to grown-up
in one drastic step.

As for Charlie, so easygoing before the war, he'd
been through plenty on the U.S.S. Carter Hall, servicing
landing craft in the invasions of New Britain, Guam,
and Leyte. He had taught himself photography, turning
the ship's boiler room into a darkroom, picking up
extra money taking souvenir portraits of the crew.
Being a machinist's mate, he also had begun to acquire
skills that could take him past his prewar job as a delivery boy. Now, home at last, he percolated with ambition, way too impatient for the soft life of the 52-20
Club. He didn't even bother applying for his GI "read-
justment allowance" for nine months. Instead, he went

down to see his old boss, Bill Gensheimer, at the sewing machine shop in Chelsea, and proposed a deal. If Gensheimer would teach him how to make attachments, he would work for free while he learned. As it turned out, Gensheimer was having trouble paying other employees, too, and one day walked through the shop offering to sell two ownership stakes for $2,500 apiece. Charlie offered to buy both and took a loan to get the money. Now, as Gensheimer's partner, he insisted on one more condition. He, Charlie, would work the counter. Gensheimer was too nice, or else too gullible, always getting talked into doing repairs for nothing.

There was just one missing piece in Charlie Greco's postwar plan: Eleanor Hatkin. All that had ended with the Dear John letter in the Carter Hall mail call. He wasn't exactly sitting home moping, not with his Navy pal Dick Gumerove also discharged and single. For a while, Charlie dated a banker's daughter, someone commensurate to his aspirations, and especially useful when her Daddy guaranteed the loan for Gensheimer's equity. He even took out an Italian girl, not his usual type, coming away muttering, "Never again." And then, sometime in the late spring of 1946, sometime after turning down Hy Keltz and his superette, Eleanor called.

When they met, when they regarded one another, they stood a long way from the teenagers they had been at Orchard Beach, a world war ago. Charlie was broader and thicker across the chest, with furrows already forming in his ruddy cheeks; his hair, freed from military restrictions, piled up in a slightly disobedient pompadour, a stray curl sometimes slipping onto his forehead. Eleanor had graduated from a coquette's enticements to a ladylike restraint. Her eyebrows were tweezed to softly curved edges, her hair gathered behind the neck and then spread curling onto her shoulders. Her pleated dress left her figure to the imagination, or, in this case, to memory, Charlie's memory.

They retraced the steps of their courtship, almost literally, dancing together again at Starlight Park, picnicking alongside the handball courts at the Castle Hill pool. They fixed up Dick Gumerove with Clare Abramowitz for a double date of bowling on Fordham Road, and amid the clamor of pins crashing a radio played Perry Como crooning his new hit, *Prisoner of Love*. Ruth Pacter's boyfriend also had come back from the Pacific, and since March she had been Mrs. Al Taylor. She and Eleanor, veterans of that all-girls weekend at Bear Mountain in 1944, returned now with their men. On the patio outside the lodge, Eleanor leaned back into Charlie's arms and just basked in the sunlight. His gaze, meanwhile, went only to her. And in all the settings, the chemistry shimmered off Eleanor and Charlie, a charged aura. *Gorgeous together,* thought Ruth. *Like they were mated,* thought Charlie's sister Marie. When a cousin of Clare Abramowitz's visited and spent some time with the couple, having heard about this daring love affair across religious lines, she was certain that Charlie was the Jew. He and Eleanor didn't need to find a song for themselves on the Hit Parade or the Make Believe Ballroom. They had the song Charlie and Bernie Dunetz had written years ago on a tenement stoop, before they could even understand the meaning of their own lyrics:

If the action takes place
Under the moon,
It's love, baby.
If the action takes place
Under the stars
Above, baby

The attraction went beyond the physical, palpable as the physical was. Where Hy Keltz had offered Eleanor modest possibilities, dependent in part on her own sacrifice, Charlie already had elbowed his way into partnership with his former boss. There was the prospect, so real with the war over, of moving up in the world. And there was also the prospect of joining a family that she seemed to accept, and that seemed to accept her, more than her own flesh and blood. Through the summer and autumn of 1946, Eleanor more and more slid into the role of Mary Greco's daughter-to-be. She joined the family for Sunday dinner, a four-hour affair thick with red sauce and conversation, so different from the abrupt meals in the Hatkin apartment, where half the time every member of the household ate on a separate schedule. At Marie's bridal shower that August, Eleanor posed for the family portrait, smiling with Charlie's arm around her, there amid Aunt Sadie and Cousin Palma and of course Mary, the matriarch.

Mary had experience in welcoming Jewish relatives to her table, especially those scorned by their own people. One of her brothers, after a failed first marriage to a Catholic, had wed a Jewish woman named Lydia. As Mary told the story, Lydia's father vowed never to set eyes on his daughter again; on his grandchildren's birthdays, he would knock on the door of Lydia's apartment, drop some gifts on the threshold, and leave. In the Greco household, Lydia was *famiglia,* and that embrace reflected ideology as much as instinct. Mary hardly could impose on others a Catholic faith she barely practiced herself. And wasn't her political hero, Fiorello La Guardia, himself the product of a mixed marriage, the child of Achille La Guardia and Irene Coen? When Charlie was a boy, Mary had told him to make friends with the Jewish kids, because in a tough neighborhood they were the ones going somewhere besides the reformatory. Eleanor, Charlie's intended, was the logical outcome of that advice. So Mary set about teaching Eleanor how to make eggplant parmesan, one of her own specialties. Just a few years earlier, she'd given the same lessons to her Jewish sister-in-law Lydia.

Up on Harrison Avenue, in the Hatkin household, Rose employed different strategies. Riding home from City downtown one night, Eleanor found a briefcase abandoned in the subway car; the notebooks inside indicated the owner was a medical student. Rose kept pressing Eleanor to call him, this future Jewish doctor, on the pretext of returning the lost property. Eleanor ignored her. When Charlie picked up Eleanor at the apartment, Rose offered him stuffed cabbage and a barbed sort of welcome. "You good friend, Charlie, I feed you," she told him. "You not marry my daughter." Everyone laughed stiffly, as if Rose were merely chiding, putting Charlie through some kind of initiation. When Charlie was gone, though, any pretense of humor fell away. "A *shande* my daughter should marry a *shaygetz*," Rose said—a shame, more than a shame, a humiliation, practically a sin. She had lost all her family on the other side, lost them to the *goyim*. How could she face the handful of relatives here in America, people like the Gartenbergs, so observant, as a mother who had raised her daughter to fall in love with the enemy?

Shoulder to shoulder, waist to waist, calf to calf, Eleanor and Charlie sat together on a pew in St. Patrick's Cathedral, awaiting the pipe organ's chord and the first glimpse of Francis Cardinal Spellman with his gold-plated crozier, these indicating the imminence of midnight's High Pontifical Mass. Until this moment on Christmas Eve of 1946, Eleanor never had set foot in a church. She barely had visited a synagogue, for that matter, in the three years since Seymour's bar mitzvah ceremony in the Jennings Street *shul,* unless she counted the time Marion Herzog snuck her into the serviceman's canteen at Temple Emanuel. Not even Emanuel, the grandest and indeed churchiest of Jewish sanctuaries, had prepared Eleanor for this cathedral modeled on Cologne and Amiens, for the granite columns vaulting to the Gothic ceiling that peaked 110 feet above, for the high altar of Siena marble, for the seventy stained glass windows from Chartres and Nantes. No, two or three Emanuels could fit into St. Patrick's nave.

They had come, she and Charlie, not to worship but to experience. As Mary's son, he was not especially religious, after all, and socially closer to Jews than Catholics. Still, this was his first Christmas back home from the Pacific, his first Christmas in New York since 1942, an occasion. He and Eleanor had spent the afternoon helping decorate the Greco tree, carols playing on the apartment radio, and inhaling the aromas of Mary's Christmas Eve feast. She always made fish six ways for the holiday—flounder, smelts, anchovies, calamari, platter after platter as belts were loosened around the table—and then dough balls with honey and liquor-soaked cherries for dessert. Lydia and her kids were there, too, one of her daughters announcing, "I'm Catholic now, when I'm with my aunties. And when I go to my other family, I'm Jewish."

It felt just about that possible to jump the fence, to migrate between worlds, this particular year. Hanukkah happened to be ending with the sunset only hours before Christmas Day would dawn, coincidence enough for the Synagogue Council of America, the most important rabbinical association in the country, to extend formal yuletide greetings to an array of Protestant and Catholic groups. "It is more important to realize what unites us," the rabbis said, "than to stress the things that separate us." Among the holiday movies was a remake of *Abie's Irish Rose,* that warhorse of interfaith romance, the comic courtship of Abie Levy and Rose Mary Murphy. New York's City Council recently had condemned five medical colleges for their pattern of discrimination against Jewish, Catholic, and Negro applicants, serving notice that the nation that had defeated fascism would no longer countenance home-grown prejudice.

So this cool, snowless Tuesday night had some magic in it. By the time Charlie and Eleanor reached midtown after 11:00 PM for the Mass, Fifth Avenue was like their private spectacle, the commuters having departed and the office parties having expired hours and hours ago. A Norway spruce, awash in ultraviolet light, towered seventy-five feet over the unpopulated ice of Rockefeller Center's rink. Bulbs burned frivolously in the display windows of the grand stores—Saks and Bergdorf-Goodman and Bonwit Teller, Cartier and Tiffany. There were silk stockings and electric shavers, diamonds and furs, the bounty of a record-breaking shopping season, the taste of what America could offer amid prosperous peace. Eleanor herself wore a tuxedo-style coat, shoulder to midcalf, of Persian lamb's paw, not a sable or a mink but a step up from her wartime chubby.

Within St. Patrick's, though, where she and Charlie sat, all was solemnity. All was ritual and procession, the stately pageantry so different from the hurried Hebrew mutterings and insistent rocking forward, *shuckeling* it was called, in the Jennings Street *shul,* one flight up from the pushcarts. Thanks to Mr. Coyle's Latin classes back before the war at Morris, Eleanor could follow snatches of the liturgy, connect those words to the sight of Cardinal Spellman, there in the middle distance, lifting the chalice and the host toward the bronze crucifix. Only when Charlie rose and filed to the altar rail for communion, for he was certainly that much of a Catholic, did Eleanor receive a reminder this was not only a lovers' outing, not only a tourist excursion from the pedestrian precincts of the Bronx, but part of a heritage that defined their difference.

Then, several minutes later, Charlie returned to her side. The Mass itself ended soon after with a reading from Saint John, and then Cardinal Spellman rose beside his archbishop's throne to deliver the Christmas message. Like obscure Charlie Greco in one of those rear pews, Cardinal Spellman was spending his first Christmas in New York since 1942. Through the war years, he had celebrated Mass in the field with fighting men as a military vicar, and his efforts had provided a spectacle of Catholic patriotism, an argument for full inclusion in America. Now, ten months after the Pope had elevated him to cardinal, Spellman was clergyman as celebrity, probably the most famous New Yorker outside La Guardia or Joe DiMaggio. He was also, it was apparent this season, an embodiment of the restive version of peace that had settled over the world, the Soviet-American friction that recently had been dubbed the Cold War. In the days leading up to Christmas 1946, the Soviet newspaper *Izvestia* had assailed Spellman for fomenting "violent hatred." This referred, most immediately, to an article by the cardinal in that unlikely ecclesiastical journal *Cosmopolitan* urging the Atlantic Charter nations to "save the cross of civilization" from Communism. Now, for the 5,000 worshippers filling every crevice of St. Patrick's, he recalled the last war's end, when "the joy of homecoming rang like the chimes of Christmas bells." And he prayed to God for the wisdom to "forever tread Thy path of peace." But he spared no sensibilities in deference to the holiday mood, saying, "Men of ill and evil will are still fighting men of good will, threatening to bear unto the world a still-born child of peace. Vengeful hatreds poison and destroy and lead mankind to war."

These were not Eleanor's kind of politics, not with her taste for Upton Sinclair and Howard Fast, not with friends like Clare Abramowitz and Ruth Taylor. This reflex to oppose anything Red sounded more like her mother's ravings; to this day, in fact, Rose often blamed Ruth Taylor for Eleanor's love affair with Charlie, explaining bitterly, "What do you expect? She's a Communist." Which wasn't even really true. And with Charlie just back from nearly three years in the military, with her brother Seymour at sixteen closing in on draft age, Eleanor could not fathom the prospect of war again, all that loneliness, all that waiting.

Sometime well past 1:00 in the morning, St. Patrick's emptied out onto the street, the worshippers spreading across sidewalks for blocks around, heading home beneath plumes of frosted breath. Charlie and Eleanor didn't need to wait for the subway and the slow rumble northward; he had borrowed his mother's car, driving being just the latest facet of Mary's modernity. For Eleanor, the grim prophecy of Spellman's message faded quickly against all the amazements—Rockefeller Center, Fifth Avenue, St. Patrick's, Midnight Mass, Charlie home and hers. Driving toward the Bronx, toward separate apartments but hopefully not for so much longer, she told herself this was the greatest night of her life.

Wearing cloth overcoats and weary expressions, Sol and Rose Hatkin entered an apartment house whose gold lettering announced it the HOMERIC. They had come in search of counsel regarding their reckless daughter, and they were seeking it from someone rooted in the Old World yet fluent with the New, Marion Herzog's mother Florence. Marion and Florence had moved to the Homeric, an elevator building in well-to-do Washington Heights, early in the war years, and they had furnished their one-bedroom unit with brand-new pieces—a striped satin loveseat, a tapestry wing chair, a credenza with a mahogany rack for their joint collection of decorative cups. The oldest piece was Marion's Baldwin Studio upright, the piano she had received as a five-year-old, the vehicle for her ascent into refinement. By this time, in February 1947, Marion had left Columbia Law School, equally bruised by a failed romance and a trusts-and-estates class, and transferred a few blocks away to Teachers College to earn a master's degree in education. She recently had landed her first teaching position in the English department of a vocational school. Florence, meanwhile, had left the Levine & Smith store on the Lower East Side to become a saleslady at the Ritz Thrift Shop on Fifty-Seventh Street, not the typical secondhand place but one specializing in furs from estate sales and movie stars' closets. All these details, all this catching up, were not incidental socializing for Sol and Rose. Florence's success, evidenced both by the Homeric apartment and an accomplished, loyal daughter, confirmed her credentials as a fount of sage advice.

Sol removed his fedora and said, "Mrs. Herzog, we are coming to you as if you are our sister." Rose started to sob. Stylish and unaccented, Florence nonetheless held a fondness for Rose and Sol, or perhaps something closer to gratitude, knowing how they had played the surrogate parents to her Marion back on Boston Road. She brought out a highball glass and a bottle of rye, and started to pour Sol a drink, pausing to ask if he wanted ginger ale in it. *"Dos iz gut zu mixen?"* he asked her, is it good to mix? She gently told him, yes, it was fine, mixing made a cocktail.

To the backdrop of Rose's tears, Sol recounted the story of Eleanor and Charlie, at least as much as he knew of it. Florence already had heard a fair amount from Marion, and shared Marion's misgivings, the conviction that such a romance could only come to a bad end. She had witnessed Eleanor's contempt for her parents as far back as Graduation Day at Morris, when the girl threw her medals at Rose. What she gathered now from Sol and Rose was the depth of their hurt, these simple, decent folk defied by a daughter beyond their understanding. Was there anything Florence Herzog could do? Sol asked. Was there any way she could change Eleanor's mind? And one more thing: Could she never, ever let Eleanor know about this visit? That would only make things worse, much worse.

Florence agreed readily to the request and the condition. Sol clasped her pale, smooth hand in his coarse workman's palms. Although Marion had not seen much of Eleanor in recent months, partly because she made it a point never to be introduced to Charlie, she looked over the newspaper listings of classical concerts in the coming weeks. She would invite Eleanor to accompany her, and arrange that they meet first at the Homeric, where Florence by design would be waiting.

Meanwhile, the love affair described a divide among all Eleanor's friends. On this matter of marrying out, every one felt compelled to take a side; neutrality and relativism were impossible; it was either-or. True to her upbringing in the Allerton Coops, where comrades married across lines not only of religion but race, Ruth Taylor backed Eleanor. Vicky Behar did, too, not surprising since she first had brought Charlie into Eleanor's circle. Vicky had dated an Italian Catholic herself, a factory worker at Burndy, even though she was serious now with a Jewish war veteran named Dave Fried. The way Charlie built to a Yiddish punchline, the way he danced the *hora* at Bill Rosenhoch's wedding reception, he was Jewish in his *kishkes*, as far as Vicky was concerned. And Rose Hatkin, to Vicky, was stupid, old-fashioned, hopeless. Clare Abramowitz took Eleanor to see a successful interfaith marriage in action—her cousin George Slayton and his Catholic wife Frances, cozily ensconced in the Manhattan neighborhood of Inwood. Eleanor told Rose all about it, how happy George and Frances were, and predictably mother and daughter were arguing within minutes.

On the other side, Marion Herzog saved her sympathy for Rose and Sol. Fannie Schlomkowitz was busy with her own life, seven months pregnant with her and Danny's first child. After more than two decades as sisters, she knew better than to try to talk rules and logic to Eleanor, anyway; Eleanor had a way of imagining facts to fit her desires. Then there was Lillian Betstadt, the one skeptic Eleanor thought she could win over. Hadn't Lillian herself had to endure a mother's opposition? Hadn't she heard all that hysterical nonsense about breaking up with Ralph because he was so sick with pleurisy he was bound to die? Lillian had persevered and married the man she loved, and along the way she often had turned to Eleanor for solace. Now, with the roles reversed, Lillian could not will herself to speak the words Eleanor wanted. As much as she hurt for Eleanor's hurting, as much as she knew the hell that 2101 Harrison had become, Lillian believed Rose would never accept the marriage. Nor, the more Lillian thought about it, would most other Jews. She had no encouragement to offer; she refused to encourage catastrophe.

Then, in the early spring of 1947, the night of the concert arrived and Eleanor stopped by the Homeric to pick up Marion. As the two chatted, Florence Herzog joined the conversation and slipped in a reference to Charlie. Eleanor must have viewed Mrs. Herzog as a potential ally, or at worst an agnostic. Just like Sol and Rose, she read into Florence's successful assimilation an appreciation of American ways, ways that included marrying for love. So much was going right, at last, for Eleanor. In the glow of Charlie, she was acing her classes at City downtown, finally performing like the Morris valedictorian. Surely Florence Herzog could appreciate that.

"You don't know how wonderful he is," Eleanor said eagerly to Florence. "Maybe you might want to meet him."

Florence weighed her words before replying.

"I don't have to meet him," she finally said. "I'm sure he must be wonderful for you to be so much in love with him."

And on that cryptic note, disapproval so subtle that Eleanor heard it as affirmation, she and Marion left for the concert. Florence had bad news for Rose and Sol Hatkin. There was no dissuading their daughter.

One late afternoon several weeks after Eleanor's visit to the Herzog household, her brother Seymour caught a ride from high school with his buddy Herbie, that rare Bronx child fortunate enough to have his own jalopy. Seymour was always thankful for a lift, which spared him two subways and several blocks of walking. For a change, he would have some time to relax between the end of classes at Gompers Vocational, where he was learning to be an electrician, and his night job bussing tables at Howard Johnson's near the Bronx Zoo. Now, at the threshold to Apartment 4D, he found himself as usual doing battle with the recalcitrant lock. When the key finally turned and the door gave, he heard voices off the foyer, from the living room. And as he entered, he beheld a most uncommon sight in the Hatkin residence: Charlie Greco.

Beside Charlie stood Eleanor, and across from them Rose Hatkin had planted herself. She wore an apron and a babushka, and she kneaded her hands together, which could mean one of two things. Either her rheumatism was acting up or she was distressed. If it was shocking for Seymour to see Charlie in the house, then it was abnormal, too, to find Eleanor there at five o'clock on a weekday. Normally, she'd have been finishing up work at Burndy, several miles away, and dashing for the subway and her night classes at City downtown. This was an especially busy term with English Literature, Essentials of Marketing, and Essentials of Retailing all piled up, seven more credits toward Eleanor's goal of graduating at last and starting the rest of her life, which seemed bound to include Charlie. From the kitchen, which was next to the living room, Seymour smelled the aromas of the lemons that Rose squeezed on her aching hands and some roast chicken or soup, as if she had set out food for Eleanor and Charlie. Rose fed company by reflex.

"Tell my mother we're getting married," Eleanor instructed Charlie, her voice even, almost pedantic.

The words lingered in the air. They lingered amid the dusty tabletops and the ragged slipcovers. They lingered amid the clothes drying on the line strung through Seymour's room. They lingered amid the china cabinet filled with Eleanor's academic medals and the framed photograph of her on the wall. It was a sepia-tinted portrait taken back before the Depression at the Blue Bird Studio on Pitkin Avenue in Brooklyn, and it showed Eleanor a few months past two in knee socks and a cotton jumper with a large creamy bow pinned to her hair. She was chunky and her short hair was straight and she was not smiling. More than twenty years later, it remained the only photograph of her children that Rose Hatkin displayed. Then and now, Eleanor was cursed with being the favorite.

"Tell her," Eleanor said to Charlie, her tone this time more urgent.

The Hatkins lived on Harrison Avenue now instead of Boston Road, West Bronx instead of East, and with two reliable salaries every payday they finally had replaced the icebox with a refrigerator and could afford meat whenever they wanted, but in most ways Eleanor's surroundings barely had changed. Apartment 4D or Apartment 21, they were small places, and small-minded. They were places to leave. Already some of Fannie and Danny's friends had moved across the Hudson to Fort Lee. A new expressway was carving an asphalt trail to the suburbs straight across the Bronx, even nicking off the tip of Crotona Park. Eleanor would be turning twenty-three in a matter of days, and she still slept on the same daybed she had as a child. On her wall just recently she had hung a painting on black velvet of a couple staring love-struck in one another's eyes. Perhaps they were meant to be Romeo and Juliet, though with a faintly Asian cast to their features. One of Eleanor's beaus, most likely Charlie, must have bought it on R&R in Honolulu.

Before Charlie could repeat the words Eleanor had already spoken, Rose began to shriek. Only a few days earlier, she had beamed at the *bris* for her first grandchild, Fannie and Danny's son Joel. Rose's *frum* uncle, Shai Gartenberg, had been the *zandek,* the person who holds the boy while the *mohel* circumcises. And Joel had been given the Hebrew name Yehuda Ariyeh, for Rose's father, one more of those slain by the gentiles. "*Zay zeinen yenneh vus hubben gekoylet mein mishpoche,*" she cried out now. Her Yiddish went far beyond the punchlines and aphorisms Charlie knew, but Eleanor understood perfectly: *They're the ones who murdered my family.* Then Rose switched into English to leave no doubt both Charlie and Eleanor would comprehend. "You can't mean it," she said, face creased with grief, hand kneading hand. She stopped to lift a single emphatic finger. "If you do it, I jump off the roof."

Now her words were the ones that lingered. They lingered near the open window, which caught the April breeze and the southern sun. They lingered four stories above the pavement, above the street sign and fire hydrant at the corner of Harrison and West 180th, above

the sedans and delivery trucks parked on this placid afternoon. Two more flights of stairs and Rose would be
on the roof. It was the same route the Hatkins took
when they wanted to pose for pictures there on the tar
beach.

Charlie bent back his arms at the elbow, bringing
each forearm along his chest, and opened his palms in
the manner of a bank teller surrendering in a stickup.
"No, no, Mrs. Hatkin," he said pleadingly. "Don't do
that." Then he backed out of the living room, through
the foyer, to the front door, blocking Rose's only path
out to the roof. As he retreated, he fixed his eyes on her,
making sure she took no step toward the window. Finally, he withdrew from the apartment.

"You're making my life miserable," Eleanor shouted.
If only her father had been here, the one person who
might have mediated, the one person in the family who
might have taken her side. Sol was a gentle man, too
gentle to watch his daughter destroyed. He would have
bent the ancient rules to restore her smile. But of course
after all those days he'd sat home without work, after
all those days he'd lumbered home luckless by late afternoon from the hiring hall, after all those afternoons,
on this one he had to be busily stitching luggage at
Galewski's factory in Manhattan, a million miles away.

Eleanor turned to run after Charlie. The sound of her
heels clicking on the tiny hexagonal tiles in the hallway
echoed for a moment, grew softer, then vanished. Seymour went into his bedroom to get ready for work, relieved to have an excuse to escape this madhouse. Rose

walked into the kitchen, her sanctuary, victorious but in no way triumphant. There was a song she'd heard in the Yiddish musicals at the McKinley Square Theater, a song called *Ikh Bin a Mame,* I Am a Mother, and she was living its words:

What does a mother ask every day
When getting up and lying down
Oh, God, I ask you . . .
To lead my daughter to the chuppa
With luck and in success
In a white dress to adorn her
To give her my blessing under the wedding canopy
To put the wedding wreath on her bright face . . .

But I am abused by God and by people
I am a mother
But where is my child?
I am a mother
I suffer because of my sin . . .

Oh, mothers, do you hear my hurt?
It is a terrible fate
To be a mother
Without a child.

As afternoon turned to evening and darkness came on, Eleanor and Charlie drove through the Bronx in Mary Greco's car, that old beater with the running board, the one they'd taken to St. Patrick's on their most perfect night. Now it was Eleanor who threatened to kill herself, and again it was Charlie who had to coax someone back from the edge. They drove all that night, crying and talking, saying things to each other they never confided to another soul. In the faint rays of morning, Charlie deposited Eleanor at 2101 Harrison, and she trudged up the stairs to the fourth floor, went past the landing table with the shared telephone, and unlocked the apartment in which only one thin wall separated her room from her mother's.

Exhausted and alone, Eleanor was left with a mystery even she could not solve. After a whole life of proud defiance, eating Chinese on Yom Kippur, mocking Mrs. Oguz, parodying the Arbeiter Ring songs, shoving the Morris medals in Rose's face, she had backed down when it came to marrying the man she loved. Was she more fearful than she cared to admit? Was she more conventional? Did she harbor some doubt about Charlie, watching him wither before Rose's dare? Or was it possible that Eleanor could not bear the toll on her conscience on the chance that Rose Hatkin, with her unfathomable bitterness, really would have leaped?

At the same time that Rose and Eleanor each threatened suicide, a very visible grudge was afflicting two of their relatives in Uruguay. It involved Rose's brother-in-law Alter David Kaczkowicz and his cousin Pinhas. For a year or more now, since a survivor had brought word of Ester Dina and her children being murdered in Treblinka, Alter David had stopped attending meetings of the Ashkenazi *kehilla,* a sort of community council of which Pinhas was a leader. Some people said that, on the occasions Pinhas did run into Alter David, he could not look him in the eye. Nobody, least of all Eleanor and Rose in the Bronx, understood why or what it possibly had to do with them and a stillborn marriage.

Two years younger than his cousin, Pinhas Kaczkow-icz had preceded him in immigrating, reaching Monte-video in 1921 and gradually becoming prominent in the *kehilla.* When Alter David arrived in 1928, he found the transition far more difficult. He was a religious scholar accustomed to reading Talmud while someone else earned the money, and abruptly he was forced into the hustling, huckstering existence of a *cuentenik,* ply-ing the cobblestone streets and stucco tenements of Villa Munoz, selling pots or towels or umbrellas on credit. A successful *cuentenik* had to learn what cus-tomers wanted and what day they got paid so they could pay him; a successful *cuentenik* shamed his debtors into compliance by writing the Yiddish word for nail, *tzvok,* on their door, because in the Uruguayan idiom an unpaid bill stuck out like a nail; a successful *cuentenik* hired a boy to serve as his *klopper,* his knocker, making the door-to-door rounds. And ulti-mately a successful *cuentenik* bought the steerage tick-ets to bring the rest of his family across the Atlantic to Montevideo.

Alter David was no such sort of *cuentenik.* He sold too little and collected too poorly. He scrambled to borrow money, perhaps from Cooperativa Israelita, a communal lending society, or perhaps from his cousin Pinhas and the *kehilla*. Regardless, he never made enough money to rent more than the single room in the Rybko family's apartment; it was Rose who paid the passage for Julius and Judis. When Alter David did have some money, he went to the poker tables or the Marona racetrack. He fancied himself a *drayer*, someone who knew all the angles, but he cut a ridiculous figure among the gamblers, with his beard and black coat and dangling *tzitzis*, the fringes meant to remind an observant Jew of the commandments. There were others like him, of course, immigrants untethered from the theocracy of the *shtetl*, alone in a land of unknown freedom and indecent attractions. They were women of virtue who wound up as prostitutes, sippers of Sabbath wine who fell into alcoholism. So the pesos that might have taken Alter David's wife and younger children out of Bialystok, taken them out in the 1930s when getting out was legal and affordable, were the pesos that Alter David squandered.

Even in Poland as a young boy, Julius Kaczkowicz had assumed the duty of supporting the family. He made money delivering meat for a butcher and making chocolate in a factory, risking firing to sneak home with stolen sweets. In Montevideo, seeing his father's blunders, Julius resumed his familiar role, working as a sausage vendor, a *klopper*, a factory hand. He intended to save the money to pay for Ester Dina and the little ones to immigrate, but all too often he instead needed to clear his father's gambling debts.

Finally, though, he accumulated the necessary pesos, hundreds of them. By this point, in the late 1930s or very early 1940s, the legal channels of immigration out of Europe had almost entirely closed. In Uruguay, meanwhile, the government had enacted several laws that tightened the nation's traditional open-door policy. Still, several hundred Jews were arriving every year. Some Uruguayan diplomats in Europe, most notably a consul in Hamburg named Florencio Rivas, simply contravened those laws out of idealism. More commonly, Jews bribed officials at the Uruguayan consulates in Prague and Vienna for "tourist" visas or bought papers from Paraguayan authorities and jumped ship in Montevideo.

Pinhas Kaczkowicz told Julius that for a certain price he would spirit Ester Dina and the children out of Poland. Julius gave him the money. The relatives, in due course, never arrived. As far as Julius could tell, Pinhas had kept the pesos for himself.

That was why, when the Ashkenzai *kehilla* convened, Alter David did not attend. It was why, when the cousins accidentally met, Pinhas did not look in Alter David's eyes. There in Montevideo were the two people whom Rose Hatkin justifiably might have held responsible for not saving Ester Dina. Except that she did not know. Instead, for their failures, she punished Charlie Greco.

On June 10, 1947, Charlie Greco's sister Marie gave birth to a daughter named Marybeth. Within the next day, Western Union delivered two particular telegrams to the maternity ward of Park Chester General Hospital. One of them, sent at 4:26 on the afternoon of June 11, was expected. CONGRATULATIONS AND A WARM WELCOME TO THE NEW ARRIVAL LOVE CHARLIE. The other, ordered at 9:20 that morning, came from a more surprising source. CONGRATULATIONS MOM HOPE YOU BABY FRANK DOING WELL BEST WISHES ELEANOR HATKIN.

In the weeks since succumbing to Rose Hatkin's threat of suicide, Charlie and Eleanor neither had seen nor spoken to one another, at least as far as any of their friends and relatives could tell. Eleanor probably heard of the birth from Vicky Behar, who would have heard from her cousin Murray Glass, who would have heard from his buddy Charlie. More than polite manners must have convinced her to send the telegram. The birth conjured memories of Marie's wedding and her bridal shower, of Sunday dinners and Christmas Eve, all those times when Eleanor seemed destined to become part of the Greco family forever. Now, for Eleanor, and for Charlie, too, their truncated love affair tingled and pricked in its very absence, the severed limb an amputee continues to feel.

Eleanor sleep-walked through her shifts at Burndy. Bernie Pacter, her boss in Cost Accounting and a kind of surrogate older brother, never had seen her so quiet, so downcast. There was some impenetrable aura around her, a force field that deflected every question, every inquiry, every joke. All that he knew, that something had ended badly between her and Charlie, he knew from a few stray ribbons of overheard conversation. With Ruth Taylor having left Burndy after her marriage, those conversations were between Eleanor and a new man in the department, Morris Laitman. A war veteran studying industrial psychology at City College, Laitman found cost accounting to be deadening work, and admired the commitment Eleanor brought to it. She, in turn, enjoyed hearing about his courses, getting a vicarious class in psychology as they ate lunch together at their desks. So when her ebullience vanished, when her face slumped, when preoccupation glazed her eyes, Morris could not help but notice. The word that came to his mind was *turmoil*.

Not that Eleanor made any effort to mask it. And yet neither did she gather the will to defy Rose while there was still time to resume with Charlie. "You get your mother on the roof and push her," urged Clare Abramowitz, but Eleanor took those words only as moral support. At a party, Vicky Behar's boyfriend Dave Fried spotted Eleanor alone in a corner, a willful wallflower, beyond consolation. He'd been a Seabee in the war, someone charged with building things, a pragmatist; he asked Eleanor why she hadn't just told her mother to take a hike. "In a way, I can't blame her," Eleanor said, her voice a strange mixture of ennui and anger. "She's ignorant from an ignorant background. I have to forgive her, but it's hard to do."

Living under the roof of the woman who had ruined her life, too paralyzed by hate and hurt to move away, furious one moment and despondent the next, Eleanor buckled. A tic that had afflicted her in early childhood, her left eye twitching, returned for the first time in twenty years. She hiccupped. As her mouth filled with saliva or phlegm, she could not get herself to swallow. Between her bleak mood and the physical toll, she sought out a psychiatrist. Hearing of the plan, Rose wailed in disbelief at this *narrishkeit,* this foolishness, of paying $7.50 an hour just to talk. *Amerikanesher dopesht.* When Eleanor did talk to the analyst, he informed her that what she had trouble swallowing was sexual desire for her father. She never went back for another session.

Charlie, meanwhile, flailed in his own ways. Some nights after work, he stalked from room to room through the family apartment, defending himself to an unseen jury. Didn't Mrs. Hatkin understand he was going to treat Eleanor right? Didn't she understand he was going to make a good living? What else was important? As Mary heard him, she contributed her own grievances. Rose Hatkin was carrying on like Judaism was the only religion that counted, like being Jewish mattered more than being happy. What about being Catholic? We have a religion, too, and we could've done the same thing.

Other times, Charlie went to visit Bernie and Anita Dunetz, nominally to see their new baby, Sandy, but mostly to brood. He stood in their living room, eyes cast to the floorboards, somber in a way Bernie had never before seen. This wasn't the serious and focused

Charlie, right after being discharged, but Charlie with some pieces broken—his heart, of course, but also his idealistic illusions. All his life, Charlie said as he stared down, he'd been so accepted by Jewish people; he'd been accepted by the Agudath Naarei Israel at the Harlem Hebrew Institute, by Bernie and Bill Rosenhoch and Murray Glass, by their families around the dinner table. Nothing, nothing had prepared him for Rose Hatkin, someone who would sooner kill herself than tolerate him as a son. Then again, he had to admit, never had he tried dating one of his Jewish pals' sisters.

In the last week of July 1947, Charlie roused himself to take a vacation at an adult resort in Connecticut called Camp Milford. There he captured the gaze of a young woman named Selma Rubenstein, a Bronx girl who had graduated with honors from Walton High and was working at a hardware export company while harboring ambitions to become a Spanish-English secretary. She thought Charlie looked like Tyrone Power. Selma was wearing a Star of David pendant, a present from her mother for the vacation, or maybe more of an amulet to ward off the wrong kind of suitor. Despite it, she was instantly attracted to Charlie, attracted enough to overcome her shyness and inexperience and start to flirt.

"There's something I have to tell you," Charlie said. "I have a girlfriend in the city. When September rolls around, I'll be getting married."

Selma said, "Goodbye, Charlie," and walked away.

The next day, Charlie bumped into Selma again. "There's a reason I'm here," he said, edging closer to the truth. "I'm not getting along with my girlfriend. That's why."

Selma smiled at him and said, "Hi, Charlie."

In the unaccustomed role of fifth wheel, Eleanor left New York for the long weekend occasioned by Rosh Hashanah, which was commencing on the Sunday night of September 14, 1947. Alarmed at their friend's doldrums, Ruth Taylor and Clare Abramowitz had booked rooms at Unity House, a resort in Pennsylvania's Pocono Mountains operated by the International Ladies Garment Workers Union. They both, though, were coming with husbands, Clare having married Hy Dickman seven months earlier, the same Hy Dickman who before the war had held such a crush on Vicky Behar. As for Vicky, she was engaged to Dave Fried, with a wedding date set for November 30. Eleanor, always the one with the choice of suitors, suddenly qualified as the spinster of the crowd.

No longer did Rose Hatkin bother objecting to Eleanor's absence from synagogue on the High Holy Days. In the wake of Charlie Greco, the stakes of religious solidarity went well beyond a headstrong teenager sneaking off to Crotona Park or eating *treif* Chinese. With Ruth and Clare and their husbands, Eleanor found herself among kindred spirits, people who read *PM* and listened to Paul Robeson and were thrilled by the speech Henry Wallace had delivered just the other night at Madison Square Garden, giving Harry Truman an earful about "breeding hate and war hysteria." For Eleanor and her friends, there was no more welcoming setting than Unity House. Stepping off the bus and into the rambling administration building, they passed the porch where the ILGWU's president, David Dubinsky, often could be found in a rocking chair, sometimes wearing his bathrobe. Around the lobby sprawled Diego Rivera's scandalously radical mural, actually the painter's copy of his original, which had been commissioned for Rockefeller Center and then destroyed on the orders of John D. himself. In one panel, a worker, a soldier, and a Negro farmer companionably greeted Lenin. On its thousand acres, Unity House offered Ping-Pong and softball, folk dancing and theater performances, including the rare recital by Marian Anderson, heroine of civil rights since her concert at the Lincoln Memorial in 1939. Unity House had a lake, too, though the running joke was that everybody was too busy playing cards to notice. Dubinsky, he was worst of all, calling for one more hand of gin rummy at double-or-nothing until he came out ahead.

Ruth and Clare had simpler hopes for the weekend: that there would be some nice single guy for Eleanor. If he turned out to be Jewish, that probably wasn't the worst thing in the world. Eleanor and her friends had been feeling more Jewish than usual lately. In the pages of *PM* and the meeting hall of the Allerton Coops, as well as in the more traditional precincts of American Jewry, much discussion and no small degree of rage focused on the plight of a vessel called the *Exodus 1947*. It had been carrying more than 4,000 Jewish refugees bound for Palestine when the British intercepted it and forced it back to Europe. When the Jews refused orders to debark in France, the British sent them, now on three smaller ships, to Germany, of all places. Barely a week ago, English troops had turned water hoses and truncheons against the refugees to drive them onto the Hamburg wharf and into trains headed for internment camps. The spectacle, with its obvious echoes of other trains and other camps, made front-page news in every New York paper. "Moral Crime at Hamburg," read the headline of Max Lerner's column in *PM*. A full-page ad in the *Post*, the other liberal daily, declared it HITLER'S TRIUMPH.

As much as Eleanor and the others wanted an escapist holiday, they could not help but talk about the Exodus episode. It felt almost personal. In her new job as a caseworker for Jewish Family Service, Clare had been shown graphic photos from the death camps, to prepare her for dealing with survivors. Eleanor was reading the new best-seller about anti-Semitism in America, *Gentleman's Agreement* by Laura Z. Hobson, which in its way helped explain why Truman was so slow to admit Jewish refugees to America. She was eight years older and far more educated in evil than the girl who had been so oblivious to the Nazi assault on Poland, on her own relatives, in the days leading up to Rosh Hashanah of 1939. For one of the first times in Eleanor's life, feeling proudly, fervently, assertively Jewish had nothing to do with appeasing an Old World mother.

Meanwhile, the odds of meeting a Jew were pretty favorable at Unity House, given the resort's connection to the needle trades. The smaller contingent of Italians generally stuck together on the bocce courts or sang along to somebody's accordion or mandolin. Eleanor had only two weeks before fall classes started at City downtown and her days would be occupied, morning till nearly midnight, by Burndy and night school. From experience, she knew better than to expect to meet any eligible man at City. The returning vets, it seemed, were all married, and the whiz kids entering from Townsend Harris were younger even than Eleanor's kid brother Seymour. As for the social life, anyone who'd lived through the Depression and the war, for that matter anyone who'd gone to the theater from Broadway to Harlem, had to find it all so puerile, Candlelight Capers and the Easter Egg Hop and the Senior Beer Party.

So the Taylors got the keys for their cabin in the grove of trees that Unity House grandly called a forest, and Clare and Hy Dickman did the same. Eleanor took a single room. They all changed into shorts and T-shirts, because even with fallen leaves spattering the lawns from the first cool mountain days, this weekend was Indian summer incarnate, the mornings all haze and dew, the afternoons almost sultry in the eighties. For some reason none of the others could grasp, Al Taylor had chosen vacation to start on a health regimen, and he led the rest out to the packed dirt of the basketball court. The effort at exercise quickly collapsed into sexy horseplay—Ruth grabbing Al around the waist on the pretense of defending him, Clare riding Hy's shoulders toward the hoop. Their antics left Eleanor sidelined, a spectator. And she felt that separation even more so when Ruth pulled her and Clare aside to whisper some rules about how to tell when she and Al didn't want anyone intruding on them in the cabin.

At dinner, Al tried to hew to his diet, this in a dining hall that served portions family-style and went by the Depression slogan, "Eat, it costs money." Through the kasha and the chicken and the blintzes the banter went on—*No, I'm not gonna eat it. But it's so delicious, Al. Don't start in with me*—until the whole table was cracking up. Al and Ruth were such a married couple already, so comfortable in their spritzing and their kibitzing. The meal over, they all went into the recreation hall for union songs and then some dancing, with Clare teasing Hy by saying yes to some stranger's invitation.

Later in the night, relaxed and danced out, they all settled down at a table, and Al and Hy started trading war stories. Hy talked about how he'd enlisted in 1940 because he wanted to work on airplanes and the civilian jobs were closed to Jews, and that was how he'd wound up in Pearl Harbor on the morning of December 7, 1941. Al had served with the Seabees in the Pacific, putting up bridges and docks behind the island-hopping Marines. It was scary enough, he said, to wait in the landing craft, a bunch of sitting ducks, for the all-clear signal to go ashore. But there was this one time it turned out the Japanese were still alive and shooting when the Seabees landed. Al's crewmates were so pissed they thought about firing at the Marines. Now, two years past V-J Day, the danger was just something to laugh about, just a story to tell.

Maybe it was then that a guest named Leonard Schulman appeared. He stood several inches more than six feet, and though he was slender, almost willowy, his shoulders spread wide and his arms were wrapped with ropy muscles. He combed his brown hair back in slight waves to show a smooth plane of forehead. When he smiled, he exposed a glistening line of teeth, set above a chiseled chin. The son of a construction foreman in the newfangled field of air-conditioning, which easily made him the best-off person in this bunch, he had grown up in an elevator building on Washington Avenue in Brooklyn, just across from Prospect Park with its museum and botanical garden. Eleanor knew the neighborhood from visits to her prosperous cousins, the Osders, who lived close by on Eastern Parkway, a neighborhood for people of means. Leonard had started college at NYU, then transferred to Cornell, no small achievement in the face of Ivy League quotas against Jews, and done a stint in the service. Now he was back at NYU, majoring in philosophy at the Bronx campus, coincidentally nearby the Hatkins' building at 2101 Harrison. He drew cartoons and loved practical jokes. Everybody called him Lenny.

With Hy and Al having finished their war stories, Lenny contributed his own. He had served in the Philippines, been taken prisoner, and survived the Bataan

Death March. Nobody needed any reminding what that was—only the most notorious atrocity against Americans in the Pacific war, the one Franklin Roosevelt himself had revealed to the nation, the one depicted by Hollywood in a John Wayne movie. The march had started on April 9, 1942, and over the next ten days the Japanese herded 80,000 Americans and Filipinos with little food or water sixty-six miles by foot and a hundred more by boxcar from the Bataan peninsula to the McDonnell prison camp. By that October, 28,500 of the captives had died. Now, Lenny described in vivid detail how he'd seen exhausted soldiers collapse on the roadside and Japanese shoot them on the spot. Anybody who had emerged alive from Bataan qualified as some kind of hero, and here was one, in the lounge of Unity House, trying mighty hard to impress Eleanor.

As the long weekend continued, Saturday passing into Sunday into Monday, the summery weather holding, the fifth wheel became half of the third couple. Together with the Taylors and Dickmans, Lenny and Eleanor canoed across the lake and picnicked on the lawn and shot baskets on the dirt court. Lenny regaled everyone with stories of his cabin-mate for the weekend, a buddy from New York who was spending a lot of indoors time with a toothsome nurse. As for himself and Eleanor, they made a fetching couple already, he lean and shirtless, sharp in his sunglasses, and she almost girlish in saddle shoes, bobby socks, and culottes. When she and Lenny sat back-to-back, arms linked, posing for Ruth's camera, Eleanor smiled in a way her girlfriends hadn't seen her smile since the day Rose Hatkin had threatened to jump off the roof.

The holiday ended in the suddenness of a thunderous downpour just after lunch on Monday. Before packing for the trip home, Eleanor pulled aside Clare and Ruth to ask what they thought of Lenny. In her yearning tone, they intuited the answer she desired. "Oh, he's nice," Clare replied, meaning, *If he wants to take you out, go ahead.* In fact, from what they could tell from these few days, Clare and Ruth did think Lenny was witty and charming, as well as Jewish, which might save a lot of headaches later on. As for Hy and Al, they had cause for skepticism. Lenny was a couple of years younger than them, somewhere in his early twenties, and logically it seemed unlikely that he could have been posted in the Philippines by 1941, when the Japanese invaded. Still, when someone was a veteran, when someone had such gruesome memories, you didn't start calling him a liar, especially on a vacation when he's sweet on your wife's friend. So Hy and Al said nothing to Lenny except so long as they all headed back to the city. Once there, Ruth got her film developed and arranged the snapshots in her album, supplying captions for each in white ink. HOLD & SQUEEZE, she jotted under one of herself and Al embracing on the basketball court. AT HOME—#411, she wrote beneath a picture of them on the front steps of their cabin. And below a photo of Eleanor and Lenny—her arm around his waist, his over her shoulder, her head nuzzled against his chest—Ruth added an inscription that hinted at one

more element of an eventful weekend. It said, THE
MORNING AFTER.

From the time he returned from vacation at Camp Milford, every single day from August through December
of 1947, Charlie Greco saw Selma Rubenstein. On occasion they strolled beside the Jerome Park Reservoir,
the closest thing to a lake in the Bronx, and after a
while Charlie would stretch across a park bench, laying
his head on Selma's lap and crying about Eleanor. In
spite of such profoundly mixed signals, Selma persevered, and as Christmas approached she dared to anticipate an engagement ring. On that day, exactly one year
after the Midnight Mass he had shared with Eleanor,
Charlie presented Selma with a set of handkerchiefs.

The fall term of 1947 was as uninspiring as any Eleanor
had known in six years—yes, incredibly, six years already and still no degree—at the downtown campus of
City College. She selected classes guaranteed neither to
tax nor to stimulate her, with one credit apiece in Art
Appreciation and Health Guidance, two more in Business News Publicity. By early November, she dropped a
course in Advanced Advertising Production and was
limping her way to a C in Principles of Finance, the only
remotely demanding class on her schedule. The night division, always the stepchild of the college, was losing en-
rollment as veterans put their GI Bill benefits into
attending the day session. Eleanor's nocturnal classmates
tended to be what City called "non-matriculants," peo-

ple who couldn't meet the normal admissions requirements but were willing to pay by the credit and were
duly milked as cash cows. The professors, meanwhile,
were rarely professors at all, more often untenured instructors or adjuncts, wearily teaching daytime and
nighttime loads for their own financial reasons. Sometimes the biggest question in the classroom was who
would doze off first.

Eleanor clearly had invested her own mind elsewhere,
in nostalgia over Charlie, hatred for Rose, ambiguity
about Lenny. After the weekend at Unity House, she did
not introduce him to Marion or Vicky or Lillian, and it
was their shared sense that Lenny was pursuing a reluctant Eleanor. It turned out, after all, that he was barely
twenty-one, two years younger than she at a time when
women invariably dated their seniors. And age had to do
with more than chronology. One evening, Eleanor and
Lenny visited Ruth and Al Taylor at their apartment in
East Harlem, partly to welcome Ruth's brother Sam
back from Washington and his service as a military car-
tographer. Lenny showed Sam a jewelry box, about the
size for a ring, and asked him to lift the lid. When Sam
did so, he found a severed, bloody fingertip. It was just
one of Lenny's practical jokes; the box had a hole in the
bottom for him to insert his finger and some red dye on
the cotton wadding inside. Sam and the rest managed a
polite laugh to mask their bewilderment.

Most evenings that autumn, like most evenings in her
six years at City downtown, Eleanor reached the college building fifteen or twenty minutes before her first

class and went up to the ninth-floor lounge to hurriedly
down a brown-bag sandwich. One course ran from
6:50 until 8:25, the next from 8:45 to 10:25, and by
that hour it was a long wait at the Twenty-third Street
stop for the uptown subway home. With its worn
chintz couches and its metal armchairs, the lounge gave
even relaxation a utilitarian cast. Maybe it was kind of
an insult to FDR that the room had been renamed in
his memory.

Sometime during the semester, though, Eleanor
chanced upon a new accountrement in the lounge, a
young man standing six-foot-four, with high cheek-
bones, full lips, and wavy dark hair. His name was Ted
Millon and he was only a few months past nineteen,
two years younger than even Lenny, but he hid his
youth well. He had reached his full height by age
twelve, and had begun wearing a bow tie at fifteen, the
year before graduating high school on the Rapid Advance track. Just recently, modeling himself upon a favorite economics professor, he had started smoking a
pipe. He liked Eleanor's look, and he felt not at all intimidated by the presumed difference in age. Through
the war years, he had worked in the Catskills as a
tummler, a combination of entertainer, cheerleader, and
social director, and had taken up with a number of female guests in their twenties. On a home front denuded
by military service of millions of eligible young men, a
bright and strapping teenager was the next best thing.

From almost their first conversation, Eleanor and Ted
had plenty to talk about. For starters, he loathed the

night session. He had entered City as an accounting major, then discovered economics and psychology, and switched almost all his classes to days. That left his afternoons and evenings free for his other collegiate passions—serving on the student government, editing for both the newspaper and the yearbook. Ted read *PM* and admired Henry Wallace. The child of a Labor Zionist household, a counselor and waiter at the movement's Kinderwelt summer camp, he had a lifelong devotion to the Zionist beliefs that Eleanor recently had acquired.

Ted began to make a habit of stopping into the ninth-floor lounge every weeknight toward 6:15, which was easy enough since the newspaper and yearbook offices were only two floors below, and chatting with Eleanor as she ate. They talked about the United Nations' debate over partitioning Palestine to create a Jewish state; they talked about Margaret Mead, one of Ted's current fascinations; they talked about how Ted's father was sponsoring Jewish survivors for immigration, helping to set them up as chicken farmers out in Jersey. They talked at such length that Eleanor often missed the first hour of her 6:50 course, finally excusing herself with the comment, "Oh, shit, that class is so boring." Indeed, Ted may well have been her most engaging teacher, because in the spring term of 1948, she registered for Abnormal Psychology and got an A.

There was one subject Eleanor didn't talk about, however, and one that Ted never raised, the subject of whether she was seeing anybody. All the palpable attraction in that ninth-floor lounge, all the musky scent of sexuality, never evolved into physical contact beyond shoulder brushing shoulder, hand briefly clutching hand. Perhaps Eleanor was more smitten with Lenny Schulman than she admitted to herself. Perhaps she could not bring herself to date a guy four years her junior, no matter how worldly and mature. And perhaps Ted, despite his wartime experience with grown women, shied just a bit from coming on to this one. Then again, neither did Eleanor ever do the usual thing for a woman with a beau and find an innocuous way of mentioning his existence to deter another man's interest. *My boyfriend Lenny . . . Lenny, this guy I've been seeing . . . I saw that movie with Lenny . . . Oh, didn't I ever tell you about Lenny before?*

Toward the end of the spring semester, as City downtown was taking reservations for its annual boat ride to Bear Mountain, Ted asked Eleanor as his date. She did not say no as much as beg off for vague reasons. He did not ask a second time. Then came summer and three months without their chats. The following autumn, when school resumed, Ted met an incoming freshman named Renee Baratz when she walked into the yearbook office to borrow a typewriter, and soon he was dating her. He told himself he was too busy with the newspaper and yearbook and student government to waste time in the ninth-floor lounge.

Meanwhile, Eleanor brought news of Lenny Schulman to at least one additional person, her mother Rose. "He's Jewish," Eleanor nearly shouted, neither pride nor surrender in her words, only the lash. "Are you happy now?"

Sol, Fannie, Rose, Eleanor, and Lenny, Aqueduct Avenue, Bronx, 1951

Four
Leaving
1948–1953

IN THE RENTED PREMISES of the New Tremont
Palace, a catering hall one flight above Nat's Pool
Room and the Triangle Detective Bureau, Eleanor
Hatkin took her last steps as a single woman. Clasping

a bouquet of calla lilies at her waist, trailing a veil and a white satin train, she stepped up the thirty-foot aisle of hardwood floor. She turned her eyes briefly down, then set them forward and pushed her mouth into a twitchy smile. A few seconds later, her lips flattened. Sol Hatkin strode on Eleanor's left flank in his tuxedo and bow tie and fedora, while Rose took the right side, pink tea roses pinned to the shoulder strap of her lavender gown. As yet uncovered, Eleanor's face showed more angles than usual, a certain tautness to the skin, as if for one reason or another she had been dropping weight lately.

At the head of the aisle the rest of the wedding party waited beneath a forest-green *chuppa,* its poles wound with strands of artificial ivy. Eleanor's sister Fannie Schlomkowitz, the matron of honor, stood in the same organdy dress that Eleanor had worn almost four years earlier, when she was the attendant and Fannie the bride. A short tubby man topped by the boxy black miter that identified him as a cantor positioned himself behind a standing microphone. He was Samuel Flaum, who owned the New Tremont Palace, and he was already clutching the ceremony's script. Beside him, in a waistcoat and top hat, attire that lengthened his lean, rangy frame, beamed Eleanor's groom, Leonard Benjamin Schulman.

This being the afternoon of Thanksgiving Day, November 25, 1948, much of the Bronx was ensconced in its apartments, carving turkey. Traffic ran sparsely outside the New Tremont Palace on the shopping strip

of Burnside Avenue and trains clattered only intermit-
tently along the El trestle two blocks away. The uncommon quiet along a usually bustling street lent a
hushed dignity to the proceedings. The stillness owed,
too, to a decided curiosity. Although Eleanor had been
dating Lenny for fifteen months, a more than respectable length for courtship, many of her closest
friends had not met him until their engagement several
weeks earlier. Her own parents and siblings had exchanged only a couple of reciprocal dinner visits with
their future in-laws. Everybody was accustomed to a
degree of secretiveness on Eleanor's part from her love
affair with Charlie. What they could not quite figure
out was why, since Lenny was Jewish and so ap-
provable, she had maintained the stealth and silence
about him.

Meanwhile, Cantor Flaum read his way through the
rites. Lenny's younger brother Alan, the best man,
handed him the wedding ring, which he slipped onto
Eleanor's finger, nestling it next to the engagement ring
that had been his grandmother's. With a flourish, Lenny
stomped the glass, Judaism's reminder of a razed temple
and a broken world. Then he lifted the veil from
Eleanor's face, closed his eyes, turned his head slightly,
and swooped onto her with a long kiss, a kiss that
looked for all the world like genuine passion.

As the wedding party retraced its route down the
aisle—Eleanor with Lenny, Fannie with Alan, and finally both sets of parents—the guests cheered and cried
and called out, "Mazel tov." These were the people of

Eleanor's life, of her twenty-four years and seven months, to the day. There were her girlfriends Marion, Lillian, Vicky, Ruth, Clare, and Hilda; there were her relatives the Schneers and the Osders, the Finks and the Gartenbergs; there was her boss and mentor from Burndy, Bernie Pacter. The ties ran through four generations, from Jack Hatkin, Eleanor's uncle, at whose wedding Rose and Sol had met more than a quarter-century ago, to Fannie and Danny's son Joel, an eighteen-month-old bounding around the reception in knee pants. Eleanor's whole life was here in the New Tremont Palace, except that it wasn't. None of her old boyfriends had been invited, understandably enough, and their absence made them palpably present, the way a teenaged Eleanor only had reminded herself more of how Hy Keltz had broken her heart by cutting him out of her snapshots.

With his religious and civil duties complete, Samuel Flaum switched from cantor to caterer, overseeing the steam tables for a buffet luncheon, featuring turkey instead of chicken in deference to the holiday. Marion Herzog chatted with Vicky Fried and Lillian Betstadt, a reunion after almost a decade of the Union Avenue Gang and the Three Musketeers, Eleanor's pals from each side of Crotona Park. Someone read aloud congratulatory telegrams from those who couldn't attend—Marion's mother Florence, recently remarried and living in Philadelphia; Eleanor's older cousin Leonard Hatkin, her academic inspiration on Boston Road, homebound with his very pregnant wife

Thelma. A combo played cha-chas like they did in "the mountains," as everyone familiarly called the Catskills resorts, and at Eleanor's request the musicians wrestled with the Israeli national anthem, *Hatikvah*, "The Hope." She had danced in the street on the night back in May when statehood was declared, and this very weekend the new nation awaited its own seat in the United Nations. Few places on earth followed the events with more intensity than the Bronx, which was home to more Jews than was the reborn Zion.

At intervals through the reception, the band supplied slow dances for the bride and groom, dances to make a sunny afternoon on Burnside Avenue feel like midnight in the Rainbow Room. *Anniversary Song*, a recent hit for Al Jolson, spoke of a wedding day "when the world was in bloom" and "angels were singing a hymn," when "two hearts gently beating were murmuring low, 'My darling, I love you so.'" Another wedding standard was *Prisoner of Love*, and Eleanor knew the words by heart. She and Clare Abramowitz had heard the Perry Como version in a bowling alley on Fordham Road a couple of years earlier, when they were double dating with Dick Gumcrove and Charlie Greco. Now, head resting on Lenny Schulman's shoulder, Eleanor must have received the words with an ironic inflection.

> Alone from night to night you'll find me,
> Too weak to break the chains that bind me,
> I need no shackles to remind me,
> I'm just a prisoner of love!

Between trips to the buffet line and the dance floor, between visits to each table by the newlyweds, Eleanor's friends took the measure of Lenny, this mystery, and shared the bits of what they knew. Fannie and Seymour, by virtue of family visits, had seen more of him than most, but even they thought of him as having sort of appeared, unanticipated, in the role of fiancé. He was definitely a young man with prospects, finishing a degree at NYU and already enrolled in podiatry school, too. He could give Eleanor the comforts, and the status, that a Hy Keltz had been unable to promise. So Fannie viewed Lenny as "a catch." And the Schulman family made him more attractive still. Lenny's brother Alan was a whiz in college, studying hieroglyphics, of all things. His father, Jack, cut a roughneck's figure with his bony face and muscled neck—even in the tuxedo now he exuded the menace of a bouncer—but his labor had put the family firmly into the middle class. Lenny's mother, Hilda, had a soft grace to her, a Mittel European sophistication, well befitting the daughter of a doctor from Vienna.

Marion had met Hilda Schulman a few weeks earlier at the bridal shower in 2101 Harrison and come away impressed and, even more than that, hopeful about the marriage. In the middle of all the usual frivolity—the girlish giggles, the crinkle of wrapping paper being undone, the appreciative oohs at *hors d'oeuvres* of pineapple and stuffed prunes—Mrs. Schulman had spoken to Marion about everything Eleanor was taking on. Here she was, going to college herself and working full-time to support Lenny while he undertook four years of podiatry school. "I admire her," Mrs. Schulman said of her imminent daughter-in-law. As for Lenny himself, from the little Marion had encountered him, he struck her as articulate, witty, and very ambitious, certainly closer to being Eleanor's intellectual equal than her other boyfriends. So even if some part of Marion suspected that Eleanor had settled, that she had run out of energy for battling Rose, then she had settled well. Lenny offered the safest way to a decent life.

Vicky Fried did not share the optimism. "Why did she do this?" she whispered to Lillian. Even physically, Lenny looked so different from anyone Eleanor had ever loved. Sure, he was handsome, but not in the earthy, weathered way of Hy or Charlie, guys who knew the street, Heathcliffs. When Lillian said, "He's beneath her," she meant not in social class, for Lenny was certainly better off than Eleanor, but in having experienced the world. Their engagement had felt so abrupt to Vicky and Lillian, a surprise, a shock, an ambush. There could be only one explanation for Eleanor's decision: She'd latched onto Lenny on the rebound.

All day long, Fannie Schlomkowitz had found herself comparing this wedding to her own, and growing more and more worried. When the wedding party was posing for pictures before the ceremony, Lenny had leaned down to kiss Eleanor on the forehead and she kept her eyes open and looked off to the side. Then when he moved toward her lips, she twisted her face so the kiss

247

landed on her cheek and sort of swatted him away. There was no love there, no desire, as far as Fannie could see, only tolerance and obligation and duty. A little later, standing beneath the *chuppa,* Fannie read the strain in Eleanor's face as she was walked down the aisle by her parents. Fannie registered the forced smile, the furtive eyes, and recognized them as something besides a bride's nerves. How that public display of dependence must have galled Eleanor, being given away by a mother she loathed. And why hadn't Eleanor, with so many close girlfriends, had bridesmaids? It only could mean that she had wanted to diminish the ceremony somehow. Fannie remembered her wedding day, the way Danny couldn't stop kissing her for a second, the way he carried her in his arms from table to table. She remembered the absolute certainty that she was marrying the one right man for her on earth.

Eleanor had her reasons. Except for Marion, every one of her close friends was already married, and Fannie already had a son, a child on whom Eleanor doted in the absence of her own. Among Lenny's forty-five classmates as podiatry school, ten had married already, a fellow named Irwin Schwartz the previous night, in fact, and five had kids. Four years down the road, Lenny would be a credentialed professional, and Eleanor would be his wife, able to stop working after a solid decade of it, able to start a family and enjoy some of life's treats. A new kind of record was just coming on the market, made of something called "vinylite," that could hold an hour of music on its "microgrooves." People were buying TVs. Just this morning, some character named "Howdy Doody" had been one of the balloons in the Macy's parade. In the *Herald Tribune,* National Airlines advertised flights to Miami, $68.90 on a DC-6. A podiatrist's wife could enjoy such luxuries.

Most of all, though, Eleanor saw Lenny as her way out of her mother's house, a Jew above objection, much less a suicide threat. A few months before the wedding, she had written an article for the Burndy newspaper about one of her friends in Cost Accounting, a transplanted Californian named Patricia Ramsey. Ramsey and a girlfriend had rented a dumpy apartment in Hell's Kitchen, a fourth-floor walkup with no heat and newspaper stuffed into window frames, and transformed it with junk-shop furniture, homemade curtains, and copious elbow grease "into three wonderful rooms that spelled HOME." This was the first article Eleanor had written in seven years, since her days on the *Piper* at Morris High, and its celebration of independence must have reflected her own longings. Unlike Patricia Ramsey, though, she was conventional enough to need to leave home on the arms of a man.

Even so, this leave-taking had included its private jabs. The night before the ceremony, Rose Hatkin had not given Eleanor an embroidered bedsheet for the wedding night, the evidence of virtue, as she had for Fannie. When Seymour asked about the oversight, Rose answered, "She doesn't need it." Eleanor already had devised her response. The satin gown she wore beneath the *chuppa* belonged to the wife of Clare's cousin Frank. She had worn it as a bride. And she, as Rose well knew, was Catholic.

By late afternoon on Thanksgiving Day, with the rancor invisible to most of the guests, the wedding reception wound toward its conclusion. Eleanor had paid for a share of the event, her new in-laws picking up the rest, and to hold down the cost they had to vacate the room in time for an evening marriage. Price had been the reason, too, for a buffet instead of a sit-down meal, and for having used the New Tremont Palace, the sort of place people complimented by saying, "It's very clean." Eleanor and Lenny had only a few nights in a Manhattan hotel for a honeymoon, since both faced college classes the following Monday. Years of frugality lay ahead, with Eleanor now supporting a husband instead of siblings. As Mr. and Mrs. Leonard Schulman departed in a hail of rice, one guest said to another, "That was over fast."

On Christmas Day of 1948, having learned several weeks earlier of Eleanor's wedding, Charlie Greco asked Selma Rubenstein to marry him. She said yes, of course, and to commemorate the moment jotted down the entire menu of the restaurant meal they were sharing when he proposed. Now that they were fiancés, Charlie had another question for Selma. Would she rather have him buy an engagement ring for her or put the equivalent money in the bank toward buying a house? Envisioning their future, Selma went with the house. Charlie did give her a present to mark their engagement, though, a gold bangle bracelet with initials inscribed. When Selma laid her eyes on it, she noticed those initials were E. R., not S. R., E as in Eleanor. Mortified by the jeweler's mistake, and assuring Selma that it really was the jeweler's mistake, Charlie had the engraving fixed.

The Rubenstein household greeted the engagement warily. When Selma first had introduced Charlie to her parents, almost a year earlier, her mother Pauline had instructed, "Tell your father his name is Grecowitz." Selma could only laugh at the absurdity. Instead, when she first brought Charlie around, her father Ralph bluntly asked, "Is he Jewish?" And after Selma said no, he issued the edict, "Don't ever see him again." But she had kept seeing him, going out dancing at Roseland with Charlie's friend Murray Glass along as sidekick and second banana. Seemingly so much less rebellious than Eleanor, so much more the obedient daughter, Selma refused to surrender to parental disapproval. Neither, though, did she insist on forcing confrontation.

Exactly three months after becoming engaged, on March 25, 1949, Selma and Charlie eloped. They went to the Municipal Building in Lower Manhattan and with a city clerk presiding and Murray Glass and Selma's friend Bettie Loeb serving as witnesses, spoke the vows joining them as husband and wife.

After their abbreviated honeymoon, Eleanor and Lenny moved into their marital home. It was a cramped, shadowy studio in a tenement that had been carved into fifteen apartments. Theirs had a railroad kitchen and a window looking onto an airshaft. The Third Avenue El rumbled less than a block away and the surrounding neighborhood of Yorkville easily could stir the discomfort in a couple of Jews; this German district had been the Bund's stronghold before World War II, the site of pro-Nazi rallies and goose-stepping parades. Even with Hitler dead and his ideology condemned, the beer halls and *wurst* shops and restaurants with waiters in *lederhosen* persisted as reminders of the Reich, all the creepier for their insistent *gemutlichkeit.*

Still, Eleanor had crossed the river to Manhattan at last, and in the postwar housing shortage it hadn't been easy. Fortunately, her friend Clare had a cousin working in the records room of a military hospital, and she discovered that a particular officer living at 234 East 88th Street was about to be transferred. A little espionage, a little key money to the super, and the man's apartment went to the Schulmans. Seymour and Danny, Eleanor's brother and brother-in-law, painted the place. The newlyweds unpacked their presents—the linens, the curtains, a toaster, a record player, and a set of Beethoven LPs. With some of the cash they received, the bought a TV. In that tiny kitchen, with its half-stove perched above the sink, Eleanor tried out a recipe for duchess potatoes on Marion Herzog, who was teaching at a vocational school in the neighborhood. She invited Fannie and Danny and Joel for eggplant parmesan, her specialty for reasons nobody else recognized.

Mostly, though, husband and wife threw themselves jointly into a regimen of long hours and self-denial. Eleanor carried eleven credits in the fall term of 1948, practically a full-time load, and earned four As in six classes; with eleven more credits in the spring term of 1949 and As in three of her four courses, she qualified at last for graduation. On June 16, 1949, nearly eight and a half years after having matriculated as an undergraduate at Brooklyn College, she donned gown and mortarboard for commencement exercises. Posing with her diploma afterward, she mustered a sheepish smile, conveying more relief than pride. Her degree in business administration, with its concentration in advertising, fell a great distance from the "achievement to capacity" that her high school principal, Elmer Bogart, had espoused. She had settled for exactly what Brooklyn College's president had castigated in higher education, "sloppy vocationalism." When the City downtown yearbook omitted any photograph of Eleanor, not even listing her name on a page of the "Camera Shy," the oversight struck an oddly appropriate note for an inconspicuous collegiate career.

Graduation let Eleanor concentrate on Burndy, where business was booming. "There's Gold to Mine in '49," went the slogan at its sales conference, and indeed Burndy was opening plants in California and Canada, sending a promotional bus cross-country bearing a curvaceous Miss Burndy. The front-office men sported pocket squares and bow ties with pin-striped double-breasted suits. In the record heat of July 29, Eleanor and the rest of the work force assembled on folding chairs on the Burndy rooftop for a ceremony marking the company's twenty-fifth anniversary, as the buttercream frosting on the sheet cake went drippy in the sun.

Burndy's prosperity brought Eleanor a raise in 1949 to $3,000 a year, almost 50 percent more than she had been earning during the war. So while the GI Bill covered Lenny's tuition at podiatry school, $400 a year, Eleanor paid for the rest, the rent and utilities and groceries, the clothes and shoes and occasional night out. A mother without daughters of her own, an aesthete married to a bruiser, Hilda Schulman showed her gratitude to Eleanor with the periodic shopping excursion. One time, when Eleanor couldn't decide between two dresses, Mrs. Schulman bought both.

Lenny divided his time between the last full year for his philosophy major at NYU and the first at the Long Island University College of Podiatry. Its suburban name notwithstanding, the school occupied a low cinderblock building in Harlem, an unlikely launching pad into the middle class. Lenny's classmates were mostly Jews, Cohen and Feinblatt and Grossman, and many were veterans as well, people who were both ambitious and impatient. For those rejected by medical schools with anti-Semitic quotas and a glut of applications from returning servicemen, or for those who simply lacked the grades, podiatry school offered a less arduous route toward that dream of Jewish immigrant parents: "my son the doctor." These young men could apply to podiatry school after just two years of undergraduate work, and four years later possess a white coat, a satchel of instruments, and a state-approved license. Along the way, they would have taken a respectable array of medical courses—anatomy, physiology, biochemistry, bacteriology—many of them taught by moonlighting physicians and med-school professors. In groups of three or four, students practiced foot surgery on cadavers in the city morgue.

For all that, podiatry college could not be mistaken for the real medical thing. The founding president, a doctor named Maurice Lewi, still held office at age ninety-one, a figure out of Hawthorne or Melville in his high-collar shirts and laced boots. He smoked a dozen cigars a day, downed a Scotch before dinner, and boasted at the school's yearly banquet, "I don't have an enemy in the world. I've outlived all the bastards." The dean, Ruben Gross, believed in hypnosis rather than anesthesia for light surgery. When Gross took the scalpel to one patient in a demonstration, the man leaped to his misshapen feet, screaming. Despite all the serious coursework, the future podiatrists were preparing to contend with nothing more life-threatening than bunions, hammertoes, and ingrown nails. They responded accordingly, ditching required shifts at the school's walk-in clinic, playing cards in a basement room used to store plaster for casts, and once sticking a cadaver foot in a classmate's coat pocket.

Lenny adopted a quiet, studious tone among his classmates, at least initially. Around school, he wore glasses with thick black frames, and they slid incrementally down his nose as he conducted examinations. The other students noticed him mostly for his cartoons, deft and skillful portraits of students or caricatures of instructors. When he did speak in class, he had ample wit to break up even the famously stoic professor Emanuel Frankel. Lenny was enough one of the guys that his classmates threw a bachelor party for both him and Irwin Schwartz a few days before their weddings.

As months passed, though, and the first year gave way to the second, Lenny began to stand out for other reasons. During a semester of neurology, he became convinced he suffered from several of the diseases. He banged out chords on a broken piano in the school basement, and classmates privately mocked his "crack-up music." Lenny drew cartoons of cherubic creatures in sexual poses, and while nobody minded dirty pictures, some of these depicted twisty, contorted positions and facial expressions than looked more painful than pleased. Lenny stayed closest to three particular classmates, Jerry Ferber, Al Glazer, and Stanley Frank. Ferber fit in alright as a regular in crazy eights games, but Frank was a slender, withdrawn guy perpetually getting to class late, trying to sneak into the back as the professor muttered, "You must be Frank." And Glazer, though married, had the habit of secreting himself in a darkened classroom with the clearest view of a nurses' residence across the street.

Eleanor probably knew little or nothing of the Lenny Schulman emerging at podiatry school. She was busy with Burndy and a household while he was going to class six or seven hours a day and giving several nights a week to the podiatry clinic. Their time together came mostly on weekends, and those weekends were, to all outward appearances, delightful. Whatever reticence Fannie had seen in Eleanor on the wedding day had vanished, and so had much of the enmity between Eleanor and Rose. Lenny and Eleanor shared Sabbath dinners and the Passover seder with the Hatkin family at 2101 Harrison. With Fannie, Danny, and Joel, they watched sailboats in the Central Park basin and admired the cherry blossoms in the Brooklyn Botanical Garden. In front of everybody, Eleanor would sit herself in Lenny's lap or cup his chin in her hand for a languorous kiss, no hesitation about it.

There was one particular day, a July day in 1949, when the whole extended family trooped to Brighton Beach. Maybe it was the joy of her grandchild Joel, maybe it was the sight of her rebel daughter safely married to a Jew; for whatever reason, Rose Hatkin carried on in a way nobody had seen in years, certainly not since the Germans first marched into Bialystok. She wore sunglasses, a flowered babushka, and a bathing suit cut low on her copious, if sagging bosom, with one strap dangling lasciviously off the shoulder. And she was acting, there was no other word for it, goofy, romping into the surf with Joel as she smiled a toothy smile, propping a sand bucket on his head as a cap. Back on the blanket, Joel placed his cowboy hat atop Lenny, and Eleanor, hair matted and glistening from the ocean, looked on approvingly. Not many grown men had the patience for fooling around with a little kid, but it was one of Lenny's winning traits. He could spend ten minutes trading silly faces with Joel, each trying to outdo the other with crossed eyes and ballooned cheeks, oblivious to the whole concept of adult propriety. Once Lenny graduated from podiatry school and set up his practice, Eleanor expected, she could quit working and have children of her own.

One morning in late 1949 or early 1950, a woman named Miriam Beyman was walking a solitary mile toward a bus stop on the eastern edge of Queens, the first leg of her daily commute to an office manager's job in Manhattan. She would wait for the Q-17, which would make its fitful way to the IND station at 169th Street in Jamaica, and then ride the subway nearly an hour to the stop at 23rd Street in Manhattan. The routine was not one she relished. So when a car horn honked and a driver hailed her at the bus stop, the Q-17 being its usual tardy self, Miriam paid attention. She recognized the man at the wheel from a neighbor's party for all the young marrieds in the Oakland Gardens apartment complex. His name was Charlie Greco.

Greco had spotted Miriam a few times before, because he drove to the same subway station in Jamaica. It turned out he rode the same train to the same stop in Manhattan, since her office at City Chemical Corporation was just a few blocks from his at Sew-Matic Attachments, as he'd renamed the old Gensheimer shop. Charlie began to offer Miriam rides in the morning and sometimes at night, too, if they happened to have taken the subway together from the city. They traded the innocuous questions of new acquaintances, and when Charlie asked Miriam where she was from, she said the Bronx. "Oh," he said, oddly pensive. "I had a girlfriend once from the Bronx."

Over a few more trips between Oakland Gardens and the 169th Street station, Charlie mentioned a few more things about the girlfriend. That he'd loved her very much. That they'd wanted to get married. But that she was Jewish and he wasn't so they couldn't. Then, one day, he told Miriam he still carried the girlfriend's picture. When they got out of the car, Charlie extracted two photos from his wallet and handed them to Miriam. One showed a slender young woman with long dark waves of hair posing in a bathing suit. The other had the same woman wearing the kind of waist-length fur jacket called a chubby. Miriam also noticed how crinkled the snapshots were, as if Charlie had pulled them out of his wallet to look at them many, many times.

"I think I know her," Miriam said. "What's her name?"

"Eleanor Hatkin," Charlie answered.

"I do know her."

"From where?" Charlie asked.

Miriam dredged up her memories of the Arbeiter Ring, Smargoner Branch Number 285, in that musty room two flights up from the Jennings Street market in the East Bronx. Eleanor had the same face then, just heavier than the one in Charlie's pictures. Miriam still could recall her wearing an apron for some class play. In fact, she and Eleanor had gone to junior high together, too, at P.S. 40. Eleanor Hatkin, right, always holding back from the other kids, like she was a cut above. Now Miriam caught a glimpse of Charlie's nails, chipped and oil-stained with labor, and figured he hadn't gone to college. She wondered if maybe Eleanor had decided she was too good for him, if that was actually what had happened. Miriam didn't offer this analysis to Charlie, of course.

The whole weird coincidence only emboldened Charlie. On their brief drives, he told Miriam about the times he and Eleanor had gone dancing. He told her about how much he'd dreaded picking Eleanor up at home, because of the way Mrs. Hatkin stared at him. Only when Miriam and her husband moved out of Oakland Gardens late in 1950, for a cheaper rental so she could quit working and get pregnant, did Charlie's confessions stop.

At dusk one evening in the autumn on 1950, Eleanor returned to the Herzog apartment in the Homeric. With Florence now remarried and living in Philadelphia, the place belonged to Marion and her new husband, Saul Maidens. A dozen years after their afternoons walking home together from Morris High, Eleanor and Marion were peers once more, both of them young married women. Marion had met Saul about a year earlier when she was handed the unappealing billet of teaching English at Machine and Metal Trades High School. He was the math teacher with a baritone voice and a swimmer's physique, conveniently standing beside Marion one lunch period in the cafeteria line. After four or five months of conversation on the crosstown bus and Friday night square dances, they became engaged. For the Maidenses' wedding on May 28, 1950, Eleanor and Lenny gave them a steam iron.

In the months since then, the couples had not managed to get together. Saul and Marion had spent their summer vacation driving to California and then back east through Canada. Eleanor and Lenny took their own brief holiday at a resort in Connecticut called Banner Lodge, submitting a snapshot of themselves arm in arm on the lakeshore to the Burndy newsletter *Howdy!* Now, belatedly, the two pairs were sitting down to spaghetti and meatballs in the dinette that Saul had painstakingly wallpapered in a Pennsylvania Dutch pattern. They traded stories of summer and work and school, laughing a lot, the whole night relaxed and jovial.

After the meal was finished and Marion had cleared the dishes, Lenny laid down a sheet of paper on the maple table and started to sketch a cartoon. He drew a snake charmer, legs crossed and turban on head, playing a wooden pipe. Marion and Saul, who never before had seen Lenny's artwork, admired the swift skill of his lines. Lenny went on to etch a wicker basket, and the first strokes of the serpent. As he finished, everyone realized that what was rising from the basket was, in fact, an erect penis. Marion and Saul locked eyes and said nothing. Eleanor laughed. Marion couldn't tell whether Eleanor really had found the cartoon so funny or thought Lenny's eccentricity was cute or was trying to apply her own sort of wallpaper to cover over a humiliating moment.

Meanwhile, the demands of the academic year, for Marion and Saul at Metal Trades and for Lenny at podiatry school, provided ample reason not to schedule another dinner. Before the spring term ended, with the Korean War underway, Saul was called up for the Army Reserve and sent to a base in Virginia. In October 1951, he sailed to West Germany to serve on a general's staff, and four months later Marion received permission to join him there. She and Eleanor resorted to letters to keep in contact. During those months, even before them, Eleanor had observed more of the Lenny Schulman who drew the snake-charmer cartoon. One time, during a visit to Fannie's family, Lenny locked four-year-old Joel in a dark room for laughs. On another occasion, he dangled the boy from Rose Hatkin's indoor clothesline. Lenny offered Danny Schlomkowitz some free podiatry care for a troublesome toenail and proceeded to cut it into jagged edges, as if he'd used pinking shears. Whether all this struck Eleanor as disturbing oddity or mere quirkiness she never confided to her sister. On the job at Burndy, though, Bernie Pacter could tell something was bothering Eleanor; he recognized the same kind of morose, distracted quality he'd seen in her after the breakup with Charlie Greco. There wasn't much time for Bernie to speak to her privately; he'd taken a second job at night selling plastic purses and tablecloths, and so he didn't stick around Burndy after office hours. Finally, too distraught to care about being overheard, Eleanor unburdened herself over the desk in Cost Accounting. Whenever Lenny peed, she told Bernie, he had this habit of bracing himself against the bathroom wall, leaving handprints behind. No matter how often she told him to cut it out, or at least to wipe off the prints, he kept doing it. And whenever Lenny went to the bathroom, Eleanor continued, meaning, you know, a bowel movement, he didn't flush the toilet. He just left the stuff for her to find.

Even so, Eleanor soldiered on, or at least kept up marital appearances. On a wintry morning two weeks into March 1952, Fannie brought her family to visit Eleanor and Lenny in Manhattan. They tromped down the slushy streets to Carl Schurz Park, set on a promenade overlooking the East River, and Lenny, Danny, and Joel built a snowman five feet tall, with a belt of dried leaves and a crown of branches. Lenny looked as handsome as ever that day in his sunglasses, bomber jacket, and banded fedora. And Fannie and Danny betrayed nothing of Eleanor's doubts, or their own, about her husband. In April 1952, with Lenny just three months short of graduating from podiatry school, Eleanor wrote to Marion Maidens in West Germany, expressing only optimism: *The end's in sight. We're going to look for a suburban practice for Lenny. At last I can think about having a baby.* Marion wrote back excitedly. She and Saul, too, were planning to start a family soon. Over the next several months, Marion didn't hear from Eleanor. She figured maybe Eleanor had forgotten to send the letter airmail.

Sometime later that spring, Eleanor phoned Clare Dickman to invite her over to the 88th Street apartment. Clare lived in the Bronx, a few blocks from Fannie, in fact, and had given birth a couple of months earlier to her second child. On many Saturdays, the two women parked their kids with their husbands and hopped the subway down to Manhattan to shop with Eleanor. This time, though, Eleanor did not suggest a shopping date, and she did not ask Clare to bring Fannie. She wanted to see Clare alone.

So on the next weekend Clare rode the Third Avenue El, and she walked down the hill on East 88th Street, and she rang the bell of that dark, cramped studio that her cousin had helped Eleanor find. She had a suspicion already about the reason for the visit. When the Schulmans and Dickmans had dined together occasionally over the past several years, Clare had observed Lenny's skewed sense of humor. Eventually, Eleanor had confided some of her anguish to Clare, perhaps because Clare had been similarly candid in discussing the bumpy times in her own marriage.

"Where's Lenny?" Clare asked now as she stepped into the apartment.

"He goes away with his friends on the weekends," Eleanor said. "That's what he wants."

Clare heard the timbre as much as she heard the

words. Eleanor's voice was flat, uninflected, devoid of emotion. Clare had heard that same voice once before, laying on their towels side by side at the Castle Hill pool in the late spring of 1947, as Eleanor described her mother threatening to jump off the roof if she married Charlie. The monotone now told Clare that Lenny hadn't been going away to pick up some money waiting tables in the mountains, the way several of his podiatry classmates did. He already had Eleanor supporting him. He had rich parents—well, parents who seemed rich if you were from the East Bronx. With a kind of fierce composure, Eleanor resumed. When Lenny returned from these weekends away, she found lipstick smears on his shirts, almost as if he had meant for her to see. She'd pleaded with him to try marriage counseling, and he'd refused. Clare didn't dare recommend divorce to Eleanor. As much of a freethinker as Clare was in her politics, she held to more conventional views about marriage, and her head was filled with stories from *Good Housekeeping* and *McCall's* about miraculous reconciliations. Maybe things could work out for Eleanor and Lenny, too. No, Eleanor said, she was getting out of the marriage. Clare waited for some rage from her, some cry, some damnation. All she got was that same veneer of resignation, cracked only by the succession of cigarettes Eleanor was smoking, the next one lit from the butt of the last.

Far from seeming ashamed of his infidelities, or even cautious about hiding them, Lenny had earned a reputation around podiatry school for boasting about his conquests. "Girls," he told one classmate, "are crazy about me." Eleanor had no way of knowing, of course, what Lenny was bragging about to the fellas in the sanctum sanctorum of the locker room. She did know, though, of his capacity for deceit, and she had known of it for the length of their marriage. On their wedding license, Lenny had listed his birthdate: May 26, 1926. Which meant that his story of surviving the Bataan death march, the story he told her with such conviction when they first met, could not possibly have been true. Oh, Lenny had served in the military, even done a tour of duty in the Philippines, in the final months of the war. But in April of 1942, as the Japanese were driving American prisoners up the Bataan peninsula, Lenny was fifteen years old and finishing his junior year of high school in Brooklyn. That memory of his about the GI being bayoneted by a Jap might have been lifted from a John Wayne movie.

For all the dispassion Eleanor exuded in speaking to Clare, her sense of betrayal must have been absolute. It was not just that Lenny had broken his vows but that he had broken her spell, the hold that her beauty had exerted over every other man in her life. She had passed up Hy Keltz and given up Charlie Greco. She had tossed aside Howard Gropper and Jack Steinglass and Ted Millon. She had chosen over all of them the one man who humiliated her, who in fact seemed to have a special genius for driving her mad. And if she had chosen Lenny to prove something to Rose, to punish her—*You want me to marry a Jew? Well, here's a*

Jew—then whom had she really punished in the end?

Sometime during midsummer of 1952, Eleanor submitted to the ultimate indignity of moving back home. At twenty-eight, she returned to the daybed of her childhood. She brought the Beethoven records from the Manhattan apartment, as well as the TV set, which thrilled Seymour, because it was one of the first on the block. She paid for a phone to be installed in the Hatkin apartment, the first private line the family ever had. She tugged the wedding and engagement rings off her finger. Lenny's mother, once Eleanor's ally, sent word she wanted the engagement ring back; it had been her own mother's, an heirloom. Eleanor hung onto it as the price of *hartzvaitig,* heartache. Seymour was twenty-two, studying hotel management at a business school in Brooklyn and dating avidly. Maybe he'd put the ring to more successful use.

Eleanor reverted to reflex and instinct, spending as little time at home as possible. By this time in 1952, Burndy had moved its headquarters from the Bronx up to the suburb of Norwalk, Connecticut, and the lengthy commute at least managed to take Eleanor away from 2101 Harrison for an extra four hours each day. There was still the matter of obtaining a divorce, two divorces actually, one each under civil and Jewish law. Sol Hatkin paid a visit to his old contacts in the Jackson Democratic Club, and looked up the one attorney the family knew personally, a man named Joseph Ranzenhofer. Rose worried about the *get,* the religious divorce decree. Without it, no rabbi would be able to marry

Eleanor; her daughter would be an *agunah*, a chained woman, and what would the observant relatives think about that? "It's a shame on me," Rose said, as always concerned with saving face. As for Eleanor herself, before even seeing a lawyer, she set about reviving her social life. She had wasted four precious years on Lenny, and summer wasn't going to last forever.

In the dappled light of a Saturday afternoon in July 1952, Dave Freedman stood on the lawn of an adult camp called Chester's, the sort of place that with its chamber music concerts and art shows stood apart from Borscht Belt neighbors like Grossinger's. At the moment, he happened to be vaguely watching a round of horseshoes in the nearby pit, when one of the metal crescents rolled on its side toward him, wobbled a bit, and flopped down beside his bare feet. Dave looked up to see the source of the errant horseshoe and traced its path to a slender, dark-haired woman wearing rolled-up jeans and a patterned blouse. "What're you trying to do, kill me?" he called, and she pulled the cigarette from her lips to laugh at his crack. The guy had a dense pile of black hair, a compact build, and forearms thick and sinewy as lamb shanks. His left eyebrow arched, as if he were taking somebody's measure, maybe hers.

When the horseshoe game ended, Eleanor walked over to introduce herself. She and Dave spent much of the afternoon together, playing volleyball and basketball, admiring each other's skill and competitive spirit. Over dinner that night in the communal dining room, they bantered through the basics. She worked for an engineering company called Burndy, loved the job but hated the daily trip to and from Connecticut. She was living in the Bronx with her folks, having been married and divorced. He was a machinist, running a shop in the small city of New Brunswick, New Jersey, with his brother Ziggy. It was a modest place for now, a storefront with the smell of sheet metal in the air, and they had opened it up with a GI Bill loan and fifteen hundred bucks Ziggy had won playing poker on the troop ship home from the war. Just lately, though, Dave had begun designing machinery for the microbiologists over at Rutgers University. He noticed that, unlike some of the women he'd dated, Eleanor didn't react as if a machinist was some kind of grease monkey, someone beneath her. Dave, too, lived at home, with his widowed mother, about forty miles from New York in a rural patch of Central Jersey. "Just a country bumpkin from the sticks," was the way he always put it. In fact, as he went on, these particular sticks turned out to contain an anarchist colony called Stelton. Dave's parents had moved there as followers of Emma Goldman; his older sister Clara had once hitchhiked to Canada to visit the great woman in exile. Dave could sense Eleanor losing interest as he talked about all the different sects in Stelton—what did she know or care about the difference between the Schachtmanites and the Lovestoneites?—but she seemed to appreciate the idea that he was a progressive. He told her all about having gone to the Paul Robeson concerts in Peekskill back in '49, seeing the

American Legion goons beating people bloody. With dinner done, and the weekend over the next day, he and Eleanor exchanged phone numbers.

Each of them, naturally, had chosen what not to say on that first weekend. Eleanor was far from being divorced; she hadn't even found a lawyer. Dave had a sort-of-girlfriend in Manhattan, a social worker named Myra who played piano well and had a knack for reading lips. He enjoyed few things more than riding the subway with Myra and having her visually eavesdrop on all the conversations. Still, he could feel the disapproval of him, this mere machinist, from Myra's mother, a doctor's wife. And compared to Eleanor, so assertive, Myra seemed timid. Then again, it was a pain to get to the Bronx just for a date. He was working six days a week in his shop, trying to build a business; that was his top priority. While he mulled whether or not to phone Eleanor, she called and invited him out.

They met for dinner in a midtown restaurant and she ordered a Manhattan. So he did the same, the first cocktail of his life. When Eleanor ordered a second, he decided not to try to keep up. As they chatted, David could tell she was well-read, intellectual, and possessed of an incredible memory. From her work at Burndy, she had an understanding of business that exceeded his own. She told him she was sure he was going to be a big success, which was more than he believed. His parents had decided early on he was the ordinary child of the household, and sent him straight to work out of high school, while his siblings all went to college. It was rare and heady for Dave to bask in someone's praise. At the same time, though, he couldn't help thinking Eleanor was stuck on herself; she'd made a point of telling him she was the smartest girl in the office at Burndy and had been a star student at City College. Myra's modesty looked pretty appealing in comparison.

So Dave wasn't quite sure what he wanted out of this divorcée, but she made for engaging company, and there was no reason to cut things off. For their next date, he even agreed to pick her up in the Bronx. The moment he entered the Hatkin apartment, he noticed the clutter, the piles of laundry, the shelves and table-tops of *tchochkes*. Rose Hatkin brought out an arm-load of Eleanor's academic medals to show him. Sol shook his hand almost in gratitude. After Rose with-drew into the kitchen to prepare a snack, Dave spotted her peering through the portal, checking him out. Later, over plates of food, Rose and Sol asked him lots of questions. Where are your parents from? Where do you live? How did you get there? Dave recognized early on in the interrogation that all this code hid the real in-quiry: Are you Jewish? He could see Sol and Rose breath in relief when he dropped a Yiddish phrase. Lit-tle did they know that David's parents, the sort of an-tireligious Jews who danced at balls on Yom Kippur, had not even had him circumcised.

Early in the autumn, Eleanor undertook the recipro-cal visit to Dave's mother, who also was named Rose. In her own young womanhood, Rose Freedman had flouted society's rules, never marrying her common-law husband Samuel. As a widow with sons, however, she enthusiastically embraced the role of *baleboosteh*, the traditional matriarch, with all of her veto power over prospective spouses. After the selfless way that Dave and Ziggy had supported Rose since Samuel died in 1941, she thought they were the finest boys in the world, which was another way of saying no girl was worthy. When Eleanor's visit ended, Rose told Dave, "She's been married before, she's no good." Without hearing that exact calumny, Eleanor sensed Rose's resistance. She later told her friend Lillian Betstadt about it, and far from being deterred by the maternal opposition, she accepted it as a challenge. Of course, first Eleanor would have to actually get the divorce she'd led Dave to believe already had been granted.

Back in July of 1950, two years before Eleanor had met Dave over a stray horseshoe, a television director named Herbert Gehr was enjoying the nocturnal companionship of his mistress in a rustic cottage when some people began rattling the screen door. Thinking they were prowlers, Gehr grabbed his .22-caliber rifle and fired. The volley killed one of the unexpected visitors, his wife Andrea, and wounded two of the four men with her. They turned out to have been private detectives, retained by Mrs. Gehr to obtain evidence of her husband's adultery. Six months later, a jury acquitted Herbert Gehr of second-degree murder. Not satisfied with merely declaring his innocence, the jurors also sent a formal message to Governor Thomas Dewey, blaming the shooting on New York State's divorce laws. JURY FREES GEHR, read the thick block headline in the *Daily News,* HITS DIVORCE LAW AS KILLER.

Now, in the early fall of 1953, the whole scandal was making Eleanor's life miserable. Getting a divorce in New York had been difficult enough before the Gehr case. In deference to the power of the Catholic Church, and the heavily Irish Catholic character of the Tammany Hall machine, the state permitted divorce only on one ground: adultery. And to prove adultery, which was not merely grounds for divorce but a crime under the law, an aggrieved spouse often had to hire the kind of private eye Andrea Gehr had, and then sit through a trial in which her humiliation was flourished before what felt like the whole world. That prospect alone scared off enough prospective plaintiffs. In the wake of the Gehr episode, though, judges and lawyers had grown leery of handling any suit based on snoops, spies, and snapshots of the unclad. For its own sake, the Democratic machine wanted quiet on the divorce front. Which meant that Eleanor was stuck.

Sol Hatkin took on the job of getting her unstuck. He started with Ranzenhofer the lawyer, a beefy and balding man in his mid-fifties, who may have been a distant relative. Sol also had kept his ties to the Jackson Democratic Club over all the years since the family had moved off Boston Road. The club had more clout than ever, because one of its longtime members, Isidore Dollinger, represented the East Bronx in Congress. Somehow, from all of Sol's backstage efforts, from all the chits he had earned in years as a loyal spear carrier for the club, a plan emerged. There was a lawyer named Maxwell Cohen with an office near the Public Library on Fifth Avenue; coincidentally or not, he had worked for many years in the same loose collection of general practitioners around City Hall as had Joseph Ranzenhofer and had lived near Ranzenhofer in a prosperous section of the North Bronx. Cohen would represent Eleanor. And there was a judge in State Supreme Court in Brooklyn named Philip Kleinfeld, who like virtually all judges in New York City had risen obediently through Tammany's ranks to his bench; he would hear the case. As for how to get around the chill on divorces, that problem remained to be solved.

A dapper dandy with a pencil mustache and penchant for hand-tailored suits, Maxwell Cohen loathed matrimonial law. He had grown up in East Harlem an ardent socialist and preferred to put jurisprudence in the service of the creative arts and social justice, often representing jazz and folk musicians of the Left. On the wall of his office hung several works by a Negro painter named Romare Bearden, whom Cohen had befriended in Harlem. By the time Eleanor walked into the room in October 1952, though, Cohen was several years into a midlife marriage and enduring the McCarthyite backlash against real or imagined Communists. He needed to take any case that paid.

The more Cohen heard of Eleanor's situation, the more he perceived a ready solution. Both she and Lenny wanted out of their marriage. There were no children at

stake and few assets to distribute. This case didn't need
to be a divorce at all. It had all the makings of an annulment. An annulment was a divorce that everybody
could pretend wasn't a divorce because it literally declared that a marriage never had existed. Annulment
satisfied the Catholic Church because it gave devout
followers a way to escape marriages without commit-
ting the sin of divorce. Annulment satisfied Tammany
Hall because it let the machine deliver an important service to its loyal constituents. Annulment satisfied
lawyers and judges because it was so simple. All you
had to do, almost literally, was follow a script. Of the
various legal grounds for annulling a marriage—that
one party was under the age of consent, or was men-
tally ill at the time, or was forced into wedlock—the
vaguest and most useful was fraud. This, surely, was the
ground that Cohen recommended to Eleanor. The fraud
was that she wanted a baby and Lenny wouldn't give
her one. Whether this was true didn't matter. As long as
Lenny didn't object and Eleanor stuck to the script, the
Democratic machine would take care of the rest.

So Eleanor and her lawyer set the plan into motion.
Eleanor switched her legal address to 263 Eastern Parkway in Brooklyn, where her affluent cousins the Osders
lived, so that the case could be heard in Judge Kleinfeld's jurisdiction. A friend of Cohen's law partner took
on the minimal role of representing Lenny. One of
Lenny's buddies from podiatry school, Stanley Frank,
consented to playing go-between for legal papers. On
October 16, Cohen drew up a summons for Lenny in

the case, and four days later, Frank handed it to him on the ironically named Amity Street. Six weeks after that, in mid-December, Cohen's partner Irwin Nussbaum asked the Brooklyn court for a default judgment, the quickest route to dissolving the marriage.

As the legal wheels churned, Eleanor could not keep selective secrets any longer. Marion Maidens returned from West Germany in October 1952, and called Eleanor the next day, seeking some explanation for six months without a single letter. Eleanor belatedly confessed to Marion about Lenny's weekend absences and lipstick stains. She explained the plan to seek an annulment. She spoke of how her lawyer had advised her not to kick Lenny out of the apartment, not to so much as put a pair of shoes outside the front door, lest she appear the aggressor instead of the victim. Marion had news, too, of a different sort. She was five months pregnant. Now every one of Eleanor's friends—every single one—was married and a mother or soon to be one. The valedictorian languished at the bottom of the class.

One evening in late autumn, Eleanor took Dave to have dinner with Ruth and Al Taylor, the latest stage in courtship. During the night, Dave overheard some references to Eleanor's court case, a case he'd been assured was all finished before that weekend at Chester's. When he later asked Eleanor just what exactly was going on, she admitted the truth. Dave wasn't bothered particularly by the fact Eleanor was still officially married, since that plainly was coming to an end soon enough, but the realization that she'd lied to him, that he couldn't reflexively trust her, that made him recoil. The more he pulled back into a defensive perimeter, the more she called him. The more she called him, the more cautious he grew. "Do you have another girlfriend?" she asked, and Dave heard in her voice something like desperation.

A new year arrived, and five days into it, Maxwell Cohen and Irwin Nussbaum blundered and missed a calendar call before Judge Kleinfeld, just plain failed to show up in court. Kleinfeld had been ready to send the case that very day to a justice named Algernon Nova, a minion who went through the charade of hearing testimony in assembly-line annulments. Instead *Schulman v. Schulman* got dropped from the court's term altogether, one more impediment to Eleanor's liberation, one more step toward turning twenty-nine as a woman alone.

The lawyers scrambled and beseeched and wangled their way back onto the court schedule for January 23. They already had drafted and filed a complaint that struck all the requisite chords for an annulment on grounds of fraud: *"Plaintiff entered into said marriage with the normal expectation that the parties would cohabit to the end that they would have children . . . defendant refused to cohabit without the use of measures and devices to prevent conception . . . upon discovery of the falsity of the defendant's statements and representations, the plaintiff left."* To augment the paperwork, Cohen planned to introduce supporting testimony. Most, of course, would come from Eleanor herself, but there also had to be corroboration. For this, Eleanor turned to her sister Fannie.

Privately, Fannie harbored little sympathy. Not only did she discount the cover story about Lenny not wanting children, she doubted whether he even had been unfaithful. Fannie figured this annulment case was the latest example of Eleanor inventing facts to suit her desires. Eleanor had proven her point—that she could marry a Jew and make herself miserable and shove it all in Rose's face, like her academic medals on Graduation Day at Morris. Now Eleanor had someone else she wanted to marry and needed a way to do it. Fannie was busy enough with her own life, trying to get pregnant with a second child, keeping books for a window cleaning company. She and Danny had recently gone to court themselves to change their surname from Schlomkowitz, convinced he was losing job offers due to anti-Semitism. From the phone book, they picked the neutral replacement Stevens. Still, Fannie placed family loyalty above all other values, and she wanted her sister to be happy, at last. If Eleanor wanted her to testify, then she would testify.

The sisters practiced one January day in Cohen's office, Eleanor and the attorney filling the room with cigarette smoke. Then, on the twenty-third of the month, they performed before Justice Algernon Nova. Cohen read his questions off a preprinted card, the sort all the matrimonial attorneys had, and Nova made the pretense of listening. In a typical day, he might hear twenty or thirty annulments, each following a virtually identical pattern. Neither Lenny nor his counsel bothered to attend. Eleanor took the witness stand in a modest plaid suit with a white blouse buttoned to the neck, the picture of propriety. For the first time since her toddler years, she wore her hair short, barely reaching her neck, as if in cutting off those dark rippling locks she was announcing some larger transformation.

COHEN: Prior to your marriage did you have any conversation with the defendant with regard to marriage, children, and family life?

SCHULMAN: Yes, I did have such conversations.

COHEN: Who was present at some of these conversations?

SCHULMAN: These conversations took place in my sister's home. My sister was present at them . . .

COHEN:What did the defendant say to you in the course of some of these conversations in your sister's presence?

SCHULMAN: We discussed the meaning of marriage, what marriage between two people entailed, and he promised me that if I would marry him, he would provide me with a home and children and provide me with a normal family life such as any woman would wish of marriage.

By design, Eleanor was speaking in a stiff, formal way, a sign that Cohen had coached her well in sticking to the script. The conversations Eleanor described were revisionist history if not outright lies, and everyone in the courtroom knew or suspected as much, and none of them cared. Falsehood provided the most efficient route to a truth, that Eleanor and Lenny wanted to pursue separate lives with separate loves. Toward that end, Cohen led Eleanor to describe another dubious conversation, this one supposedly between her and Lenny shortly after his graduation from podiatry school the previous June. Eleanor averted her eyes as she testified, and ever since childhood Fannie had recognized that as the sign her sister was skirting the truth.

> COHEN: At that time did you request him to provide you with a child?
> SCHULMAN: Yes, sir. At that time I told him that I had believed him all this time, and that now that he had graduated, and there was no reason to delay having children, it was time for us to have the child that he promised me.
> COHEN: What was his response?
> SCHULMAN: At that time he told me he did not intend to have children and never intended to have children. He said he wanted the life of a professional man, he wanted to be free, and he did not want to be tied down with children.
> COHEN: Was this the first time that you learned of the defendant's true views and intentions?
> SCHULMAN: Yes, it was the first time.

Having established fraud, or established it well enough to suffice in a case lubricated by political influence,

Cohen soon concluded his questioning of Eleanor. Presently, Fannie Stevens took the witness stand, and, under the lawyer's prompting, reiterated several conversations that in all probability never had occurred.

COHEN: Did you hear what the defendant told the plaintiff?

STEVENS: Well, yes. They were discussing marriage, and I heard him say that if she agreed to marry him he would provide her with a home, children, and a normal family.

COHEN: After the marriage and after the separation did you have occasion to speak to the defendant?

STEVENS: I did . . .

COHEN: What did he tell you about that?

STEVENS: Well, he said he never intended to have children but had merely promised this to my sister to make her marry him.

Ten days later, on February 2, Justice Nova issued a provisional ruling in Eleanor's favor. It annulled the marriage "because of the fraud of the defendant, as prayed for in the complaint." There was, however, one catch. The "interlocutory judgment" would not take effect for another ninety days. Eleanor was not yet free of Lenny. And in spite of the preordained result, in spite of Lenny's disinterest in contesting the case, she emerged from it far from unscathed. As a matter of law, her marriage to Leonard Benjamin Schulman soon enough would be expunged. It never would have existed. As a matter of fact, she had lost four years being his wife, paying his way through school, sitting through his jokes and cartoons, wiping off his handprints, flushing his toilet, and, despite all that, pining to start a family together. The law couldn't restore those years and it couldn't restore her dignity. That phrase in Nova's ruling—"prayed for"—was mighty right. Eleanor prayed, impossibly, for the calendar to roll backwards, for a second chance.

Selma Greco was driving past the 7-11 store on Jericho Turnpike on Long Island when she noticed her husband Charlie standing in the phone booth outside, absorbed in conversation. That struck her as pretty peculiar. Why would he be using a pay phone two blocks from their house? When he got home for dinner a few minutes later, Selma asked him. He was too surprised by the question to finesse the answer.

"Eleanor called me," he said.

"Why?"

"She said if she gets divorced and I get divorced, she'll marry me now."

It turned out, as Charlie went on, that Eleanor had been phoning him at work. That was how they'd arranged the call from the 7-11. As Selma heard it, she felt buffeted, knocked all unsteady. Was Eleanor going to barge into her life? Was Eleanor going to ruin it? Selma and Charlie had two children of their own by now. They were living in a house that had its financial origins in the engagement ring that Selma had agreed to do without so the money could be set aside for a down payment.

"What did you tell her?" Selma asked.

"I told her I have two children and I'm not going to leave my wife," Charlie said. "It's too late now."

The rabbi's car rolled slowly down the lumpy asphalt of Poplar Lane as he searched for the right house, fifth one on the left past the corner, he'd been told. The anarchist colony of Stelton was unfamiliar territory for a clergyman from the affluent suburb of Livingston, thirty miles away in the hills west of Newark, and an unlikely place indeed for a religious ceremony. Here the landmarks included a library named for Peter Kropotkin and a street called Freedom Avenue. For the last two days, people in Stelton had been talking about little beside the execution of Julius and Ethel Rosenberg, atomic spies only if you believed the reactionaries. Still, the rabbi had a *chuppa* and poles, and he had a *ketuba*, the Jewish wedding contract, consecrating the marriage of Eleanor Hatkin to David Freedman.

It was almost three on the Sunday afternoon of June 21, 1953, two hours past the summer solstice, and hot as a blowtorch, ninety-four degrees. Dave waited in the living room of his mother's home, dressed much as he had been when Eleanor met him at Chester's—shorts, T-shirt, bare feet. Eleanor wore a loose lavender skirt and a light blouse, casual attire for a second trip to the altar. They had invited mostly family members, and not even all of them could attend; Seymour was working at the front desk of the Waldorf and Rose had warned him not to miss a day or he might get fired. With even the modest number of guests filling the living room, Dave threw open the windows to capture whatever breeze stirred.

At last the rabbi spotted the house, parked, and walked past the beds of irises and zinnias up the front steps. He had Danny Stevens and Ziggy Freedman sign both the civil license and the *ketuba* as witnesses. He arranged the *chuppa*. He took off his own suit coat in surrender to the heat. Then he read the vows in Hebrew and English, and waxed philosophical about how Dave and Eleanor might be a little different from other couples but nonetheless had religion in their souls. As most of the guests knew, it was more like the pair had atheism in their souls; suspicion of organized religion was one of the values they shared. The icons of Rose Freedman's living room, that temple of art and reason, were a Steinway upright and a painting of Homer. Dave and Eleanor had decided to permit the religious ceremony solely as a concession to her parents. Dave even had gone to the trouble of bribing a different rabbi to issue Eleanor a *get,* a Jewish divorce decree.

For all the enervated informality on this torrid afternoon, Dave felt apprehension, both about marriage in general and this marriage in particular. "Scared shitless," was the way he privately put it. All through the spring, and especially after the annulment was granted in early May, Eleanor had pushed him and pushed him and pushed him. He found out she was already telling friends they were engaged before he'd so much as proposed, and once again he doubted whether he could trust her. But when he resisted her pressure, she pleaded, "Things will be better when we get married. You'll see." At thirty-two, he wanted children, that was true. The demands of building his machine shop into a scientific instrument company left little time for a bachelor's rambling. He admired Eleanor's intellect, her confidence, her zip. So, ultimately, he consented.

As Dave looked at Eleanor now beneath the *chuppa,* she appeared so certain, so gung-ho. Maybe what he saw, though, was closer to a profound, encompassing relief. Dave was her ticket out, out of the marriage to Lenny, out of the breadwinner's burden, out of the suffocating Bronx, out of her mother's reproach. After all her promise and all her yearning, she had settled for escape. She had settled for settling.

The relatives sweated in the crowded living room, and the curtains rippled with the gusts of an oncoming storm. Dave slipped a gold wedding band onto Eleanor's ring finger. Then he tugged on a pair of shoes so he wouldn't cut himself when he smashed the glass.

The weekend after the wedding, Dave and Eleanor entertained their friends—Marion, Lillian, Vicky, Ruth, and Clare among them—at a luncheon reception in a Manhattan hotel. Later in the summer, they drove across country, national park to national park, for their honeymoon. Two years, three months, and twelve days into their marriage, they had their first child. In memory of Dave's father, they named him Samuel.

Eleanor, Sam, and David, Bar Mitzvah Day, October 1968

Five

Dying

1974

THE MORNING AFTER my freshman year of college ended, I embarked on a fitful route home. I intended to delay my arrival as long as plausible, because I knew to what I was returning. First I spent a couple of days in

Chicago, hitting bars and record stores with an editor from the college paper. Then I took the Greyhound down to South Bend to meet my hometown friend Tim, who was finishing his own final exams at Notre Dame and ready for some joint celebration. From there, we drove east over two leisurely days with Tim's father, the only Republican I knew, debating about Nixon and Watergate the whole way. It was just about twilight on a prematurely sultry evening, May 16, when I dragged my duffel bag up from the curb and through the front door, rousing my mother from her copy of the *Times* at the kitchen table.

When she rose and turned to greet me, I could tell right away her condition was even worse than I'd anticipated. A sheen of sweat coated her face, and her face was bloated. My father had warned me to expect that effect from the cortisone, but it was another thing entirely to see it up close. Every pore on her cheeks gaped wide, as the existing flesh struggled to stretch to these new unnatural contours. She had deteriorated so much in the three weeks since her fiftieth birthday party with its illusory joy. Or maybe she had lost the strength to keep up the front. My mother could see me inspecting her. She told me she hated looking fat when she wasn't; she hadn't been fat since she was fourteen. And she hated how her skin went dry and scaly in some patches and pimply in others. "I'm fifty years old," she said beseechingly. "I shouldn't have acne." She caught herself starting to tear up. "I must be the only one," she muttered.

Casting her glance down the hallway toward the garage, she started talking about the car. A few months earlier, my father had bought her an Opel, thinking a subcompact would be easier than the old Plymouth wagon for her to maneuver, less strain on her cracked rib and the scar tissue from her lumpectomy. He paid extra for an automatic transmission so she wouldn't have to wrestle with a stick shift, and for air-conditioning because her hot flashes were unbearable in the muggy Jersey heat. Well, the Opel was all mine for the summer, if I wanted it, she said brusquely. It had been nothing but torture to her. With all those options overburdening a four-cylinder engine, the car bucked and fought. She barely could turn the steering wheel without wincing. And if she forgot to turn off the radio when she parked, then the battery went dead overnight. "I hate that thing," she said.

From the kitchen, she climbed gingerly up the stairs to my bedroom, to show me her welcome-home surprise. All year long, I had been mailing home my articles from the college newspaper. She had laminated every one and put the collection in a spiral notebook. "You shouldn't've done it," I said, not in humility but reproach. Back in my Madison dorm, I'd been mounting the same articles differently, gluing each onto a sheet of typing paper. I wanted them the way I wanted them. Not that it mattered much how they were displayed. I had tried and failed to land a summer job on a newspaper, had collected rejection letters everywhere from the *New York Times* to the New Brunswick *Home*

News. The best I could manage, and this with family connections that I was ashamed to use, was part-time work writing press releases for Rutgers. That would occupy my afternoons. Every morning but Friday I would be taking Spanish at the local community college, the coward's way to fulfill my foreign language requirement. As a family, we had no plans for a vacation, no successor trip to last summer's tour through Greece. We didn't dare venture too far from my mother's doctors. We didn't dare ask too much of her diseased bones, brittle as crockery.

I was still in my bedroom when my father came home from work. "How's Samuel Gary?" he asked me in his jocular way, tugging on one of my earlobes. I squirmed loose, the way I always did, and told him I was okay, glad to be back, all the standard replies. Then we closed the door and picked up from where his last letter to me had left off. After gaining my mother several years and one prolonged remission, the chemotherapy and radiation were no longer working. The cancer was spreading—breast, lung, liver, bones. The only remaining options were experimental treatments, one at the National Cancer Institute, another at the University of Chicago, possibly surgery to remove the pituitary gland. My father had all the right contacts in oncology circles from his business, but contacts alone offered no guarantee. My mother would need a biopsy first for the doctors to determine whether she even had a chance of benefiting from the risky regimens. I asked my father if he knew how long she had left, and he said, as he had said every other time I asked the same question, there was no way to tell. My fingertips went cold.

The next night, I was kneeling in front of the television set in our den, turning the dial away from the third-place Mets, when I saw the house on fire. A special report must have interrupted the program on whatever channel this was, because instead of a sitcom or game show the screen was filled by a frieze of calamity. There were flames, smoke, rifles, snipers, and at the center of it all a stucco bungalow. I deduced pretty quickly that this bulletin had something to do with the Patty Hearst case. A group of revolutionaries calling themselves the Symbionese Liberation Army had kidnapped her back in February and gone underground until reappearing a day earlier, shoplifting from a sporting-goods store in Los Angeles and escaping behind a cloud of machine-gun fire. Now it looked like the police had found them. I retreated to the easy chair and turned off the air conditioner to hear better.

Ever since Hearst had been abducted, I had been following the saga with a very particular fascination. I had a crush on Patty Hearst, at least on the pictures of her in the papers, sexy in that waifish hippie way. I hated that at nineteen she was living with one of her prep-school teachers, because that just reminded me of my own tongue-tied futility with girls at college. It was like last Thanksgiving at my Uncle Freddy's house, when one of his faculty buddies from Case Western showed up with a student lover, so fetching in her peasant dress and Judy Collins hair.

The scene on the television now transfixed me, the soaring flames, the fists of smoke, the crackle of gunfire. Stripped to my boxer shorts, I felt the whole year of college receding. I was home again, home to my dying mother. And as she was dying, so was our whole life as a family, the sum of twenty years. This sensation kept rising in me, this compassion for whoever was trapped in that bungalow on TV. I thought to myself, I know the feeling of a burning house.

My mother stayed behind in the hospital, suffering from a breast infection, for several days after I was sent home as a newborn. My father gave me my first bath, and I peed in his face, no good deed going unpunished. We lived then, in the autumn of 1955, in a garden apartment just off the main street in Highland Park, walking distance from my father's machine shop across the river in New Brunswick. Within months, my mother was pregnant again, delivering Carol in August 1956. Since the business was improving, my parents bought a two-bedroom house with forsythias and rhododendrons in the yard, up the hill from a county park. Ken was born in February 1959, sending Carol and me into a finished attic as roommates.

Early on a Saturday afternoon in what must have been 1960, my mother pulled into our driveway in the secondhand gunmetal gray Volvo that she called Trustable Combustible. She was back from her half-day of classes at Rutgers University, where she was studying for a master's degree in education, and she was carrying a sack of McDonald's hamburgers for our lunch. Maybe I had been playing on the swing set in the back-yard, or maybe helping my father nail together a wooden shed, his first effort in a long, futile quest to make me a fraction as handy as he was.

That moment was the oldest in my memory, the point at which I first became aware of my mother's life coinciding with my own, the beginning of my conscious sense of our existence as a family. It blurred and merged with other images—my mother sitting cross-legged in the living room practicing the classical guitar, frying up hamburgers to pack for lunch at Sandy Hook, giving me a sip of beer for my thirst while waiting on line at a Labor Day picnic for a free ride on the municipal fire engine. She called a beer a *brrr,* because of how cold it felt on the kind of day she invariably pronounced a *scorcher.*

We had a small outboard boat during that period of my childhood, and on weekends my father loaded our family aboard to cruise the brown waters of Raritan Bay and picnic among the dried seaweed and horseshoe crab shells on the beach at Morgan. On July 4, 1960, a certifiable scorcher, we brought along another family with three children of their own, and set out for New York Harbor and the Statue of Liberty. An approaching thunderstorm churned up the water, dropping our boat onto an unmarked, sunken tug, and swamping it within minutes. After bobbing terrified for some time in the waves, we were rescued by a passing fisherman, and from a waterfront tavern we hitched a ride back to

Highland Park, where our station wagon sat alone at the moonlit marina. That night was the first time I heard my parents argue.

As I grew into a greater cognizance of their lives, I began to see the divergent paths of my parents. Although he always told us "I was the dumbest one in my family," the one sent to work so his siblings could go to college, the father I knew was a smashing success. I did not recall his first machine shop, a storefront in downtown New Brunswick, but rather the block-square factory he built on the city's edge, across the road from a golf course. I loved playing hide-and-seek with my brother and sister amid the rows of kick-presses and welding torches, the air pungent with the aroma of greasy machinery. This playground produced equipment for microbiology research, pollution control, and ultimately cancer research. Professors and scientists called on my father in our house, business associates visited from Germany and England and France, and sometimes he would sketch out his latest invention right there on a napkin.

My father's talents brought our family prosperity. We moved from the two-bedroom house to a brick colonial twice its size on the side of town where the Rutgers professors lived. We ate out on weekend nights, and I could order surf and turf if I wanted. My father drove an Imperial, then a Delta 88, then a Cadillac, and he hired a series of housekeepers to help my mother, to free some of her time for classes or jobs. We took family vacations in Stowe and Hawaii; in the summer of 1968, the first summer when all of us children were in sleepaway camp, he whisked away my mother to Europe.

Amid the comfort, my father never lost the sense of himself as both a working stiff and a radical. He kept a basement workshop with tools hanging off a pegboard and nails and screws sorted into pickle jars; he bowled every week on a team he called The Flintstones, once or twice rolling a 300. He reared my siblings and me on the Weavers, Tom Lehrer, and *That Was The Week That Was,* and could sing a robust *Internationale.* He forbade me from patronizing the nearby amusement park owned by a family of John Birchers. We renounced our membership to a local swim club because it was segregated. The worst insult in my father's vocabulary, the way he let you know you'd really failed him, was to say you were bourgeois.

My mother went through interests and jobs and hobbies the way she went through cigarettes, lighting the next off the stub of the last. She studied guitar, painting, sculpting, creative writing. She read books two at a time. She sold ads for a small radio station and a local weekly newspaper and told people she had majored in journalism at City College, even though her concentration actually had been in public relations. She volunteered for the PTA and the League of Women Voters, served as den mother when I was in the Cub Scouts. For one fulfilling year, when I was in seventh grade, she tutored children in the Title I program, including a boy who ran away from home for several days, living off table scraps at Burger King. Then the funding was cut and she was looking for work again. Of the many stories and articles she wrote and tried to sell, she placed only one, a feature for the New Brunswick paper about the family of gerbils my brother and sister were raising. I'm pretty sure she didn't even get paid.

Most of the time, my mother appeared optimistic, energetic, full of plans. She taught me Latin roots. She introduced me to the dictionary and the tennis court. She could remove my undershirt without taking off my top shirt, whispering in conspiratorial tones, "That's a trick I learned in the striptease." When she was fighting with the electric company over a service problem, she took us children to the main office with instructions to run amok among the mechanized floor displays until she got satisfaction. Then there were those other times, like during the Cuban missile crisis, when she was crying that the whole world was going to get blown up, or when she complained that my father was away on business too much, which made me feel guilty since she was saying it to me behind his back. One day during high school, I noticed my mother carrying a paperback with the title *Diary of a Mad Housewife*. I asked her what the book was about. She looked at me and said flatly, "The story of my life."

During one of my parents' arguments, I said to them, "Why don't you just get divorced?" To my shock, they laughed at the question. They laughed as if to say that, no matter how precocious I was in the classroom, I didn't know the first thing about marriage. I did know that they loved to talk to each other. They talked about

civil rights and opera and the war and the morning
Times and how religion was sectarian and materialistic.
Sometimes, when they didn't want us children to understand, they talked in Yiddish. Not infrequently, my father would say to me in a rapturous way, "Your mother
is so goddamned smart." They never got along better
than they did after my mother got sick. That was going
to be their great common cause, saving her life.

From my seat in the aluminum bleachers, I peered
down to the football field, covered with folding chairs
containing the senior class of Highland Park High
School. On this sticky and overcast June afternoon, five
weeks since my return from Madison, I was trying to
pick out my sister Carol in her white mortarboard and
gown, searching for the telltale sign of her waist-length
black hair. My father and my brother flanked me in the
stands. Moments earlier, we had deposited my mother
in the front aisle, having driven her the two blocks from
our house, rolled her in a wheelchair across the pebbled
and rutted jayvee baseball field, and lifted her up into
the bleachers. She had cursed and cried at the prospect
of attending the ceremony in a wheelchair—the whole
damn town would know something was seriously
wrong with her—but it was the only way she'd be able
to watch Carol graduate at all.

At the periphery of my vision, I noticed my favorite
teacher, Mr. Stevens, moving down the front aisle and
reaching the place where Mom's wheelchair blocked his
path. He was a dapper man in charcoal slacks and a

navy blazer, and normally graceful in his movements, even on the occasional days he smelled of gin. As he turned himself sideways to slide behind the wheelchair, though, he must have bumped hard against it with a foot or leg. Suddenly, as I sat helplessly three rows away, the chair pitched to its left, the right wheel lifted, and my mother started to fall. I thought in those few seconds that if she toppled over, she would shatter into pieces, and I would shatter, too. Somehow, she hurled her weight against the chair's momentum. It rocked back and forth a few more times, wobbly as a bowling pin, and finally settled.

My mother hardly needed any more humiliation. Her cracked rib still ached after months. A few weeks earlier, she had broken a toe sliding off a stepladder while taking down towels from the linen closet. Then, just the other night, she had slipped on some water our pet dog splashed out of its dish, crashing to the unforgiving kitchen tile. The fall had cracked a bone at the base of her spine and made it agony to walk. That was the reason for the wheelchair. My father already had warned me not to expect any of these injuries to heal, because the cancer was so advanced.

The summer felt claustrophobic, heavy and enveloping. My best friends, Jimmy and Tim, both had girlfriends to occupy them. Mark, another buddy, was leaving soon for a backpacking trip to Europe and Israel. My brother Ken would be spending the summer as a counselor-in-training in a New Hampshire camp. My own solitary routine was established: Spanish in the morning, Rutgers public relations in the afternoon, look around for a pickup basketball game after dinner. On weekends, I went to bars with a few high school classmates. We heard bands play Eagles covers and mutely gazed at girls in platform shoes and halters, too paralyzed to flirt, or I was, anyway. Sometimes we had to stop the car on the way home for somebody to vomit, if he'd been mixing Quaaludes with tequila sunrises.

No matter how late I came home on those nights, I usually found my mother at the kitchen table, slumped face down into the pages of the *Times*. I gently jostled her awake and told her to quit waiting up for me. She said between yawns, no, she wasn't waiting up, she'd just dozed off reading the paper. I believed that less when there was a glass next to her, an inch of unfinished Manhattan at the bottom. I didn't blame her for drinking. She knew what was happening to her. I wound up drunk myself so many nights, because I, too, knew.

As I looked across the long remaining weeks of summer, I saw only one highlight, one reward, one compensation for all the misery. On the night of August 8, Crosby, Stills, Nash & Young were bringing their reunion tour to Roosevelt Stadium in Jersey City. I'd already spent the requisite predawn hours on line at a Ticketron outlet to buy seats for myself, Tim, his girlfriend Lorraine, and a mutual friend named Marty. Tim had introduced me to Neil Young after mistakenly ordering *Harvest* from a record club, thinking it was by

Neil Diamond. During my freshman year in Madison, I'd decided my own favorite of Young's records was *After the Goldrush*. It wasn't just the spare and plaintive songs I loved, or the quavering tenor voice, it was the cover photo of Neil Young—stalking down a city street in full scowl, his aloneness heightened by print's steely tone. I fancied myself that way, somber and isolated, valiantly detached, when in fact I was tethered to my mother in her wheelchair.

On the last weekend of July, I drove with my parents to visit my brother Ken at summer camp in New Hampshire. He was the star water-skier of the place and had a French girlfriend named Sylvie. In summers past, we always had enjoyed these reunions, even the six-hour drive north, when my father passed me the *Times* and said, "Read me Tom Wicker, old boy." This year had gone badly from the start, when we inadvertently left New Jersey without a new and essential piece of baggage, the painkillers my mother required several times a day. Although she could limp along without her wheelchair by now, her broken bones remained broken. The cancer was spreading ever more deeply into her organs. She drank gimlets at lunch.

By the time we returned to the motel late Saturday afternoon, Ken needing to resume his counselor-in-training duties, my mother was moaning in pain. "Dave, you've got to get more," she said of the painkillers. "I can't take it. I just cannot take it." From the motel room, my father tried reaching her oncologist and internist, but the best he could do in the middle of a summer weekend was leave messages with each doctor's answering service. He phoned our usual pharmacy in Jersey to try to convince the druggist there to call a New Hampshire colleague and vouch that my mother really had a prescription for the medicine, that she wasn't some kind of dope fiend. We sat in our room then and waited and waited and waited for somebody to call back. We didn't dare leave the telephone to eat dinner. Eventually, after darkness had fallen, the internist rang. We raced in our car to a nearby strip mall with a pharmacy, and my father dashed inside to place the order before the store closed.

In the front seat of our car, my mother whimpered. Tears rolled down her face, each cutting a trail through her sweat. Never, ever, not in almost five years of her cancer, had I seen or heard her so utterly reduced. I had witnessed tears of anger and disappointment from her over the years, tears that came in gales. These were different tears, tears of defeat.

"When you're like this," I said in a soft and halting voice, "do you ever, y'know, think about just ending it?"

No sooner had I spoken than I regretted every word. But they were already there, hanging in the air between us. And this was the question I'd been asking inside my own head all summer.

"Not as long as there's one more great book to read," my mother said. "Not as long as there's one more great play to see."

I sat in the back seat and said nothing. I looked out the window, trying to find the silhouette of my father inside the plate glass front of the pharmacy. That had been our favorite thing, reading and talking about the same books. I had come home for the summer with a new one, from my class in Third World Literature, a book called *In the Castle of My Skin*. It was all about a teenaged boy who realizes he must leave home. My mother didn't like it as much as I did.

When my father returned to the car with the drugs, my mother unscrewed the cap with shaky hands and swallowed two pills dry. I knew then we would survive the weekend.

As we headed back to the motel, I counted off the days. Twelve more till the Crosby, Stills, Nash & Young concert. Nineteen till I went back to Madison for my sophomore year. I already had arranged a midway stop in Chicago with my editor from the college paper, who'd promised to introduce me to the best chili joint in town.

I pressed the transistor radio flush against my ear, and twisted the dial to raise the volume, and still I strained to hear the voice. Around me in Roosevelt Stadium on the night of August 8, tens of thousands of other college kids were roaring, and off in the middle distance on a stage near the center field fence, Crosby, Stills, Nash & Young were howling a song called *Immigration Man* into the swirling wind. Bending down, head and radio between my knees, I finally heard what I'd been anticipating, Richard Nixon telling the nation "I shall resign the presidency. . . ."

"He quit! He quit!" I shouted to my companions, Tim and Marty and Lorraine, and to everyone nearby in the crumbling cement stands behind home plate. Nobody seemed surprised or impressed. Tim leaned over to shout in my ear that Graham Nash had already made the announcement—several minutes too early, in fact—which was why the crowd had been celebrating while I was tuning in the speech. Somehow, in being the only one in the stadium to get the moment of victory right, I felt like the village idiot. There was nothing to do except toast Nixon's demise by pouring myself another cup from the Styrofoam jug of vodka and Hawaiian Punch that I'd concocted for our foursome.

Since we'd arrived hours before the concert to grab the best of the general-admission seats, I had downed most of the punch myself. I wanted to be in festive and addled spirits for Nixon's resignation. I'd been following Watergate since my senior year of high school, and last year at college my dorm friends enjoyed nothing better than smoking some pot, turning the Darkness and Contrast knobs on the television to the most extreme settings, and seeing only Nixon's eyes and teeth glowing from the black screen as he groveled for his political life. In one letter to me at college, my mother had mentioned her favorite anti-Nixon bumper sticker: IMPEACH THE COX-SACKER.

A song or two after Nixon's resignation, I staggered off to the stadium bathroom. The next morning, that was the last thing I could remember. I didn't remember Neil Young singing *Old Man* and *Ohio* and *Cowgirl In The Sand,* songs Tim told me about later as I pretended to recall. I was wickedly hung over, starving because I hadn't eaten anything since a couple of hot dogs on the Jersey Turnpike the afternoon before, and yet too nauseous to contemplate food. This day, a Friday, was scheduled to be my last on the Rutgers job. I roasted under the sun as I watched an ROTC unit perform a marching drill, then dragged myself to the office to type up a press release. When I came home, my mother was at the kitchen table, dying a little more each second. These last days had summed up the summer, all right. I forgot the things I most wanted to remember, and I remembered all the things I so desperately wanted to forget.

A week after the concert, I drove back to Madison, and autumn arrived on Canadian winds. I lost myself in the campus newspaper, history classes, raucous football weekends. Carol was starting college at the University of Iowa and she was the immediate object of my mother's concern. For almost ten years, Carol had suffered from epilepsy—or, as we delicately called it in the family, from "spells"—and she was going through an especially severe period now with *petit mal* seizures that clouded her awareness and shivered her legs. My mother, though, was too weak to lift a suitcase; she had to cushion her cancerous bones with extra pillows in order to sleep. So she turned to Fannie to accompany her to Iowa City, relying on her kid sister, marveling as Fannie pulled the bags off the airport conveyer, "Gee, you're strong." My mother treated Carol's roommates to dinner, trying to get friendships off to a start, while leaving her own steak untouched. She and Fannie helped Carol navigate the steep hills rising from the Iowa River. Back home after the trip, she mailed Carol heel cushions, extra sweaters, Simon and Garfunkel tapes. When Carol described in a letter how a married grad student had tried to invite her to his room, my mother answered, "How happy I am that you are able to say NO because it could prevent you from getting stuck with a clinker or a premature marriage."

In the mail I received, I could not help noticing my mother's script tilting and slumping on the page, as if she were losing control of her fingers. One letter started out with the uncharacteristic admission, "This will be short because I really am exhausted." When I regaled her with stories of my birthday night in Madison, six bars and six drinks, she wrote back, "Go easy on the booze, love—it can get to you after awhile, as you well know. I guess the liking runs in the family, but it has to be done in style & at the right time or it gets to be a struggle." I was trying that fall to sell my first freelance articles to large newspapers and magazines, and getting turned down every time. "Boy, do I remember my rejection days—they're no fun," Mom wrote. "Actually, if I hadn't become ill, I'd probably still be masochistically sending out stuff just for the pain of the rejection. But those writing days were lots of fun, anyway, & already you're way ahead of me." These pieces of advice, like the advice to Carol about falling for the wrong guy, seemed different than the usual maternal meddling. They sounded like last bits of wisdom.

Meanwhile, my mother and father drove to suburban Washington, flew to Chicago, called the Mayo Clinic, following every lead about an experimental protocol. Some of the tips ended in cold trails. Then a biopsy proved that pituitary surgery would not arrest my mother's cancer. For good measure, the incision refused to heal. Fluid started to accumulate in her lungs. The rib, toe, and tailbone remained broken. My mother's father had died several years earlier, and until this point, she had avoided telling her mother about her own illness, expecting and dreading a histrionic reaction. But the old woman was beset with mice and muggers in her housing project, and so my mother invited her out to New Jersey for a visit. Stepping through the front door, Rose took one look at my mother, locked herself in the bathroom, and burst into tears.

Still, my mother went into New York with her friend Mira to hear a debate between the Senate candidates. She saw Jason Robards and Colleen Dewhurst in the revival of *A Moon for the Misbegotten*. She undertook one final art project, a bust of Golda Meir. Through the massacre of Israeli athletes at the 1972 Olympics, the Yom Kippur War the following year, and most recently the United Nations debates on the resolution equating Zionism with racism, she had come to see Golda as a heroine, a prime minister tough as a street Jew from the East Bronx. Besides which, she loved the process of shaping clay into the expressive lumps and creases of Golda's face, etching the bun of wiry gray hair strand by strand with a toothpick. One Saturday in October, my mother called on Fannie again to be her arms and lug the finished sculpture to a foundry for casting. "If it comes out good," she wrote to Carol, "who knows, I may try to sell some."

Two Sundays before Thanksgiving, my parents pulled up to a tidy brick and fieldstone home in Teaneck, New Jersey. As far as they knew, they had come to have lunch with Marion and Saul Maidens, just the four of them. Waiting inside, though, were two surprise guests, Joe Lempert and Hy Kraft, classmates from Morris High School whom my mother had rarely if ever seen since the commencement exercises in January 1941. For months, no doubt feeling her time dwindling, my mother had been telling Marion how much she'd like to see some of the old crowd. Marion did not reveal that by coincidence she and Hy had rediscovered each other only recently, when he joined the math department at Kennedy High School in the Bronx, where Marion taught English. The first question Hy had that day was, "How is Eleanor?" Marion answered that Eleanor was terminally ill.

Standing at the door on this fall afternoon, though, she did not look that way to Marion and Hy and Joe. She looked smart in a deep green velveteen outfit, her hair dyed black as it had been in high school. She was holding a Boston fern in a ceramic planter, a little gift for Marion. And she looked gleeful, giddy even, as the first wave of recognition washed over her, and she saw behind the eyeglasses, the gray streaks, the receding hairlines, the smooth faces of two teenaged boys from a long time ago.

Over quiche and apple cake, they caught up, which meant going back to Hy's military service in North Africa, Joe's in the Pacific. They ran through all their classmates from the Goodwin honors program—Bernie Solomon teaching Chinese at Queens College, Mel Goodman a psychiatrist in Texas, Ernie Kaplan running a jewelry and watch store in the Diamond District, not bad all in all for a bunch of poor Jewish kids from the tenements. They talked about how Buddy Rashbaum, Eleanor's nemesis in the election for class president, had married his Morris sweetheart, Charlotte Harrow. Word was he'd done very well for himself in the *shmatte* business. As for Joe, he had gone into insurance, and was deeply involved, too, in Jewish philanthropy. Just tonight he was delivering the keynote speech at a fund-raising dinner; his tuxedo was in the car. Hy had become a teacher and for a time the assistant principal at Morris, a very different place these days. The East Bronx was now called the South Bronx and it was infamous for arson, fires by the thousands. Eleanor's childhood home, that U-shaped apartment house at 1461 Boston Road, had burned down a few years earlier. There was nothing left worth seeing in the old neighborhood. It was much happier to hold a reunion in Teaneck and let memory paint the picture of the Bronx.

As the daylight faded, Hy and Joe said their farewells. Saul Maidens lit a fire in the living room hearth, and my mother asked him to mix her a Manhattan. On this occasion, one was enough; one was just right. In the soft light of the flames, my mother's face looked sweetly rounded, not bloated as it truly was. Eventually, the time came for my parents to leave, and my mother embraced Marion, her friend since kindergarten. Something must have made her think of graduation day, nearly thirty-four years ago, the day she won all the prizes and threw them at her mother as Marion and Florence Herzog looked on, envious and aghast. "You know, Marion," my mother said, "you were the one who deserved the French medal. I did a point better on the Regents, but you really had a feeling for the language." Marion laughed, maybe to hide how touched she was, and said, "Thanks for that, Eleanor. You've just made my mother very happy."

Then Saul and Marion walked my parents out to the car. My father helped ease my mother into her seat. And they drove off together into the night, the inescapable night.

Through the misted windows of our motel room, my sister and I stared out into the blizzard. The switchboard was off. The restaurant next door was closed. A half hour earlier, the state police had shut down the Ohio Turnpike, stranding us halfway back to our respective colleges from Thanksgiving at home. It was the Sunday afternoon of December 1, 1974, and nobody knew where we were. We felt the isolation especially keenly because our mother had gone into the hospital a few hours after we had left Highland Park on the previous afternoon. Peering into the storm, the snow blowing nearly horizontal on the howling west wind, I made out a phone booth beneath a streetlamp by the restaurant. I slogged to it and placed a collect call home.

My father reassured me in the same way he had reassured me before our departure. This was going to be a very normal procedure, just draining some pleural fluid from my mother's lungs. The oncologist would be doing the tap himself. It wasn't even scheduled until Monday. And we shouldn't worry. My mother, after all, had willed herself to host Thanksgiving dinner for the extended family, this less than a week after making a second visit to Carol at Iowa.

None of my mother's efforts and none of my father's calming words meant the long-term prognosis had turned any less forbidding. During the holiday weekend, she had suffered through headaches and weakness; between cooking and serving, she gasped for breath. Our family dared think no farther ahead than Christmas break, hoping Mom lasted long enough for a vacation in the Caribbean. My father and mother had one more plan, unknown to us children. He had bought her a cassette recorder. In the first week of December, she intended to start dictating tapes, an inheritance of sorts, telling us all about her life.

Carol and I awoke on Monday morning to clear skies and plowed roads and we got back on the interstate. The plan was for me to drop her at O'Hare Airport in Chicago for a flight to Iowa and then continue myself to Madison. By the time we reached O'Hare, Carol was twenty hours late for her ticketed flight, so she lined up at the counter to see about going standby. When I reached my dorm in Madison, more than two days after having started from New Jersey, I told myself nothing could be worse than that trip.

Then I saw the note from my roommate to call my father. When I did, neither he nor my brother was home. An unexpected voice answered—a French graduate student named Odile, who had been staying with us for a few days because she was a friend of one of my father's business associates. Her English consisted mostly of murmuring, "Yes, ah yes," to whatever anyone said. Now she managed to enunciate her way through a phone number I was supposed to call. It started with the area code 212, meaning New York City. This time, my father picked up on the other end. He told me my mother had died. The doctors had botched the lung tap. She had bled or choked or something, right there on the table. I couldn't help thinking, even in that moment, that maybe this medical mistake was a tiny bit of mercy.

My father asked me to find Carol and bring her home. I was the eldest. It was something only I could do. So I phoned Carol's dorm in Iowa City and heard from her roommate that she hadn't arrived. I called the airline at O'Hare and had her paged to no avail. I threw my duffel bag, still packed and zipped, back into my car, and I drove eighty-five with all the windows open for the entire hundred miles to O'Hare. It was past ten at night by the time I arrived, and I ran up and down the empty, echoing concourses, searching for Carol at any gate, any ticket counter, any phone booth. Breathless, I dialed Iowa City again. She was there. She knew.

I arranged to meet Carol's flight from Iowa the next morning and then continue together onto Newark. For now, I drove to a hotel close to the airport and asked for a room. The only one vacant was the executive suite. Inside it, the heat blew incessantly and the curtains refused to close. I lay awake all night, listening to the drip of water from the wet bar's faucet. I only wanted it to be tomorrow in the airport, to be able to hold my sister, to have someone for whom I could be strong.

On that last Monday afternoon of my mother's life, my father and brother had driven to Montefiore Hospital in the Bronx from Highland Park. When they walked out of the elevator onto my mother's floor, they saw my father's sister Clara sitting next to a vending machine in the waiting area, streaming tears. "You know, I was right there," she told my father. "And I heard something going on. I went right into the room. A mask was being put on her face, and she was saying, 'My God, I'm dying, I'm dying.'"

Dad and Ken dashed into my mother's room. Her body still lay in the bed, head tilted back, chin jutting, plastic tube protruding from her mouth. Ken touched her hand. Soon an intern entered the room and started to explain what had happened. The oncologist hadn't come in as promised to tap the lung. The intern had done it. Something had made the lung start to bleed. He couldn't get the bleeding to stop. And then she'd stopped breathing. My father grabbed the intern by his shirt. "You fucking idiot," he shouted, eyes narrowing. "How could you do this? Look what you've done! Look what you've done!" Ken had to pry my father's hands off the intern.

In the succeeding days, the medical examiner conducted an autopsy that acknowledged the inexplicable bleeding but nonetheless listed the cause of death as carcinomatosis. The document also informed us that the original breast cancer had spread over the years into my mother's spine, liver, lymph nodes, lungs, spleen, pituitary gland, and calvarium. At the time of her death, she was fifty years, seven months, and seven days old.

In the days between my mother's death and her funeral, my father went to the family safety-deposit box to retrieve her will. She had executed it on July 18, 1974, barely a week before that night in New Hampshire when she told me she wanted to live as long as there was one more great book to read. The will itself was the typically arid and precise legal document that a will is meant to be, filled with language like *bequeath, trustee, foregoing powers,* and *fiduciaries.* The envelope containing the will bore her essence, etched in pencil.

Do not open before my death
Diamonds in the safety deposit box are marked
Silver coins can be saved or turned in & amount
   shared by kids
If I die before Bubbe & there are services, I would pre-
   fer that she not attend.
I have fantastic children & they helped give me a good
   & happy life
Love—forever

My father did not honor her wish to have my grandmother banned from the funeral. I delivered a eulogy, as
did Dad, Carol, Ken, and Aunt Fannie. After the ceremony, the hearse carried the coffin to a crematorium
near Princeton. Perhaps my mother had chosen to be
cremated as a testament to her insignificance. Or perhaps it was one last, posthumous slap at Judaism,
which prohibits the practice. Either way, as the plain
pine box was rolled into a chapel for a brief period of
contemplation before being incinerated, my grandmother hurled herself onto the casket, wailing, "Ellie,
Ellie, *hub ich doss gedarft derleben?*" Ellie, Ellie, did I
have to live for this?

   In our secular way, we sat a version of *shiva* over the
next few days. Our visitors included Marion Maidens
and Vicky Fried. Condolence cards appeared in the
mail, from Lillian Betstadt and Hilda Saltzman Wachtenheim, from the local chapter of the League of Women
Voters and the Carolier Lanes Mixed Bowling League

and Highland Park High School's vice principal, the one we had nicknamed Maude the Broad. People planted trees in Israel in my mother's memory, contributed money to the American Cancer Society in her name. "So gutsy and uncomplaining," someone wrote in a condolence card.

Shortly after my mother died, her brother Seymour tracked down Lenny Schulman at his podiatry office and told him. We never heard a word in return. Nobody among our family or friends had any idea how to locate Hy Keltz. The news did reach Charlie Greco, probably through Vicky Fried, always the go-between. While Charlie was too circumspect to contact us directly, one day he was driving with his wife Selma down Route 1, past the cemetery, when he asked out of nowhere if she minded if he stopped to visit Eleanor's grave. Shocked though she was that Charlie knew where it was, Selma consented. When Charlie himself died in 1987, she found a photo of my mother among his belongings.

For my own part, after the mail thinned and *shiva* ended and the neighbors stopped popping over with covered platters of dinner, I returned to Madison to catch up on a week's missed assignments and prepare for final exams. It never even occurred to me to ask for an extension under the circumstances. A girl in one of my classes had noticed my absence, though, and somehow determined the cause. I found a card from her waiting in my room. Her stationery had a pink border and a pattern of spring flowers.

dear sam:

when you are sorrowful look
again in your heart, and you shall
see that in truth you are weeping
for that which has been your delight

sam, i'm so sorry about your mother—
you are in my prayers—

love (♥)
teresa
from meteorology

Eleanor, Miami Beach, 1964

Epilogue

ON A STIFLING, sun-bleached afternoon in July 2004, I brushed the vines away from the marker of my mother's grave. With each sweep of my sweaty hand, the raised lettering of the simple plaque became visible, showing her name and the inscription, and also a line in between, 1924–1974, such a brief time. It had not taken me long to find the marker. I would have found it quickly enough by memory even if the site had not been identified by a canvas canopy and a mound of freshly excavated earth. I had come for the burial of my sister's husband George, like my mother dead too soon from cancer.

As I approached the family plot, I had felt a tremor of panic, thinking at first that the gravediggers had piled the loose dirt atop my mother's plaque. Instead, as I soon saw, the marker was visible right at the foot of the folding chairs where Carol, Ken, and my father took their seats. I stood beside the grave, reading poems by Frost and Tennyson in George's memory. After we finished and the mourners began walking back to their cars, I stayed with Aunt Fannie and Uncle Seymour and several cousins to place pebbles on the plaque in the Jewish tradition. "You have Eleanor's movements," Uncle Seymour said to me as he turned to go. "The way you walk, the way you lean."

Now that I knew who my mother was, I had earned the right to stand at her grave. Or perhaps what I mean is that I have reclaimed the right that I abdicated by assembling a self that shoved her aside in life and ignored her in death. If I understood even back in 1973 how selfish I was to have pretended my mother was a stranger when she sat in on my classes, then I now recognize in such a gesture the full measure of my capacity for emotional brutality. I assumed back then that she had enjoyed a college experience of her own, so I resented her for intruding on mine. Now I have learned just what she surrendered in going to work full-time as a teenager and leaving Brooklyn College for City downtown at night. Now I have learned she went to work so her mother wouldn't be reduced to picking garbage. So when I recently reread the letters she wrote to me at Wisconsin and found a sentence saying, "Boy, college was never like that for me," a simple little sentence that flew right past me at age eighteen, I was harrowed by the casual cruelty of that son.

Yet I conclude this mission with more than shame and apologies. To the degree I anticipated at the outset what my search ultimately would reveal, I thought it was the story of a bright and plucky daughter in a smothering immigrant household and how she battered her way into the wider world, emerging bruised yet unbowed, and finally triumphant. In some ways, I had guessed right, more right than I could have imagined at the start. But in the largest way, I was wrong. I was much too optimistic. The story of my mother is the story of someone whose life peaked at seventeen. And if there's anything sadder than dying at fifty, then it's having peaked at seventeen and living to fifty with that knowledge.

Early in this book, I recalled the day my mother stormed out of a potluck lunch at the Workmen's Circle, and my father's explanation that she was moody from quitting smoking. There were other moments in my childhood, less often moments of lightning temper than of enveloping melancholy. I know now they had little to do with a craving for cigarettes. I recognize that alcohol eased her journey into darkness, but alcohol was not the darkness. The darkness abided in her, sober as well as drunk. I remember the intent way my mother watched the children's movie, *The Red Balloon,* as a crowd of hooligans chases and stones the balloon. I remember her inviting me to stay up late the night before my last day of fourth grade to watch the brooding British movie about a soulful misfit, *The Loneliness of the Long Distance Runner.* I remember, out of all the paintings she made in years of classes, one particular canvas. It showed a peddler, seated dejectedly on a vegetable crate, in front of a fancy fruits and vegetable store. That canvas, those movies, they bespoke a sadness I neither could comprehend nor penetrate as a boy. Now I can do both, and to possess such awareness is poignant and burdensome all at once.

There are so many different reasons my mother died unfulfilled. She died unfulfilled because her father was such a failure at supporting the family that my mother had to mortgage her dreams to assume his duties. She died unfulfilled because the society in which she came of age squelched ambition in women and opened few doors for them besides teaching or nursing. She died unfulfilled because her mother considered religious fidelity more important than love or happiness. To put it another way, she died unfulfilled because Rose Hatkin blamed Charlie Greco for what Hitler did to, and what her brother-in-law Alter David didn't do for, her beloved sister Ester Dina.

My mother died unfulfilled also, however, because of her own judgments and decisions. As I interviewed her relatives and friends, I repeatedly asked why my mother, who so gloried in flouting her mother, succumbed when it came to breaking off with Charlie Greco. None of them could unlock the enigma. Eventually, I arrived at an answer, or at least the most educated guess I could venture. I think she needed to hate her mother more than she needed to love Charlie. She needed the grudge. She needed somebody to blame, not just for Charlie but for every lost dream. In a short story my mother wrote late in her life about how she had refused Hy Keltz's marriage proposal, she cast her mother as the villain, when in reality it had been she herself who passed up genuine love when it carried the price of being a grocer's wife. That need to hate her mother deformed my mother's life. It propelled her into a miserable marriage to Lenny. It cut her off from whatever might have been nourishing or affirming in her parents' experience and values. It made her try to banish her mother from her funeral. I cannot help but gasp at the sheer waste of hating for so long, even hating someone unworthy of love.

For all my grandmother's fears and superstitions and faults, I have come to see, there was something valiant in her. Alone in her family, she comprehended the doom that was falling across the Jews of Europe, and to the limits of her abilities and at real cost to her own children, she tried to rescue her family in Poland. She deserved some modicum of regard and respect, some of that deep, compassionate pity that Yiddish calls *rach-manes,* from my mother, and from me, too. From be-yond her grave, my grandmother has made the Holocaust palpable to me, taught me who and what my own lineage lost, taken the massiveness out of mass murder and turned it personal. In researching this book, I met the distant relatives in Uruguay who are the grandchildren of Ester Dina, and we cherished our re-discovered bond. When I look today on my mother's bust of Golda Meir on the shelf in my living room, I imagine in the furrowed, creased face a suggestion of Rose Markiewicz Hatkin.

Finally, my mother died unfulfilled because she lifted her vanity so far above her intellect. She wanted every man, I think, to love her, or at least to want her. And she took her intelligence so much for granted that when she moved from high school to college and suddenly could not coast along on native brains and a prodigious memory, her grades never recovered. I can tell now how deeply that mediocrity embarrassed her. She let every-one in our family, just like all her friends back in the 1940s, believe she had graduated from City *cum laude.* My father and I both flourished the credential in our eulogies for her. When my mother attended graduate school during my boyhood, earning a master's degree in education and being elected to an academic honor soci-ety, she was engaging in an act of redemption, of prov-ing her academic prowess had not been lost. One of the many tragedies of her cancer is that it stalked her and felled her right at the point in her life when we children were growing older and she could be free enough of household chores to take up a profession. Watching the feminist movement take shape in the early 1970s, she would often sigh, "I was born twenty years too soon."

That is true and not true. Her desire—the desire to be desired—may have cost her life. I never will know what would have happened had she agreed to a mastectomy when her cancer was first diagnosed. Maybe it was too late already, the diseased cells already sown in her lungs and lymph nodes. Or maybe she would be alive today, joking that her left breast, the artificial one, doesn't sag like her real, right one. But she could not have foreseen what advances in reconstructive surgery later would make possible. All she saw were the men all around her, the men whose appraising stares gratified and ratified her.

During my teenaged years, she sometimes gazed across the street from our home at the house where my friend Jimmy Lyons lived. Jimmy was an athlete, a Catholic of Irish and Italian stock, and he had a careless flip in his sun-lightened brown hair. He always had a girlfriend, too, and my mother often would say in a dreamy, faraway voice, "Jimmy Lyons really knows how to treat a girl." I realize now that in Jimmy my mother saw another version of Charlie, while I was like her egghead classmates at Morris, and I think her reverie betrayed more than bittersweet nostalgia. She wanted every head to turn, even the head of my buddy. On our family trip to Greece the summer before my mother died, we took a cruise around the Aegean islands. One day, while she was on the toilet, a deck steward mistakenly entered her stateroom. In the diary she kept on the trip, a diary I discovered just a few months ago, she wrote approvingly of how the man, far from being abashed, told her he wanted to spirit her away for a week's romance. I felt a wave of vertigo as I read those words. Not because they showed my mother as a sexual being, but because they confirmed my sense of her as someone of insatiable vanity, juvenile vanity. If indeed she paid for narcissism with death, then I cannot imagine a more terrible bargain.

When my mother wrote on the envelope containing her will that my brother and sister and I "helped give me a good & happy life," I have come to believe, she was writing those words to offer solace rather than to speak truth. A loving parent regarding imminent death, she must have appreciated that in her eternal absence we children needed to believe that we had been her life. So she told us what we wanted to hear—a final kindness, a final lie. We children provided consolation; I appreciate that. But I am not convinced we were consolation enough for all the other dreams and desires and ambitions unrealized.

As I recognize now, my mother hurtled into marriage to my father and thus into our life as a family as a damaged and desperate person. Growing up, I understood that she and my father had had a brief courtship. I believed then and for a long time after that it indeed had been a courtship, not the unsentimental mixture of pressure, falsehood, attraction, and mutual convenience their road to wedlock actually was. Some part of me hates to relinquish the romantic fantasy, the ideal that they had married for love. Another part appreciates that, from such an unpromising beginning, they somehow lasted together for twenty-one years.

After thirty years as a professional journalist and nearly half as many as a journalism professor, I cling to a fundamentalist's faith that there is such a thing as truth, and that I can achieve it through facts. So the reporter in me feels somehow defeated to admit that despite all my research, all my sleuthing, all my sleepless midnights wrestling with what I had learned, I never can know with absolute, 100 percent certainty what was happening inside my mother's head and heart at every second of her young womanhood. I wish I had discovered exactly when Charlie first kissed her or what she thought on her wedding day to Lenny. She was no diarist, my mother, and some of those who might have known those answers are themselves long dead. And maybe I'm not quite as skilled as I like to think I am.

Still, the son in me believes that I have come to understand my mother's essence, that I have approached her soul. For a long time in my years of research, I searched futilely for my mother's high school yearbook, ripping apart my father's attic and basement three times over in obsessive pursuit. I envisioned that yearbook with its personal inscriptions as the Rosetta stone, the translation of her person, at least during one formative stage of her life. Two weeks after I finished my first draft of this book, my sister remembered that the yearbook had been sitting on her shelf all along. When I borrowed it and read through it, read through every message from teachers and classmates, I realized they told me nothing I didn't already know.

I dare to believe, then, that I know the exact time and exact place when my mother was happiest, happier even than at Midnight Mass with Charlie. It was on that September afternoon in 1941, when she and Fannie climbed to the roof of 1461 Boston Road in their swishing dresses and posed like Claudette Colbert in *It Happened One Night*. I think of my mother at that moment in her life. She was the valedictorian. She was beautiful. She was coveted. America was at peace, however tenuously, and the Depression was loosening its grip. She was a freshman in college, just seventeen, every possibility ahead of her. Never again did the planets align so magically. When I finger my copy of that snapshot, I am so deeply thankful that I was an insecure, lonely mess at seventeen, because that way my life only could improve. To her dying day, I firmly and sadly feel, my mother never stopped trying to recapture seventeen.

I do not love and miss my mother any less for having discovered her self-absorption, her misjudgments, her readiness to bend or break the truth, because in my search I also rediscovered what I had forgotten since her death, all the vigor and curiosity and heart, all the zest. I only can love and miss the real person, the flawed person, and that is the person I have exhumed. For more than three years now, since my quest began, I have felt my mother's presence more profoundly than I did when she was alive. I have welcomed her presence instead of trying to escape it. I have imbibed what she has had to teach me, about herself and her family and her times. Each detail I located—her prom date, an article from *Howdy!,* a summer housemate on Coney Island—became something precious we shared. It brought back my days in high school when, rather than joining my friends in the cafeteria, I walked the several blocks home so I could eat lunch and talk with my mother. It has been priceless these past few years to pick up where we left off.

On that torrid July afternoon in the cemetery, after I had placed the stone on my mother's grave, I remembered the African violet. When I was nine or ten years old, I took the money I had saved from my allowance and snuck off to the local florist to buy her an African violet for Mother's Day. I must have overheard her say once that African violets were her favorite. Within two or three weeks, the plant had died, and I was despondent, so despondent I almost cried. My mother drew me to her and said not to feel bad. Some flowers, she told me, are just harder than others to keep alive.

Now my work is over, my task complete, my odyssey at its destination, and I have no choice but to bury my mother again. This time, I can mourn truly. I can weep unshackled from thirty years of regret. I have given all I could give, the best I had in me, this imperfect, impermanent reincarnation.

Fannie and Eleanor, the roof of 1461 Boston Road,
September 1941

A Note on Methods and Sources

AT A PERSONAL LEVEL, this book took me on a search into my mother's past. But I also had a professional agenda in the process. As someone who writes nonfiction and who teaches it at Columbia University, I have grown troubled over the past several years about the seeming license that the terms "literary journalism," "family history," or "memoir" give for an author to bend, blur, or altogether ignore the line between fact and fiction, reality and invention. One can acknowledge that any writer's version of truth is bound to be challenged by others and yet hold fast to the ideal that producing nonfiction means making one's utmost effort to get as near to the truth as is humanly possible.

Except in some very small sections, this book is not a memoir, because most of the events occurred long before my own memories begin. Nor is this book a retelling of family lore, because my mother shared little of that lore with me or with our family. Rather, I approached this book with the same kind of research methods as I have my other books, especially *The Inheritance,* which followed three working-class families and their political beliefs over the twentieth century. Once more, plumbing obscure lives, I have engaged in what Herbert Gutman famously called "history from below."

Certainly, I relied extensively on interviewing living informants by the score—my mother's siblings, high school friends, college classmates, former boyfriends, and colleagues on various jobs. Some of these people I knew about at the outset; many others I located through Internet services such as Locateplus.com and Switchboard.com and by sending out letters to 1,000 alumni from City College's downtown campus. My informants also provided me with documentary evidence in the form of letters, diaries, yearbooks, autograph books, home movies, souvenirs, military records, and photographs, many of them dated and inscribed. My mother wrote a number of short stories about her childhood, and by circulating these among her closest relatives and friends I was able to determine the facts woven within the fiction. Both my sister and I kept the letters we received at college from our parents.

I availed myself of period photographs and films of the Bronx, as well as the oral histories collected at Lehman College and in the magazine *Back to the Bronx.* I consulted innumerable back issues of the *Bronx Home News,* the borough's daily newspaper until its demise, as well as the *Forverts, Herald Tribune, New York Times, New York Post, Daily News,* and *PM.* Quite deliberately, I did not draw on the many wonderful literary accounts of Jewish immigrants in the Bronx by Kate Simon, E. L. Doctorow, et. al. Although I have read many of those books for pleasure, I did not want their versions of the territory to creep into the Bronx of my mother and her family.

My information about Bialystok comes from the *Bialystoker Stimme,* the bilingual monthly magazine of Bialystok émigrés in New York, as well as from the ground-breaking scholarship of Rebecca Kobrin and the correspondence between my grandmother and her Polish relatives. I spent a week in Uruguay conducting research there, assisted by a translator and two historians.

Thanks to genealogists in New York and Montevideo, I was able to locate every relevant immigration record, and many relevant census records, regarding my relatives. I also obtained the Social Security records for my mother and grandfather, giving me details on their earnings for every three-month period from 1937 through 1953, as well as my mother's City College transcript. Her high school records were destroyed in a fire and flood at Morris High School in the 1980s, but I was able to find the transcripts of Marion Herzog, Bernie Solomon, and other classmates in the Goodwin honors program. I found the legal records of my mother's annulment proceedings, including transcriptions of testimony, in State Supreme Court in Brooklyn. The corporate archive of Burndy, housed at the Massachusetts Institute of Technology, included photographs, employee newsletters, job descriptions, and other primary-source material. The archive of the Catholic Archdiocese of New York contained a highly detailed account of Midnight Mass in 1946, including the verbatim text of Cardinal Spellman's message. I obtained my mother's medical records from Einstein Medical Center, which has absorbed Montefiore Hospital.

Despite my efforts, there remained some gaps I never could fill, some questions I never could answer. Nowhere, however, have I tried to pass off surmise or invention. As I sometimes told my agent during the process of writing this book, if I wanted to just make it all up, I would have written a novel.

A full bibliography is posted on my website, *www.samuelfreedman.com*

Acknowledgments

I COULD NOT have undertaken this book without the consent and support of my father David, my brother Ken, my sister Carol, my aunt Fannie Stevens, and my uncle Seymour Hatkin. These are the living people who were closest to my mother, and they trusted me to venture into an unexplored family past and to reveal honestly what I found there. All of them enhanced my efforts with their own memories and artifacts, and I am most especially grateful for the patience and insight that Fannie and Seymour, as well as their spouses Danny and Evelyn, showed to me over the last three and a half years.

Of my mother's surviving friends, Marion Maidens was the first among equals in sharing her recollections, her memorabilia, her affection, and her English teacher's unerring radar for correct grammar and usage. I also deeply appreciated the time and thoughts of Vicky Fried, Lillian Betstadt, Clare Reeves, Ruth Manners, Hilda Wachtenheim, Bernie Solomon, Joe Lempert, and Bea Fleischman. Hy Keltz not only reopened his youthful heart but shared inscribed photographs and his wartime diary, all of which were invaluable.

Charlie Greco died nearly a generation ago, but his widow Selma spent many hours graciously answering my questions about him and providing essential links to Charlie's surviving relatives and friends, especially his sister Marie Connor. Similarly, with my mother's dear friend

Ruth Taylor deceased, Ruth's surviving relatives gave me access to period letters and photographs, as well as their ample memories of her.

My research in Uruguay was underwritten by a generous grant from the Legacy Heritage Fund, Limited, created by Harry and Bella Wexner and overseen by Susan Wexner. Carole Agus helped introduce me to the fund. I am deeply thankful for her efforts and the Legacy Heritage Fund's show of confidence in my work.

In Uruguay, I relied in numerous ways on Carolina Aguerre, Nuria Sanguinetti, Raquel Cuenca, Miguel Feldman, and Teresa Porzecanski. Dawn Weiner and Casey Woods translated scholarly material and personal correspondence from Spanish. My relatives Rebeca and Guillermo Bronstein and Dina Berlinblau were wonderful hosts and guides. Becky Rottenberg, Francisco Ravecca, and Alberto Brause provided helpful contacts and introductions.

For the Bialystok portion of the research, I am enormously grateful to Rebecca Kobrin, an excellent historian and author in her own right. Liel Leibovitz translated significant portions of the *Bialystoker Stimme*. Chana Pollack was an extraordinary help in translating passages from the *Forverts*. Chana Mlotek and Fern Kant of YIVO helped decode the songs and plots of the Yiddish theater for me. The late Jonah Krakowski painstakingly translated a series of Markiewicz family postcards for me, unveiling a vanished world. Jenna Weissman Joselit walked me through the intricacies of immigrant fashion, deepening my understanding of my forebears' experience. Lucille Gudis efficiently tracked down immigration and census records of my forebears.

In my research on newsreels about the Holocaust, I relied on Raye Farr, Regina Longo, and Lindsay Harris of the Spielberg Film and Video Archive at the United States Holocaust Memorial Museum. In reporting on Midnight Mass of 1946, I was helped by a number of present and former staff members of the Catholic Archdiocese of New York—Joseph Zwilling, Sister Marguerita Smith, Bishop Patrick Ahern, and Tom Young. Barbara Young and Patrizia Sione at the Kheel Center at Cornell University ably fielded my requests for archival material involving labor unions. Anne Battis afforded me use of the Burndy corporate archive, which is maintained at the Dibner Library of the Massachusetts Institute of Technology.

Brad Tuttle brought his acute eye for the telling detail to his role as research assistant, and Christian Red genially fulfilled the tedious job of addressing and mailing a thousand letters to City College alumni. A few of those letters yielded pearls.

At City College and Baruch College, I benefited greatly from the help of the public information officers Zane Berzins and Charles DeCicco and the archivists Sandra Ross and Sydney Van Nort. Janet Butler Munch of Lehman College opened its collection of Bronx oral histories and documents. Michal Goldman screened her archival film footage of the Depression-era Bronx for my benefit. At Morris High School, I was aided on many occasions by Claralee Irabunda, Fernando Alvarez, and Jose Ruiz.

I thank Vice Dean David Klatell and Professor James Carey for helping to secure a research grant for me from the Columbia University Graduate School of Journalism, my pedagogical home for fourteen years now.

For other favors, kindnesses, and forms of assistance, I wish to acknowledge Arthur Gelb, Jonathan Sarna, Riv-Ellen Prell, Judith Laikin Elkin, Houston Person, Joshua Freeman, Eric Foner, Rabbi Avi Shafran, Yossi Klein Halevi, Roslyn Bernstein, Scotti Williston, Barbara Fasciani, Lloyd Ultan, Miriam Robinson, Deborah Wassertzug, Sachiko Onishi, Michael and Beth Norman, Joe Berger, Peter Edelman, David Krajicek, Sam Norich, Sara Barrett, and Bill Harms.

In writing this book, I find myself yet again in the debt of Alice Mayhew, the greatest of editors. Alice has let me follow my peripatetic path from book to book, bringing her restless intellect and literary wisdom to bear on each one. She improves all that she touches. Elsewhere at Simon & Schuster, I appreciate the collaborative efforts of Emily Takoudes, Roger Labrie, Victoria Meyer, Rachel Nagler, Miriam Wenger, Kathleen Rizzo, Linda Witzling, Michael Accordino, and Elisa Rivlin.

I continue to learn about researching and writing by teaching those crafts to my students at Columbia University. During the course of working on this volume, I was engaged and educated by the members of the Book Seminar in the spring semesters of 2002, 2003, and 2004. Their efforts remind me never to let up my own.

My longtime friends and fellow authors Kevin Coyne and Ari Goldman read and commented on the manuscript-in-progress, and the finished work is the better for their advice. Michael Shapiro, who has been at the next desk for almost thirty years, provided a fresh set of eyes at the end of the process. Barney Karpfinger, my agent over twenty years and four previous books, was steadfast as ever.

Carolyn Starman Hessel of the Jewish Book Council has been a guardian angel of my writing life ever since we met four years ago. She is reader, advocate, advisor, and friend all at once.

With their love and diversion, my wife Cynthia and my children Aaron and Sarah kept my life in balance as I made this deeply personal journey into the past. I hope that, for them, this book has provided at least a bit of the mother-in-law and grandmother they never knew. My stepmother, Phyllis Freedman, gave me unstinting support and unearthed memorabilia hidden away in the Highland Park closets. My mother-in-law, Elaine Sheps, who is my mother's contemporary, was a valuable sounding board.

Finally, I want to thank the secret sharer of this book, Christia Blomquist Fieber. We met twenty-eight years ago in a college class entitled "The Literature of Death and Dying," taught by Professor Evelyn Beck, the kind of class nobody takes except for a very private and intimate reason. Chris, here's to the day we all see the colors again.

S.G.F., July 2004

About the Author

SAMUEL G. FREEDMAN is the author of four acclaimed books, each of which either won or was shortlisted for a major literary prize. His last book, *Jew vs. Jew: The Struggle for the Soul of American Jewry*, won the National Jewish Book Award for Nonfiction in 2001. His previous book, *The Inheritance: How Three Families and America Moved from Roosevelt to Reagan and Beyond*, was a finalist for the Pulitzer Prize in 1997. *Upon This Rock: The Miracles of a Black Church* won the Helen Bernstein Award for Excellence in Journalism in 1993, and *Small Victories: The Real World of a Teacher, Her Students and Her High School* was a finalist for the National Book Award in 1990. A former reporter for the *New York Times*, Freedman continues to write for the newspaper on a freelance basis, and he contributes op-ed columns regularly to *USA Today* as a member of its Board of Contributors. As a professor of journalism at Columbia University, Freedman has been selected as one of the nation's outstanding journalism educators by the Society of Professional Journalists. He is a board member of the Jewish Book Council. Freedman lives in New York City with his wife and children.